Arthur Williams

SHOTGUN DIGEST

Fourth Edition

Edited by Jack Lewis

DBI BOOKS, INC

About Our Covers

Exciting new things are happening in the shotgun world, and the covers of this Fourth Edition of SHOTGUN DIGEST showcase prime examples from one of America's best-known gunmakers—Remington.

Our front cover highlights the rebirth of the over/under shotgun from Remington, the Peerless. Chambered for 12-gauge 3-inch shells, this new field gun is offered with 26-, 28-, or 30-inch light contour barrels and each comes with three Rem Choke tubes for Imp. Cyl., Mod. and Full constrictions. The gun has a single selective trigger system with an amazingly fast lock time of just 3.28 milliseconds, and selective automatic ejectors. Set up for field shooting, the Remington Peerless has an American walnut stock with 14^3/$_{16}$-inch length of pull, and 20 l.p.i. checkering on the grip and forend. With 26-inch barrels, the Peerless weighs just 7^1/$_4$ pounds.

The autoloader is the Remington 11-87 Sporting Clays model that features a target-grade, cut-checkered American walnut stock that's ^{3}/$_{16}$-inch longer in length of pull and ^{1}/$_4$-inch higher at the heel. The butt pad is radiused at the heel and rounded at the toe for easy gun mounting. For added performance, the new light contour barrel has a lengthened forcing cone, and carries a medium-high, 8mm wide ventilated rib with stainless mid-bead and Bradley-style front bead sight. Rem Choke tubes are supplied in Skeet, Imp. Skeet, Imp. Cyl., Mod. and Full. This fast-handling auto comes in the new two-barrel, custom-fitted hard case.

On our back cover, you'll see three equally exciting shotguns from Remington. On top is the new SP-10 Magnum Camo, the world's only gas-operated autoloading 10-gauge. This handsome brute is wearing new clothes in the form of Mossy Oak Bottomland overall camouflage for real concealment. Also new is the fast-handling 23-inch barrel with ventilated rib and, naturally, it comes with the excellent Rem Choke tubes. A great complement to this gun is the new Nitro Steel Magnum ammo for long range performance on heavier, high-flying waterfowl.

In the middle is the legendary Remington Model 870 Wingmaster pump shotgun. This one is chambered for 12-gauge, but is also available in 20- and 28-gauge and 410-bore, most with Rem Choke tubes to handle any hunting chore. Target-type twin-bead sights atop the ventilated rib, polished blue receiver, twin action bars for smooth cycling and more all add up to the reason why this gun has been America's most popular pump shotgun for over 40 years. To boot, the Model 870 is available in an amazing variety of finishes and models to suit nearly any need.

Remington's impressive line up of Special Purpose Synthetic shotguns is well represented by the 12-gauge Model 11-87 SPS Deer model with overall black matte finish. This impressive gun comes with a 21-inch barrel, a bead front sight and fully adjustable rear sight. Since the barrel is fully rifled, no choke tube is fitted. The stock of the 11-87 SPS Deer gun is checkered black synthetic, and it comes with swivels and a black sling. An excellent choice of ammunition here is Remington's new Copper Solid shotgun slug, just below the gun.

Photos by John Hanusin.

EDITORIAL DIRECTOR
Jack Lewis

ART DIRECTOR
Rueselle Gilbert

PRODUCTION DIRECTOR
Sonya Kaiser

PRODUCTION COORDINATOR
Nadine Symons

PRODUCTION EDITOR
Russ Thurman

COPY EDITOR
Julie Duck

PUBLISHER
Sheldon Factor

Produced by

GALLANT CHARGER

OUTDOOR GROUP

ISBN 0-87349-137-8
Library Of Congress Catalog Card Number 74-80333

CONTENTS

INTRODUCTION

WHEN ONE glances at a rack of shotguns in his local sporting goods store, the initial thought usually has to do with "sameness." There are basic shotgun models — autoloaders, pump-actions, side-by-sides and over/unders — and none of them seem to change all that much.

On the surface, that is largely true. Shotguns are designed for some specific uses, but in this day and age those purposes are changing and that means new innovations in gun design, including the materials used and, perhaps, more important, in the ammunition that is being introduced.

Today, with continuing encroachment of our open areas by housing developers, more and more states are insisting that hunting of deer — particularly the whitetail — be done with shotguns that will handle short-range buckshot or slugs. With increasing pressure for the reduction of lead shot use, steel has become the standard, if not necessarily the shot of choice. However, there is a new substance on the horizon which may come close to equaling the performance of lead — Bismuth. That potential is investigated in great detail in this volume.

Sporting clays is the continuing rage among the shotgun sports and new equipment, ranging from loads to traps, is being introduced and evaluated. These pages are meant to bring you up to date on what is happening in this demanding sport and what is ahead.

No book — or anything else — is going to be "all things to all men" (or women), but the contributors to this volume come from a broad spectrum of scattergunning activities and each has provided thought and introspect on those various subjects. I hope each of you will find information in these pages that will prove of value and improve your own shotgunning.

Jack Lewis
Capistrano Beach, California

CHAPTER 1

HIGH PERFORMANCE SHOTGUNS

Maximum Scattergun Performance Requires A Careful Combination Of Factors

Backboring can improve the performance of any smoothbore, but is more important when steel shot is used since hard pellets do not deform. If forced through a too-small choke, steel shot can cause damage.

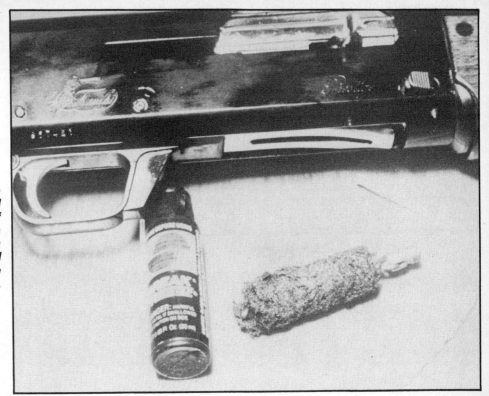

Burnishing a bore can be accomplished with normal cleaning, if you're one of those savvy shotgunners who scrubs the bore with 0000 steel wool wrapped around a bore brush. The process is faster with Nailon.

IT'S PROBABLE different scattergunners will have a different definition of what constitutes "high performance" in a smoothbore. To a trap shooter, it might be the ability to reach out and smoke the tough twenty-seven-yard handicap targets. For the upland gunner, it might be the right combination of fluid handling and open patterns that can catch and drop a streaking close-range grouse or woodcock.

Ask Larry Nailon what he considers high performance, however, and you'll get a more simple answer.

"The high performance shotgun," he states, "is the one that delivers the best downrange performance, regardless of the load used or the distance at which it is fired.

"To put it another way, it is the gun-and-load combination that delivers the maximum number of pellets in the shot charge at the point of impact simultaneously, while producing the largest usable pattern with no gaps or holes that a bird or target could slip through."

How is that high performance achieved? To Nailon, it's rather simple.

"High performance is downrange performance. To get that you must get every pellet, or as many as humanly possible, through the bore and out of the gun in a perfectly smooth, round and undeformed condition," he continues. "Round pellets fly true and will arrive on target together. Deformed pellets become flyers at the edge of the pattern and often lag behind the main pattern — sometimes, far enough behind to be of no practical use. You may as well not even have fired them for all the good they will do.

"It doesn't really matter how many pellets you start with in a given load. What really determines downrange performance is how well you take care of what you start with. When we build a high performance shotgun, our goal is to get as many pellets as possible out the bore in perfect condition."

Nailon, president of Clearview Products (3021 N. Portland, Oklahoma City, OK 73107) apparently has been accomplishing that goal quite well for quite a period of time. Indeed, among top-level sporting clays shooters, his custom barrel work and carefully machined choke tubes are considered state-of-the-art.

Yet, Nailon doesn't consider what he does to be particularly new, innovative or startling.

"There are a number of modifications one can make to a shotgun barrel," he claims, "that will result in a certain degree of performance enhancement. All we do is combine each of these proven modifications. That careful combination is what results in such a dramatic increase in overall performance: Each modification, combined with the others, compliments the other modifications and yields a larger increase in performance."

According to Nailon, there are four key areas in any shotgun barrel that play a significant role in the overall performance of that barrel. They are the chamber, forcing cone, bore and choke. Certain modifications to any of them can increase performance. What Nailon does, however, is refine all four to work in perfect harmony and provide the maximum performance increase. Here's how Nailon "tunes" a barrel.

Chamber: "It is possible to get a chamber on a factory gun that is a little off. It's not real common, but we do check it," he notes. "The most common problem we find is a chamber that is a little short."

The problem with a short chamber, according to Nailon, is that it sometimes allows the unfolded crimped portion of the shell to protrude into the forcing cone, resulting in a restriction of the wad/shot charge as it moves forward. This increases chamber pressure, recoil and shot deformation, all of which detract from performance.

7

While each component of a shot shell is important, the most vital is the pellet charge. Everything Nailon does in tweaking a barrel for maximum performance is intended to "baby" the pellets out the barrel in an undeformed state.

"This may be a little thing," he states, "but I like a chamber about .060-inch longer than normal specifications, especially if the shooter is reloading his shells. As a shell is reloaded and fired, it tends to stretch a little and a slightly longer chamber is an asset."

Excessively overlength chambers, however, are a drawback.

"Many people," Nailon explains, "ask about firing 2¾-inch shells in a three-inch chamber. It works okay, but downrange performance suffers, because the shot column has a one-quarter-inch run to the forcing cone at its highest pressure point. Side pressures here tend to beat the pellets more than a chamber of proper length."

Forcing Cone Length: Just ahead of the chamber is the forcing cone. As its name implies, it is essentially a funnel that guides the wad/shot charge from the chamber into the bore. The mormal length of factory forcing cones is between one-half- and five-eighths-inch, depending upon the gauge. Nailon says this is much too short.

"The shot column length," he explains, "is between one inch in light loads, and over 1½ inches in heavy loads. As the lower pellets in that shot charge are rammed into the upper pellets, outward pressure is tremendous at the moment the shot charge moves from chamber to forcing cone. Since the shot column is moved through a cone one-half its length, with as much as 10,000 psi behind it, it becomes obvious that many pellets are deformed before they even get into the bore."

Nailon's solution is to lengthen the forcing cone, a standard gunsmith tactic. How much he lengthens it, though, may surprise some folks.

"I feel 1½ inches is the minimum," he states, "and my own tests, which involved both stationary pattern board testing, and tests conducted at our moving pattern board (where precise target speeds can be set and shot strings of up to sixteen feet in length can be accurately measured) indicates that cones of over 2½ inches will help, not hurt."

If longer forcing cones are an asset, why don't more factory guns have them?

"It's simple and cheap to make a short forcing cone," Nailon notes, "and there still are some of the old paper over-wad shells out there, where a short and abrupt forcing cone is needed to make a good gas seal. But with modern plastic wads, the short cones are obsolete. All they do is raise pressures, increase recoil and deform shot."

Some of the biggest offenders in the short forcing cone area are the mid-priced Italian and Spanish shotguns, because many shooters in those areas still rely on the old paper over-wad shells.

Bore: Larry Nailon is a big believer in backbored barrels. Backboring, for those not familiar with the term, is the deliberate overboring of the bore to a point larger than standard industry specifications for true cylinder bore in that particular gauge.

To understand why Nailon considers this an important component of the high performance barrel, a disertation on choke is required.

As used by shotgunners, the term choke describes two dissimilar, but related measurements: (A) The exact inside diameter (ID) of the point of maximum constriction at the muzzle end of the barrel, and (B) the percentage of pellets in the shot charge arriving within a thirty-inch circle at a

Clearview makes a variety of custom-machined choke tubes that are matched to the ID of the gun's bore. Longer tubes are favored for excellent performance.

range of forty yards for all gauges, excepting the .410, which is measured at thirty yards.

The first measurement is made in thousandths of an inch increments (i.e., a choke construction of .719), while the second is expressed in terms of percentages, as in a seventy percent pattern.

The seventy percent would equal the current industry standards for a full choke. If the shooter wanted to put a full-choke tube into a 12-gauge, he would reach for one of around .695-inch. The reason is that industry standards list "full-choke" muzzle constriction at .035-inch over specified bore diameter. In a 12-gauge shotgun, specified cylinder bore diameter is .729-inch. A constriction of .695-inch would produce the required .035-inch muzzle constriction to deliver full-choke patterns.

Choke is the relationship between the bore diameter and the amount of constriction at the muzzle. One achieves precise degrees of choke by installing an equally precise amount of muzzle constriction in relationship to the bore diameter.

But while those who make choke tubes can control the inside diameter of their product down to a thousandth of an inch — plus or minus — what happens if the barrel maker is wildly off on his equally important bore dimensions?

What happens is that whatever degree of choke is marked on the choke tube now becomes nothing more than a rough idea of the pattern percentages that particular tube will produce.

It is not uncommon — indeed, it is common — for factory barrels to vary considerably from specified industry standards.

None of the above explains why Nailon favors backboring. But this will:

"The degree of pattern control you exercise through the use of screw-in choke tubes is dependent upon the degree of constriction difference between the bore diameter and the ID of the choke tube. If you have a factory barrel with a bore diameter of .725-inch and you install a choke tube with an ID of .715-inch, you have an improved cylinder choke," Nailon explains.

"If the barrel has a bore diameter of .750-inch and you want to install an improved cylinder constriction of .010-inch, all you need to do is put in a choke tube with an ID of .740-inch. You have the same amount of constriction with either setup and you'll get the desired improved cylinder pattern.

larger barrel/tube combination."

Why? Easy to figure! The goal of the high-performance shotgun is to get the pellets out of the barrel undeformed, and that's easier to do if the pellets have a bigger hole to go through as they leave the barrel!

"Once your shot charge enters the choke constriction, the pellets, if they are lead, can only do one of two things," Nailon claims. "They either can reposition themselves to pass through the smaller area (one pellet moving ahead or behind another) or they will be deformed. There's no other option. With the backbored barrel and the larger choke tube in use, the pellets have more room to reposition and fewer are deformed."

With steel shot, the situation changes. Pellets can either reposition — or damage the choke! Steel shot doesn't have the option of deforming as easily as lead. That's one reason why backboring is even more important for waterfowlers than other shooters.

As a personal note, in my own battery is a Franchi Prestige 12-gauge with a twenty-six and a twenty-eight-inch barrel. One of the first to be imported into the country, the barrels had fixed chokes and were fitted quickly with Tru-Choke tubes. The gunsmith who did the fitting mentioned that the twenty-eight-inch barrel had an ID larger than the shorter tube. My patterning test showed that with identical loads, and the exact same choke tube, the twenty-eight-inch barrel delivers patterns about ten percent tighter than the twenty-six-incher, and they are much more uniform! Backboring works!

How far to overbore depends upon the individual barrel. Nailon feels most will take between .010-inch and .015-inch without difficulty. Going over .015-inch can result in a slight velocity loss, although it does tend to produce larger useful patterns. Nailon, who has one 12-gauge back-

Larry Nailon has spent years searching for maximum performance from a shotgun. His work is respected.

bored to .750-inch (.021-inch) over industry specs, reports that one-ounce shot loads lack the pellets to fill the larger pattern properly, but that this gun shoots marvelously with 1⅛-ounce loads.

To be most effective, Nailon finds it best to machine his custom choke tubes in precise increments of .005-degree over backbore diameter, allowing a fine degree of pattern control.

For those who don't want the backbore option, Nailon's custom tubes are matched to the existing barrel ID. This requires the barrel be sent to him for precise measurements, so the exact degree of choke constriction over the bore diameter can be maintained.

One additional step Nailon takes is to burnish the bore.

"If the bore isn't perfectly mirror smooth," he has found, "it tends to accumulate fouling, especially plastic fouling from the wad itself, at a much higher rate. This fouling acts to increase friction as the wad/shot charge moves through the barrel, decreasing velocity and increasing recoil. In extreme cases, it can actually impede the performance of the wad and cause pellet deformation."

Most makers only finish the bore to "near smoothness." Complete polishing is a time-consuming step and time is money in mass production. Even if your bore is chrome-lined, that's no guarantee it is smooth. Chrome is only as smooth as the surface over which it is applied, and if the metal wasn't polished to mirror smoothness before the chrome was applied, you'll still have a rough bore!

If you're one of the savvy shotgunners who cleans his bore with 0000 steel wool wrapped around a bore brush, you're doing a little burnishing every time you clean the gun; in time you'll have it burnished. Nailon speeds up the procedure with a series of specially designed hones running down to 800 grit.

"A mirror-smooth bore," Nailon notes, "is just one of those small things that combines with others to increase overall performance, and it makes cleaning a much easier task."

Once Nailon has tweaked the barrel this far, all that remains is the choke. Again, he disagrees with the manufacturers.

"Once the pellets enter the choke constriction," he contends, "they can either reposition or deform. Our goal is to give them the maximum opportunity to reposition before they begin to deform.

"Most factory choke tubes," he continues, "are about 1½ inches long. That requires the shot to reposition in a limited amount of space. If you double the choke length, you double the time and distance you have for that. All other factors being equal, longer choke tubes deform less shot, and, remember, deforming the least amount of shot is our goal when creating a true high performance shotgun barrel."

Nailon combines three-inch tube length with an inner taper that combines a cone, plus parallel surfaces, instead of the traditional cone style that places the maximum constriction at one extremely short point. The addition of the parallel surfaces is a further aid in allowing the shot to reposition itself.

Making his custom choke tubes is considerably more difficult than producing the standard factory tubes. It is more time consuming and expensive because, as a machinist's rule of thumb, you cannot — in high-speed production — hold precise tolerances when boring over two times the length of your diameter. To make his tubes, Nailon must rely on a series of precise fine cuts, instead of accomplishing it all in one pass.

What the customer receives in a set of tubes bored in precise increments of .005-inch over the measured bore diameter of his barrel, giving the shooter the ultimate degree of pattern control.

While some casual shooters may feel Nailon is chasing the elusive nit, the net effect of each modification raises the overall performance of the gun/load combination.

That becomes quite clear when Nailon takes one of his high-performance barrels to his specially designed moving target that allows precise measurements of the load's shot string.

"On moving targets," he claims, "the length of the shot string determines the number of pellets that can strike a moving target with a properly placed shot, and that is the only true measure of performance on moving targets. It's simple mathematics: The velocity of a thirty-five mile-per-hour target is 616 inches per second. At that speed, it requires only 4.8 hundredths of a second to pass through a thirty-inch pattern. With a six-foot shot string like that produced by many gun/load combos at forty yards, you would require a pellet velocity of 1500 fps to allow all the pellets to arrive before the target passes through the thirty-inch pattern. That's not possible. In fact, the average #8 pellet has slowed to about 660 fps at forty yards and would require a shot string of about thirty-two inches to deliver all the pellets before the target crosses the pattern.

"That," he continues, "assumes that one hundred percent of the pellets are in the pattern and that doesn't happen. Full choke performance is around seventy-five percent and forty yards, so a six-foot shot string with only seventy-five percent of the original shot charge in the thirty-inch pattern will only deliver thirty percent of the starting shot charge before the target passes at thirty-five miles per hour. That's why the shortest possible shot string is critical to downrange performance.

And that's why Nailon endeavors to get every pellet out of the barrel undeformed, because what constitutes the shot string is the pellets that were deformed upon firing!

For those interested in a more detailed examination of the subject of high performance, Nailon has produced a couple of informative, technical booklets on the subject. They are available for a nominal fee from Clearview Industries. — *Rod Hunter*

CHAPTER 2

INS AND OUTS OF SCREW-IN CHOKES

Screw-in choke tubes afford tremendous versatility.
Many clay target shooters find this allows them to
use the same gun in the field as well as on the range.

Understanding These Tools Can Make You A Better Wingshooter

THEY HAVE been called one of the greatest innovations for shotgunners since the plastic wad cup, and they may well be. Thanks to the interchangeable choke tube, gone are the days when a shooter desiring to change the performance of his shotgun had to change barrels, or hang a bulbous device on the end of it.

Now, armed with a handful of small metal tubes and a wrench to install them, the one-gun hunter can slip in any degree of pattern spread he so chooses, and that range of pattern control can be far greater than that ever achieved with fixed chokes.

Most of us grew up accepting the fact that when we purchased a shotgun, we had a limited range of pattern control available. Traditionally, you could get a cylinder bore (forty percent pattern at forty yards), improved cylinder (fifty percent) modified (sixty percent) or full (seventy percent). Skeet shooters also had a special "skeet" choke as an option that fell somewhere between cylinder and improved cylinder (about forty-five percent). That was it, and a shooter had to live with his choice. Not so today.

Interchangeable tubes are considered essential by expert sporting clays shooters who routinely face a varied array of targets. The ability to quickly tighten or open a gun's patterns pays large dividends in this most demanding game.

Thanks to the interchangeable choke tube, not only does the shooter have the option of selecting any of the above degrees of choke, but also skeet II (about fifty-five percent), improved modified (sixty-five percent) extra full (seventy-five-plus percent) as well as some specialty tubes that help open patterns quicker than straight cylinder choke.

For the one-gun hunter, the range of versatility is tremendous, allowing him to quickly and inexpensively select the optimum pattern for anything from fifteen-yard woodcock to fifty-yard geese!

Unfortunately, for every shooter who is realizing this degree of versatility, there are many who are not, and that often stems from a basic misunderstanding of what "choke" actually is and how it is achieved.

What we refer to as choke is a term used to describe two different but related shotgun functions: (1) The actual measured constriction of the shotgun's bore at the muzzle and (2) the actual degree of pattern spread. The latter usually is measured in terms of the percentage of pellets the load will place in a thirty-inch circle at a range of forty yards (thirty yards for the .410).

The actual muzzle constriction is measured in thousandths of an inch, and knowledgeable shooters often refer to these increments as "points of choke." For example, a constriction of .005-inch would be five points, while .019-inch would be nineteen points.

The degree of constriction needed to produce different chokes varies from gauge to gauge. And, translating this into more commonly used choke terms — using the 12-gauge, as an example — we find the American standard bore and choke dimensions call for a 12-gauge bore of .729-inch, with no constriction producing a cylinder choke; .005-inch for

When armed with a proper selection of choke tubes, a shooter can use one gun for many shotgunning chores.

Skeet I; .009-inch is improved cylinder; .012 inch, Skeet II; .019-inch, modified; .025-inch, improved modified; .035-inch, full, with extra-full and super-full chokes running from .045- to .089-inch.

From the above, it would seem a simple matter to select any degree of choke the shooter desires just by screwing in

Special steel shot choke tubes allow the use of ultra-hard shot for waterfowling without fear of barrel damage.

a choke tube of the proper constriction. Install a .019-inch tube, and you should get a modified pattern that puts sixty percent of the pellets into a thirty-inch circle at forty yards. In reality, however, it doesn't always work that way.

The degree of constriction of the choke tube is called the choke, but that alone does not determine the actual amount of constriction being produced. What does determine that is the true bore diameter of the shotgun.

It is the relationship between the constriction in the tube and the bore size (inside diameter or ID) that determines how much actual constriction is produced.

If that is confusing, let me attempt to clear it up, using the 12-gauge as an example. If a shooter has a 12-gauge with a true .729-inch ID and he installs a choke tube with a .710-inch ID, then you have a true nineteen-point constriction and a modified choke.

A number of companies offer aftermarket shotgun tubes designed to produce extra-full patterns. They are popular with turkey hunters and card shooters.

Quick opening tubes, like skeet 1 or straight cylinder, are ideal for close flushing quail and woodcock.

If, however, that barrel ID is actually .745-inch, your .710-inch tube now is giving you thirty-five points of constriction — or a full choke. It makes no difference that the tube is marked "modified." Shot charges can't read, they only respond. You have thirty-five points and a full choke!

Should the barrel have a true ID of .720-inch, then the .710-inch tube is providing only .010-inch constriction or about an improved cylinder.

Sound farfetched? Not at all! In fact, in conversations with a number of gunsmiths who specialize in the instal-

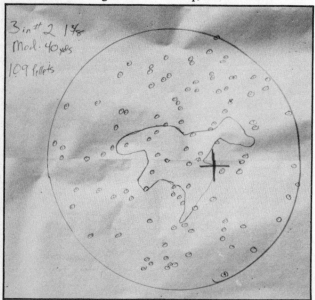

lation and manufacture of interchangeable tubes, I have been told it is quite common to see 12-gauge barrels with true ID measurements running from .710- to .750-inch!

My own Franchi Prestige model is an excellent example. I purchased this gun when it first was imported into the country — and before interchangeable chokes were offered as a factory option. The gun came with twenty-six- and twenty-eight-inch ribbed barrels, and the first thing I did was to send them off for installation of the then popular Tru-Choke system.

When the barrels were returned, the gunsmith who had done the job included a short note informing me that the twenty-eight-inch barrel had a slightly larger ID than the shorter barrel. That made a significant difference at the patterning board.

With the full choke tube installed in the twenty-six-inch barrel, Federal 3 dram #7½ trap loads delivered patterns of seventy-three percent, standard for full choke. Screwing the same tube into the twenty-eight-inch barrel produced eighty-three percent patterns with the same load! That relationship remained constant with each tube in the set. The longer barrel, with its larger ID, delivered patterns averaging nine to ten percent tighter than had the twenty-six-inch barrel with the same tubes.

A handicap? Not as long as I am aware that those tubes are throwing patterns one choke tighter than marked.

Interchangeable choke tubes can deliver ideal patterns with steel shot. In most cases, shooters should select a tube with less constriction than needed with lead shot.

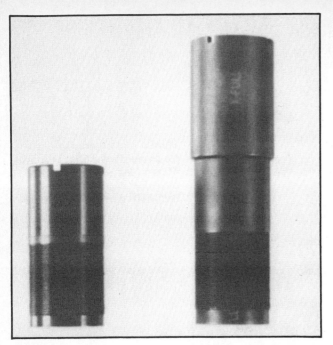

While flush-fitting tubes are a good choice for lead shot, some makers suggest external tubes for steel.

Actually, the patterns from the twenty-eight-inch barrel are generally more uniform and evenly distributed than those from the twenty-six-inch barrel. This brings up another point concerning interchangeable choke tubes.

As a general rule, it has been found that barrels with oversize IDs do not require as much choke constriction to produce the same pattern percentages as barrels with standard or undersize IDs. In simple terms, this means there is a larger hole in the muzzle for the shot to exit, and this tends to help reduce shot deformation and the number of flyer pellets in the pattern. As a result, they tend to deliver more uniform patterns.

The larger bore diameter also reduces friction in the bore as the shot charge hurtles down it. This tends to increase shot charge velocities and reduce recoil.

Many savvy shooters have their barrels reamed to a larger ID — a process called backboring — in order to gain these advantages. With such a barrel, it is not uncommon to have an improved cylinder tube deliver improved modified patterns!

Barrels with undersize IDs produce the reverse: more friction, more recoil, more deformed pellets and, generally, poorer patterns. Such guns also are common, especially if they are a model not originally intended for the American market. Much of the world still relies on the old fiber wad system which does not seal propellent gases as well as do

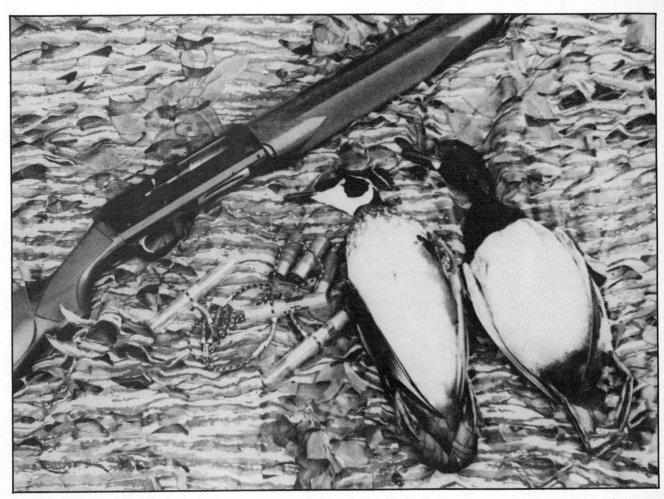

Every major gunmaker now offers interchangeable choke tubes as factory items. However, many shooters who are looking for the maximum in versatility often purchase additional tubes offere by aftermarket manufacturers.

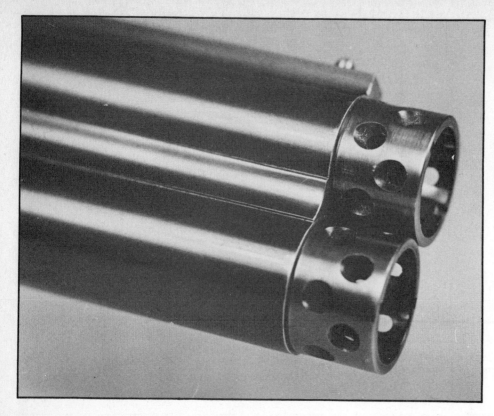

Muzzle brakes are featured on some choke tubes today. These Clearview tubes help diminish muzzle flip by redirecting propellent gases.

plastic wad cups. A "tight" bore is an advantage here, and you will find a number of such 12-gauges with IDs in the .710- to .720-inch range.

What this means to the user of interchangeable choke tubes is simple: You'll know the ID of your tubes, but unless you know the ID of your barrel, you cannot predict pattern performance accurately. Smart shooters pattern their tubes to learn what they are really getting.

The problem with varying barrel IDs is common enough that one company, Clearview Products, Inc., 3021 N. Portland, Oklahoma City, OK 73107, offers what could be termed a "custom" choke tube service. They require the customer send them the barrel, which they carefully measure to determine the exact ID. Then the tubes are machined for *that* gun to provide exact degrees of constriction based upon the barrel ID. These tubes have become extremely popular with sporting clays experts, who face targets at widely varying ranges, as well as with discriminating shooters who demand precise pattern control.

If the problem of varying barrel IDs and their effects on choke tube performance is enough to cause confusion, there are other factors that can cause your tubes not to deliver the pattern percentages marked on them. Most important is hardness of the shot within the shell.

Round, undeformed shot flies more true than shot that has been flattened partially and deformed by set-back pressures that occur upon firing. Deformed pellets usually become "flyers" that leave the main pattern and rob it of uniform density.

Hardening shot requires antimony, which is not an inexpensive substance. As a result, ammomakers attempting to keep prices down may scrimp on this, especially in their low-priced, promotional or field loads.

The difference in patterning performance between "soft" shot (two percent or less antimony) and "hard" shot (five to six percent) can be significant.

In one test, I patterned several Federal 3 dram #7½ Champion trap loads from the full-choke tube of my twenty-eight-inch Prestige barrel and got an average of eighty-three percent. Opening several shells and replacing the shot with low antimony bagged shot from the loading bench dropped the patterns to sixty-eight percent — a fifteen percent decrease. Opening a few more and replacing the shot with hard Lawrence Brand magnum shot brought the patterns up to eighty-one percent. The only variable was the hardness of the shot in the shell, yet it changed the patterns considerably.

Shot size also can play a role. You generally find larger shot patterns a bit tighter than those fired with smaller shot. This fact has not been lost on many top sporting clays shooters who frequently shoot an entire round with an improved cylinder choke. They select loads of soft #9s for close shots to open patterns quickly, and 3 dram #7½ trap loads to tighten patterns enough to reach out and break forty-yard-plus targets.

Shotshell velocity is another factor. The higher the velocity of the load, the more pressure and set-back will be realized, and the more the shot will be deformed. The better high-velocity loads use extremely hard shot — often plated with copper and nickel and buffered with ground plastic — to control deformation and produce good patterns. The cheaper high-velocity loads with plain black shot seldom pattern well. If this is what you are using and you're blaming poor patterns on your choke tubes, you may have the wrong villain.

Each of the previously mentioned factors also will affect shotguns with fixed chokes in the same manner. Factors such as barrel ID variations, shot hardness and velocity are not restricted to screw-in tubes. They can screw up the patterns on any shotgun!

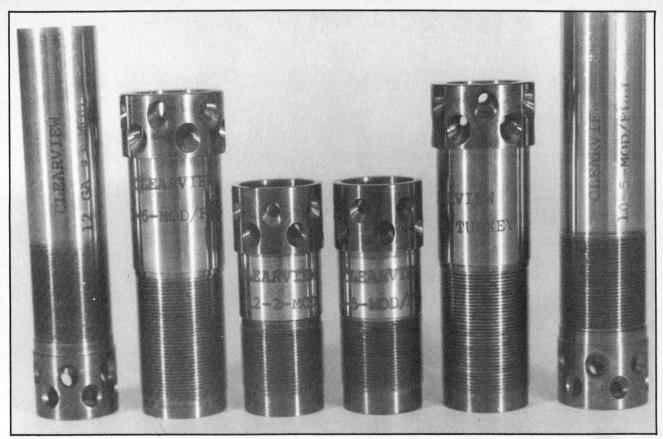

Clearview tubes are available for many guns, but one must specify the manufacturer and model of his shotgun.

But the shooter armed with interchangeable choke tubes, at least, has an inexpensive means for correcting them and still obtain effective patterns. The fixed-choke shooter is pretty much stuck with what he has.

When it comes to selecting choke tubes, shooters have a wide range of options. If your present gun is not fitted to accept them, a number of companies perform that task well. In addition to Clearview Products, both Hastings Company (Box 24, Clay Center, KS 67432) and Pro Port Ltd. (41302 Executive Dr., Mount Clemens, MI 48045-3448) install tubes. Clearview uses their own system for 10-, 12-, 16- and 20-gauge guns, while Hastings and Pro Port use the Briley system that can be installed in all gauges.

Several years ago, Hastings installed the Briley system in my Mossberg .410 pump and increased the versatility of the little gun immensely! Screw-in systems are not confined to the larger bores.

Shooters who already own guns threaded for any of the various factory choke systems may find the factory-offered tubes are rather limited in scope. Clearview and Hastings also offer replacement tubes covering the full range from cylinder to extra-full that fit the popular factory thread systems.

There are a number of different systems in use and not all of them interchange. This requires shooters to specifically state the make and model of their gun to be assured of receiving the correct tubes when ordering aftermarket tubes.

In actual use, interchangeable choke tubes are simple items, but there are a few do's and don'ts that shooters must adhere to or risk damage to the gun.

Most important is installation of the tube into the barrel. The tube must be installed fully and bottomed out in the threads. It should be firm, snug, hand tight, and not over-torqued.

If a tube should back out even slightly, there is a real risk of gun damage. Remington's Rem Choke system is notorious for backing out with heavy recoiling loads and shooters using this system are advised to check the tube tightness frequently! The other systems are not known for such problems, if they are snugged down hand tight.

Tubes should never — I mean, *never* — be installed without lubrication on the threads, and standard grade gun or light machine oil is not acceptable lubrication. They offer no real support to the threads. Far better choices are Never-Seez, or Lubriplate or one of the many specific choke-tube lubricants incorporating either of these ingredients.

Threaded barrels never should be fired without a tube in place, since such activity can damage the threads or worse!

It also is a good idea not to leave tubes in the barrel indefinitely. At least once a year, the tube should be removed, cleaned and the barrel threads also cleaned of old lube, before the tube is re-lubed and returned to the gun. Leaving tubes in place for a few years and just "forgetting about them" sometimes can result in a stuck tube that will require the services of a gunsmith to remove.

Other than that, there isn't much required to get the full benefit from these modern pattern control marvels. Just don't forget them when you head for the field! — *Chris Christian*

When chronographing shotshells, use a benchrest to ensure your aim is directly through the skyscreen triangles.

YOU CAN CHRONOGRAPH YOUR SHOTGUN

Here's A Method That Tells You How Fast Those Pellets Travel To The Target

EVER WONDERED about the ballistic performance of shotshell loads? Sure, how they pattern and whether they bring down birds are the ultimate measures of effectiveness. But what about the velocity of the shot itself and the energy delivered?

All that most of us know about the exterior ballistics of a shot string is what we read in catalogs or loading manuals. Such data is developed in special heavy pressure and velocity barrels, not the kind of tubes that grace the guns we use afield.

But there are those who have inquiring minds and want to know these things. John E. Ross is one of them, so we went to him to learn what his investigations had turned up in the way of solid fact.

Shortly after chronographs became readily available to those of us in the thin wallet crowd, I wanted to clock the velocity of shot from scatterguns. But I've been reluctant to set a couple hundred dollars worth of electronic gadgetry in front of the muzzle and fire away. With my luck, a stray pellet would punch through the transistors and diodes and that would be the end of my chronograph.

Oehler's Model 35P chronograph system eliminates my worries. The machine's electronic heart sits at my elbow on the shooting bench. Only its eyes — the Skyscreens — are out in harm's way.

These I protected with three-quarter-inch plywood shields, cut to cover the screen and light diffusers, but open, of course, over the shooting area. A piece of 2x4 separates the shields from screens. The plywood shield is nailed to the 2x4 and then bored with a five-eighths-inch drill to fit over the half-inch thinwall conduit which supports the screens.

In the bottom of the 2x4, perpendicular to the five-eighths-inch hole, drill a pilot hole with a 3/16-inch bit. Use a hex-head two-inch by one-quarter-inch sheetmetal screw in the pilot hole to lock the shields in place. The shields keep the diffusers from being hit by shot wads during testing.

The firm's Model III Skyscreens provide an ample "window" for clocking shot columns. The shooting area is a more or less truncated triangle thirteen inches wide at the top, twelve inches high and four inches wide at the bottom.

Shields of 3/4-inch plywood are easily constructed and fixed to the chronograph's rail. It important to protect unit's screens and diffusers from stray shot and wads.

According to Oehler, the screens give 103 square inches of shooting area, three times as much as the system with the next largest window.

The Model 35P employs three screens, providing a proof channel which helps check the accuracy of each shot that's recorded. For most applications, including measuring velocity of shot, Oehler recommends four-foot spacing for the primary screens. The proof screen is placed in the middle of the spread.

With the proof channel, the chronograph will alert you when the difference between the primary velocity and the proof velocity exceeds one percent if screens are set with four-foot spacing. In the case of shotshells, the chronograph will let you know if the difference between primary and proof channels exceeds about twelve feet per second. That's accuracy!

If the difference is larger than one percent with four-foot spacing, the reading will flash on the screen and will be marked with an asterisk on the paper printout.

Oehler also recommends that, when clocking shot columns, the first screen be placed three or four feet from the muzzle. In my tests, I located the center of the spread ten feet from the muzzle. I was concerned that the awesome muzzle blast from the 3½-inch 12-gauge shells I wanted to measure would trigger the Skyscreens.

I needn't have worried. James Bohls at Oehler said the structure of the muzzle blast from a discharging shotgun is much different from that of a rifle or handgun. Consequently, while muzzle blast from a shotgun will "blow the screens around," as Bohls puts it, the blast will not trigger them.

The following steps are all you need to begin chronographing shotshell velocities with the Model 35P:

1. Shoot from a supported rest on a bench. It is important the shotgun be sighted like a rifle so the charge passes through the measurement area of the screens.

2. Place a target (a bullseye pistol target works well) at fifty yards for a consistent aiming point.

3. Set up the Skyscreens using four-foot spacing, and place the first screen three feet from the muzzle.

4. Align the screens so that, when you look down the rib or over the shotgun sight, the bead is just under the bullseye and centered within the "triangle within a triangle" pattern made by the three Skyscreens.

5. Plug in the screens and you are ready to go.

6. Test a minimum of five rounds — ten is better — for each load you chronograph.

I tested a dozen different loads in a variety of shotguns. Three of the guns were pumps — Mossberg's Ulti-Mag Model 835 with twenty-four-inch and twenty-eight-inch barrels, a Remington 870 Express and a Winchester Model 12 with a twenty-eight-inch modified tube. I also tested the system with a Parker Reproduction Steel Shot Special. A side-by-side double, the Parker was the acid test of alignment of barrel and Skyscreen window.

Shooting shotguns from a bench can be cruel punish-

A heavy wad from a 12-gauge shattered this plywood shield, but the diffuser was unhurt.

ment. A "slip-on" rubber recoil pad helps, but not much. A sandbag also can be placed between butt and shoulder to dampen recoil. But the best technique is just to hold on tight and take your medicine.

I encountered only one problem in chronographing shot shells. About three-quarters of the way through my initial test with the center screen ten feet from the muzzle, a velocity reading flashed on the machine and was starred on the tape. This is an indication of a suspect velocity.

At the time, I was shooting 12-gauge, 3½-inch Federal factory shells loaded with 1-9/16 ounces of Ts. Velocity variation was about four percent, instead of one percent between proof and primary channels. The mean velocity for the five shots was 1218 fps out of a twenty-eight inch barrel.

Later tests with the same ammo in a twenty-four-inch barrel yielded a five-shot mean velocity of 1208 fps with no indications of suspect velocity. In discussing the siutation with Bohls, he said the purpose of the suspect velocity message is only to call one's attention to a possible error, but that the shooter must decide whether or not the reading is reasonable.

Measuring the velocity of shot charges with a Skyscreen system is less precise than using Skyscreens to check the speed of a single projectile. You know when a bullet triggers the system. But with shot columns, one needs to question precisely what is being measured and where the reading is being taken.

As it leaves the muzzle, a shot column contains pellets, a wad and a few unburned granules of powder. The shot

For his tests, author used Federal and Winchester ammunition and (l to r) a Remington 870 Express with 28-inch barrel, a Winchester Model 12 with 28-inch barrel and a Mossberg Model 835 Ulti-Mag with 24- and 28-inch barrels.

column is at least as long as the wad and probably longer. Shot charges, of course, contain many projectiles, all moving at about the same speed. But some are traveling faster than others. The difference in velocity of shot pellets causes the shot charge to string out on its way to the target.

As it passes through the first screen, a lead pellet probably turns on the chronograph. But which pellet triggers the middle or the proof of channels? And which one turns off the machine at the third screen? Is it the same pellet? Or is it a different one? I don't know.

To minimize the effect of the length of the shot column, place the first screen three of four feet from the muzzle as Oehler recommends. The closer the screens are to the muzzle, the shorter the shot string and the more accurate the reading.

If the chronograph is being triggered by the first pellet, which must be the fastest in the charge, are the machine's readings an accurate measurement of the velocity of the entire shot charge? According to Bohls, the timer is probably reading the velocity of the first pellet which may be two to five percent faster than the average speed for the whole charge.

Oehler's two to five percent figure is based on their comparison of velocities clocked by Model 35Ps and disjunctor coil systems used by ammo manufacturers and ballistic labs to measure the average velocity of shot columns. Oehler Research makes both types of chronographs.

Bohls explains that disjunctor systems generally include a three-inch-diameter pipe mounted with two coils spaced three feet apart. A shot charge is fired down the pipe from a pressure and velocity barrel. As the charge passes under the coil, the center of the mass of shot triggers the induc-

tance of the coil, thus sending the signals that operate the chronograph.

So much for background. Let's look at a practical application of the chronograph to measuring shot velocities. I've been, and still am, a fan of the 3½-inch, 12-gauge Super Mag introduced jointly by Federal and Mossberg. It is, I think, the most efficient and effective shotshell for hunting geese.

But I was curious about the actual velocity of the pellets. According to Federal's catalogs, the muzzle velocity of a 1-9/16-ounce load of BB shot in their 3½-inch, 12-gauge shell is 1365 fps. But five shots out of a twenty-eight-inch Mossberg Ulti-Mag barrel fitted with an improved cylinder tube averaged 1240 fps, according to the Model 35P chronograph. The difference, when the instrumental velocity is corrected to muzzle velocity, is about 120 fps.

Five rounds of 12-gauge, 3½-inch shells loaded with 1-9/16 ounces of #2 shot produced a mean velocity of 1252 fps. Same load with "T"-size shot generated a mean velocity of 1218 fps, all significantly lower than the advertised 1365 fps.

And if Oehler is right and velocities recorded on the 35P actually are higher than what the load produces when measured with a disjunctor coil system, then the difference between my readings and actual velocity is greater still.

For control, I chronographed five rounds of Winchester's AA Plus, light trap 12-gauge loads, using a Model 12 with a twenty-eight-inch modified barrel. The mean velocity of these rounds was 1150 fps, more or less on the money for a target load. The same ammo in the twenty-eight-inch Mossberg barrel clocked 1146 fps, even though the Mossberg bore diameter of .775 inch is .045-inch larger than the .730 bore of the Winchester Model 12.

For a further check, I clocked ten three-inch WW Steel 1¼-ounce loads of #1s through the twenty-eight-inch tubes of the Parker Reproduction. Velocities averaged about 1367 from the modified bore and a little less in the improved cylinder barrel. These velocities also are close to advertised figures of 1375 fps.

In an attempt to shed light on the discrepancy between reported and actual velocities with Federal steel shot loads, I talked with Mike Larson at Federal. He said bore diameter plays a big difference in velocity and that Federal's velocities were developed in special pressure and velocity barrels.

For shooting shotshells through Oehler's Skyscreens, author used a 25-yard pistol target as an aiming point.

This was confirmed by Paul Escherick at SAAMI. He said temperature, barrel length and bore diameter effect shot velocity. He reported that test barrels are typically cylinder bore. Escherick also said that steel shot load velocities are less consistent from shot to shot, or have a higher standard deviation than lead loads. He would not be specific on the range of standard deviation SAAMI was finding among steel shot loads.

How significant is the discrepancy between actual and advertised velocities? The question is one of delivered energy. A steel BB-size pellet which leaves the muzzle at Federal's advertised velocity of 1365 fps delivers 7.1 foot-pounds of energy at fifty yards.

Determining delivered energy for a single shot is not a simple task. According to Les Roane, a ballistics engineer at H.P. White Laboratory, the premiere ammo-testing facility in the country, a shot pellet leaves the gun at a supersonic speed (in excess of 1070 fps, more or less), but passes through the transonic zone (sound barrier) and becomes subsonic before it hits the target.

Think of the transonic zone as a wall of Jello. At supersonic and subsonic speeds, velocity loss is more or less directly proportional to distance traveled. But in the short transonic zone, velocity loss is much greater. A graph on page 578 of *Hatcher's Notebook* (3rd Edition) shows what happens.

To compute delivered energy, the downrange velocity must be known or a fairly sophisticated mathematical model must be constructed. Reluctant to set the chronograph up at fifty yards and fire at the Skyscreens with steel shot, and unable to afford to have H.P. White labs create and apply the mathematical model, I'll hazard a guess at delivered energy of a Federal "BB" in the 3½-inch, 12-gauge loads.

Let's assume that, in determining the delivered energy of a BB pellet with a muzzle velocity of 1365 fps, Federal either clocked its speed downrange or computed the terminal velocity with a model similar to the one Roane at H.P. White suggests.

If so, then we can make this rough comparison: The speed of the pellets I measured is about nine percent slower than Federal's. If the weight and form of the pellet do not change, then velocity and delivered energy should be directly proportional. Thus, the delivered energy of a BB pellet with a muzzle velocity of 1240 fps would be about 6.4 foot-pounds.

Where does this leave us? The difference of a less than foot-pound of delivered energy is significant as hell to scientists. For a hunter, it may mean nothing at all — if he keeps his shots at waterfowl within fifty yards. Beyond that distance, as we know, pattern density falls apart and more birds are crippled than killed.

While I wish that manufacturers would report velocities from field guns and not special pressure/velocity barrels, I doubt that such will be the case. There's simply too much variation from gun to gun to obtain reliable comparisons.

Chronographing shotshells is a valuable aid in understanding the differences in the performance of one load from another. I'm looking forward — with a little painful dread — to clocking my handloaded steel shot cartridges.

But real performance comes in the field, when sleet spatters on your parka as that huge honker sees you come up out of the pit and tries to outrun your swing. — *John Ross*

CHAPTER 4

A FITTING SOLUTION

It Doesn't Take Big Bucks To Custom Fit Your Shotgun!

Sporting clays shooters are fanatics concerning proper gun fit, and many ranges have instructors who will fit guns to their clients. A gun that is fitted properly to the shooter gives him a distinct edge in this demanding game.

A gun that is fit for one type of shooting can be poor for another. These skeet shooters favor guns that center the pattern at the point of aim. Yet, these guns would be poor choices for the trap range where quick-climbing targets are best handled with guns that place their patterns up to 18 inches high at 40 yards.

NOBODY GIVES it a second thought when they see a rifleman or handgunner making careful adjustments to his sights. In fact, not only is it considered a perfectly normal occurence, but it's a sign of a shooter knowledgeable enough to understand a gun that won't put its payload to point of aim is relatively useless.

Yet, let a shotgunner start tinkering around with his gun, and he is generally branded as some kind of nitpicker who is dabbling in the black arts and probably will screw up a perfectly good scattergun.

Nothing, however, could be farther from the truth. In fact, when a savvy shotgunner begins altering the dimensions and balance points of his favorite smoothbore, he is doing nothing more than the rifleman or pistolero: adjusting his firearm to place the payload at the point of aim.

Unfortunately, he is engaging in the mystic art of shotgun fitting — a relatively simple endeavor that, over the years, has taken on the aura of magic and should be left to the "professionals."

Bull waste!

There is no doubt a shotgun — carefully fitted to the dimensions of a particular individual by someone skilled in that operation — can improve that individual's shooting, but I'm convinced not every scattergunner requires the services of a pro to achieve proper gun fit. In fact, I believe any reasonably experienced shooter — with basic understanding of what the various dimensions on a shotgun stock are intended to accomplish — not only can do a good job of fitting his gun, but possibly do a better job than an outsider. After all, the shooter is the one who will be shooting the gun, not the fitter.

To understand why one should take the time to fit a shotgun, it's necessary to understand exactly what a fitted shotgun is.

Anyone with even below-average hand/eye coordination can stand on a skeet field, have a target launched and smoothly — without any real effort — raise an arm and track the target with his index finger. One doesn't have to consciously work the index finger into position, you just focus on the target with the eyes and the index finger will find it everytime! Were the index finger "loaded," you'd probably break that target every time.

Put a shotgun in the shooter's hands and the picture changes. Now you have a foreign object that must be placed in proper position against the body with contact at four separate spots before you can even consider tracking the target with it. And unless it comes into position in exactly the same manner each time, it won't be looking where you are looking each time. If you and the shotgun aren't "looking" at the same spot, you won't hit much!

The purpose of fitting a shotgun is to turn that foreign object into your index finger. That is done by making the key stock dimensions on the gun match the dimensions of your body.

To understand why you may have to change the dimensions of a perfectly good shotgun to fit your dimensions, it's necessary to know the nomenclature of a stock, and the basic dimensions built into it by gun makers.

Figure A shows how to properly measure these points with the gun placed on a flat surface with any sight beads beyond the end of the surface, or else they will throw off the angles of the critical rear measurements. What we have then are:

Comb Height: (The area between the Es) is where the cheek contacts the gun, and can, to a great extent, determine whether the gun places its shot charge high or low. Consider it to be the elevation adjustment on a rear sight.

The higher the comb height, the higher your eye is above the bore and the higher the gun will shoot. The lower the comb, the lower your eye and the lower the gun will place its pattern. The "universal" comb height for a flat-shooting field gun, which is intended to place the shot charge right where the front bead looks, is 1½ inches. Trap guns and

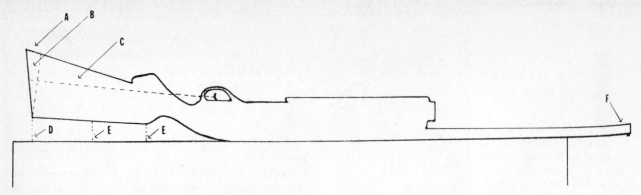

FIGURE A — *It's important to understand the parts of the stock and how they affect the way smoothbore shoots.*

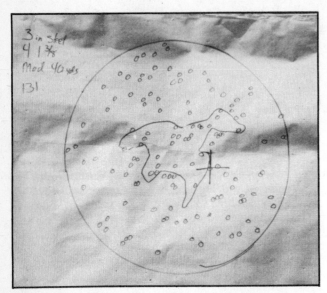

A gun fitted to a shooter will shoot where the gunner looks. That's important if you intend to be on target.

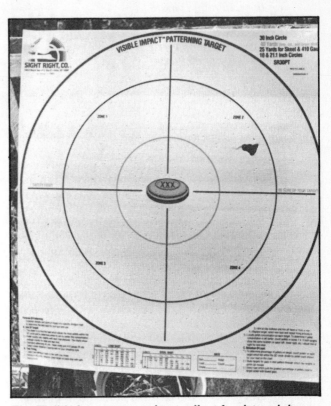

The Visible Impact target is excellent for determining precisely where your gun shoots. It will take a number of shots before a central impact point is "blown out."

those guns fit for live pigeons have a drop at comb of about 1⅜ inches — about one-eighth-inch lower. This elevates the pattern around one foot above bead at forty yards to provide a built-in lead.

That's fine if your face is "average." Shooters with full, fleshy faces may find the extra padding raises the eye farther above the comb and makes the gun shoot higher for them.

Thin-faced shooters may find the gun shooting lower. It has nothing to do with the standard stock dimensions. It's just that our body dimensions aren't standard.

Length Of Pull: Dotted line C is the basic stock length. On factory guns, it falls most commonly between fourteen and 14½ inches.

If your sleeve length is around thirty-two inches, and you commonly shoot with light clothing, this is actually pretty close to the proper length for you — but that's a big, big if!

Suppose your sleeve length is thirty-four to thirty-six inches, or, if a woman or an adolescent, maybe it's twenty-eight inches. Is this the right stock length for you? Not hardly! And, there's no reason why you should have to live with it.

A stock that is too short for your body often will make the gun shoot high. Frequently, it causes you to bang your nose with the trigger hand on firing, and in general, make you crawl around on the stock before you can get a decent gun hold.

A stock that is too long causes problems in mounting the gun, can make it shoot low, increases muzzle weight and impedes your ability to swing on hard, crossing targets.

So why do you need to shoot a stock length that someone else figured was "standard?" The answer is that you don't, and as soon as you stop, your shooting will improve!

Comb height — or more correctly "drop at the comb" — and length of pull are the two most critical measurements on a shotgun stock. Shooting problems often can be corrected with these two alone.

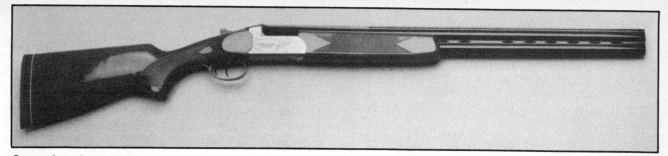

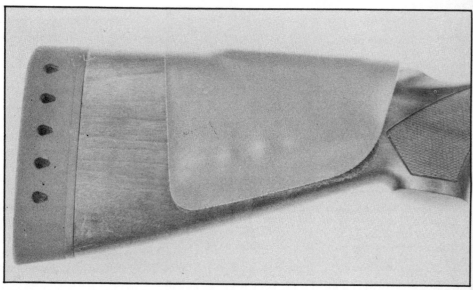

Gunmakers have no idea who will buy their product, so they must build firearms with standard dimensions. This Italian over-and-under (above) will fit some shooter, but it may not be the person who purchased it.

When the author increased the length of pull on one of his favorite guns by installing a thicker recoil pad (right), it caused the gun to shoot low. That was corrected with a stock pad.

There is a relationship between the two that must be understood. Look at the shotgun comb, and you'll see that it slopes downward to the rear. If you alter the length of pull, you automatically will alter the comb height to some extent, and hence affect the elevation of the pattern.

Increase the length of pull and you slide the eye farther down the comb, lowering the pattern placement. Shorten the stock and your eye goes up the comb to raise pattern placement. Any change you make to the length of pull will raise or lower the pattern, requiring you make a change of some type in comb height.

Performance can be improved by altering the above two measurements alone. But, there are some others that also need to be considered.

Pitch: Dotted line B is the angle at which the butt stock meets the shoulder. It is measured by placing the butt pad flush on a hard surface and moving the gun over to an intersecting ninety-degree surface until the top of the receiver touches the surface. Gunsmiths use an L-shaped bracket to provide a horizontal and vertical intersecting ninety-degree surface, but a wall and a floor works fine.

The distance the muzzle is from the vertical surface, in inches, is the pitch measurement. Normal pitch is two to 2½ inches and is called down pitch.

Pitch is a misunderstood function on a shotgun, even by experts. Some consider it far more important than it actually is.

Increasing the down pitch often can help heavy-chested males and well-endowed females by providing a better fit into the shoulder pocket. Decreasing the pitch measurement aids some shooters on flushing birds and quick-rising

trap targets. Some feel a straighter pitch angle also helps reduce muzzle jump on recoil.

Once a shooter has dealt with length of pull and comb height, experimenting with pitch can fine tune the gun further. To increase down pitch, back out the screws holding the recoil pad and insert some cardboard shims at the heel and replace the recoil pad. To decrease pitch, put the shims in at the toe. If you find a particular change in angle helps, leave the shims in place then have a gunsmith measure and cut the butt stock on the new angle.

Heavy-chested shooters also can benefit from cast at toe.

One of the problems with a smooth gun mount is that shotgun butts are made straight up and down, while the shoulder pocket they fit into slants at an angle. Cast at the toe — common in Europe but seldom seen here — addresses this by relieving material from the inside portion of the recoil pad at the toe. That's the left side of the pad for right-handed shooters.

Slender shooters can find this an aid, but it's most advantageous for heavy-chested shooters. It reduces gun canting, gouging, and can improve the swing.

Cast Off/Cast On: Cast off is a slight lateral bend of the butt stock that moves it *away* from the shooter's face. This aids in putting the shooting eye in direct line with the rib. The Europeans use this extensively, but it is absent from standard American guns. United States shooters have learned to compensate by bringing the cheek over the top of the comb, then inclining the head down and forward slightly.

Cast on means there is too much wood on the comb. This

The Convert-A-Stock pads give shooters great leeway in adjusting a pattern's point of impact. Removable shims will raise the comb height and allow a shooter to turn a flat shooting gun into a high shooter quickly.

places the eye out of line with the rib and causes the gun to shoot to the left for a right-hand shooter. This seldom occurs, unless the shooter has a fleshy face, or if the comb height was lowered and the original taper at the top of the comb was not maintained. Consider cast off/cast on to be the windage adjustment on your rear sight.

These are the basic dimensions you will alter in order to fit a standard gun to your non-standard body. Before making any changes, however, you have to know what needs to be fixed — or where your gun is shooting for you now. Standard patterning techniques are not the best way to do this, because when a shooter pre-mounts the gun, he subconsciously crawls around on the stock to position himself on the gun. This defeats the purpose of fitting the gun to you, since you are fitting yourself to the gun!

A better way is as follows: (1) Put up a forty-by-forty-inch target with a small, quail-size central aiming point. (2) Using light loads of 7½ through 9 shot with a full-choked tube in the gun, back off to about twenty to twenty-five yards. (3) Take your normal foot position with the gun butt off the shoulder, lock your eyes on the aiming point, mount the gun and fire quickly. Do not settle the gun into position. Mount and shoot in one fluid motion. (4) Repeat this several times, until you've torn a large, visible hole out of the target.

Some experts use a bed sheet for a target, since it takes a number of shots to punch a hole. I like the Visible Impact Targets (Routes 5 and 20, East Bloomfield, NY 14443), because they're cheaper than bedsheets and do about the same job.

The reason for firing a number of shots is they give you a better indication of how the gun now fits than does just one round. The full choke provides a tight, easily discernable impact point pattern.

Don't attempt to shortcut this procedure. Do it right, and take your time. How well you accomplish this will affect every dimensional modification you make.

Now that you've shot the target, here's what that information will tell you and how to use it:

If there is no single impact point and there are several different "groups," you are not achieving consistent gun mount. This could be due to a stock that is grossly over or under length. Take the shotgun in the trigger hand, assume a grip on the pistol grip/trigger — make certain the gun is unloaded first — then bend the arm upward to form a ninety-degree angle between the forearm and upper arm. Place the butt in the crook of the elbow. If the butt is far short of the elbow crook, the stock is too short. If you can't get the butt in there while maintaining a shooting grip, it is too long.

If it fits well, the problem likely lies in the recoil pad catching clothing and not finding a consistent place on the shoulder. Round off the top of the pad, and you might also consider some cast at the toe. You should not make any drastic alterations, however, until you can punch one hole in the target.

If the gun shoots high, this isn't always bad. Trap shooters, live pigeon shooters and those who pursue fast-flushing birds often fit their guns to pattern six to eighteen inches high at forty yards. Their targets are rising fast, and, in order to hit them with a flat-shooting gun, they would have to swing up and through the target, covering it. With a high-shooting gun, these shooters can keep the bead below the bird where they can see any last-minute erratic moves and let the built-in elevation do the rest.

Before correcting a high-shooting gun, consider the use to which you'll put it. If the pattern center is only three to four inches high — or less — you might find this an asset.

If you're using it for skeet, sporting clays, dove and ducks, you may want a flat-shooting gun. The easiest way to bring the pattern down is to lengthen the stock. A few leather shims slipped under the recoil pad will let you experiment with increased length. Most shooters can handle a longer length of pull without problems, and many experts feel the longer length helps keep the head on the stock better. If the shims work for you, a gunsmith can replace them with permanent spacers.

If you increase stock length to an uncomfortable point without achieving the desired pattern lowering, you'll have to lower the comb. If the wood is of great quality, you may want a stockmaker to do it. If not, you can do it with sandpaper.

Keep the original contour or you may create cast on. And do not go overboard. A change of just one-eighth-inch can alter impact points up to a foot at forty yards. Once you get the comb height down, it can be refinished with Birchwood Casey or similar products available just about anywhere.

An excessively high shooting gun is common if you have cut down a shotgun to fit a woman or child. Since lengthening the stock in this situation is impractical, you'll have to lower the comb.

If the gun shoots low, you can shorten the stock to slide the eye farther up the comb. That's if the stock is overlong. If it's comfortable, it's best to raise the comb height. Moleskin is an effective means for this and many shooters use it.

Proper gun fitting should also take into account the clothing normally worn when using the gun. Heavy clothing will increase the length of pull and often cause a gun to shoot low.

A cheekpiece like the Meadow Industries Convert-A-Stock Pad (P.O. Box 754, Locust Grove, VA 22508) is an inexpensive, soft pad that fits to the comb via velcro strips. I've had one on a gun for years and know they last.

The pad features removeable inserts that allow one to vary the comb height beyond that of the basic pad. Some shooters use them to make a flat-shooting field gun shoot high for trap or on flushing birds. As a side benefit, the soft pad cushions the face during recoil. If you want to correct a low-shooting gun without stock work, this is the best way to go.

If the aesthetics of the pad are unappealing, comb height can be increased with moleskin, then taken to a gunsmith who can use that to build up the comb with glass or inlet a piece of wood to create a new comb.

When a gun shoots to the left for a right-hand shooter, it could be a bent barrel, which a gunsmith can check. More often, though, it indicates a need for cast off. Carefully removing wood from the side of the comb will bring your eye more over the rib and correct the problem.

If your gun shoots to the right, this is not a common problem, but a real bear when it occurs. Again, a bent barrel is a possibility, or it could indicate excessive cast off that is allowing the eye to move too far into the gun. It also could be an excessively low comb that the shooter is compensating for by bringing his head too far over it. This is most common with the old hump-back Browning designs on which increased drop at comb and heel makes the shooter keep his head more erect on the gun.

Obviously, the eye must be moved to the left — if a right-hand shooter. Begin adding moleskin to the cheek side of the comb and see how much effect this has. If it works, it can be made permanent with fiberglass. If it doesn't, experiment with comb height as well.

Lateral pattern placement problems also can be caused when the dominant eye is not on the same side you shoot from. If you're a right-handed shooter with a left master

eye, you will cross fire as the master eye takes over barrel alignment.

Determining your master eye is easy. If a right-handed shooter, hold out the right arm, extend the index finger and, with both eyes open, point it to a spot on the wall about ten feet away. Now, close the left eye. If the finger stays on target, your right eye is dominant. If it moves, you have problems.

This is a more common problem than is realized. A number of shooters don't have their dominant eye on the same side from which they shoot. They have a limited number of options to correct this problem.

The easiest answer — although it sounds the hardest — is to learn to shoot from the other side. It'll take practice, but it is the best bet in the long run, because the gun can be properly fitted, and once you make the switch, you should find your shooting improving.

Some shooters have had success with special shooting glasses that blur or partially blot out the offending dominant eye, allowing the other to take over. You also can order a special cross-over stock, a strange looking affair with tremendous cast off that puts the offside eye over the barrel. As one might expect, such a gun kicks like hell with heavy loads, but it will let you hit!

Fitting a shotgun properly takes time, and a shotgun fitted for one type of shooting may not be the best bet for others. So too, can a shotgun fitted for one type of clothing.

If your goose gun only sees service when you are bundled in heavy layers of Gore-Tex, it doesn't make much sense to fit it while wearing a lightweight summer skeet vest. The extra clothing will lengthen the length of pull.

This is why I feel the shooter is his own best fitter. He understands his requirements far better than a stock tailor.

Whether proper fit is worth the time and effort depends on how badly you want to hit your targets. If you're serious about your scattergunning, you'll find this a fitting solution. — *Rod Hunter*

GOOD THINGS COME IN THREES

All Remington's Over-And-Unders Have Garnered User Friendliness

An experienced hunter, the author took grouse with this Model 32 Remington that was made in the 1930s.

WHEN "REMINGTON" rings in the average shotgunner's ears, the name doesn't conjure up thoughts of over-and-under double-guns. When most of us, especially shotgunners, think about the Remington name, we immediately envision the company's venerable pump-action Model 870, their soft-shooting Model 1100 semi-auto — or both.

Today, the Model 1100 semi has been replaced largely by the Model 1187, the gas-operated semi that is capable of handling target ammo right up through three-inch magnums, without any adjustment. The Model 870 continues to be one of the most sought-after, reliable and best-designed pump guns. Millions of each have been produced and sold over the years.

While the shotgun legacy of Remington has been personified in its 870 and 1100 models via their preponderance in availability, the company's over-and-unders can hardly fall into the category of success stories. They are not even close. The 1100 experienced sales of well over three million in about three decades. It took the 870 about four decades to turn a four-million statistical sales trick. In contrast, the first Remington over-and-under, the Model 32, ran a scant 5000-plus finished guns.

But like a number of models that were introduced at or shortly after the Great Depression, which started in 1929, Model 32 sales were doomed from the start. Thus, the 32 had about as much chance of being a sales barn-burner as I did of becoming president. First, no matter how many swooned over the thought of owning a 32, no one had the few necessary bucks to buy one.

Second, the mind set of that period had swung away from double-guns to the increased firepower of pumps and semi-autos. Those were the days when guys carrying a Model 12 Winchester, as an example, had the plug out and the magazine tube filled to the gills. And many six-shot volleys were loosed at quail, ducks, geese and such.

At that time, "it was the thing to do!" Limiting one's shooting to two shots hadn't entered many minds then. But history tells us that wild game was wonderfully abundant. Evidently, the mind set of the gentry was to shoot, shoot, shoot. And pumps and semis, with their ample magazine tubes, offered the firepower they wanted.

But as weakly as the Model 32 was accepted when it was introduced — in 1932, when the starting price on standard 32s was $75 — this first Remington over-and-under has strong interest of late. In the early 1970s, these unique

These Remington Model 32s, the skeet (left) and the trap, are dependable performers despite their maturity.

This is the Field version of the Model 32 Remington. This shotgun is void of a rib and has a slender forend.

over-and-unders sometimes could be had for say one-half the price of a Parker. Eventually, the shotgun-buying world discovered there were nearly 200,000 Parkers and only 5000 32s, so the price on 32s escalated appreciably. Scanning a recent list, I saw Model 32s for $1300 to $1400. So the public's gun-buying eye has caught up with the worth of the 32.

The 32 was ahead of its time. So that's another factor that kept buyers at bay. Another was that World War II came along, and the Remington facilities quit making sporting guns, where there has traditionally been scant profit, to produce weapons of war.

The first cosmetic feature that put the 32 ahead of its time was separated barrels. To the 1930s shooter, these barrels simply didn't "look" right. History has proved

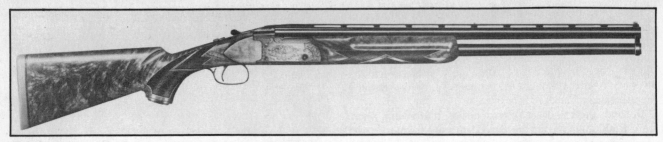

The Remington 3200 "1 of 1,000" Skeet features a high-grade walnut stock and a custom scroll engraving pattern.

Remington correct with their then-new concept, because separated barrels are highly popular today. Why? First, quicker heat dissipation, important to tournament shooters who bang away hundreds of times a day. Second, less wind resistance. On the hard, crossing shots of skeet and sporting clays, the fast-swinging gun is less encumbered by air resistance, if the barrels are separated. On a windy day, a gun with non-separated barrels can be pushed where the shooter doesn't want it to go. But the world was not ready for separated barrels, and that's a pity. They're a far better idea than non-separated barrels.

The Model 32's designer, Crawford Loomis, came up with a sliding top breech cover, the gun's second significant innovation. When opened, the breech cover retracts over the top of the receiver. Upon closing, this breech cover moves forward over the top barrel to lock the barrels in place. John Browning designed his Superposed with an underlocking lug, but this required more depth to that gun's receiver.

The 32's receiver is more shallow in comparison. It was a good enough system for the Krieghoff, a shotgun that sells for about a zillion dollars, or it might as well be that high, since most of us can't afford one. The Swedish-made Valmet (now made in Italy) relies upon a similar top

breech cover system. But this lock-up looked *different* to the 1930s buyer, so he didn't buy. At least, most of them didn't.

The 32 was made in three versions, one for the field, one for trap, one for skeet. The Field 32 is a semi-lightweight. Wonderfully responsive, this model falls within the mould of the traditional game gun. Weight with twenty-eight-inch barrels on a Field 32 owned by my friend, Leonard Reeves, is 7½ pounds. It was offered in three barrel lengths: twenty-six, twenty-eight and thirty inches. I remarked to Leonard how light it felt the first day I hunted with it. I couldn't believe it later that evening when it weighed 7½ pounds on my baby scale. Normally, I carry a 6¼-pound Franchi 48/AL for grouse, but the Remington 32 felt only slightly heavier. It's the gun's great balance that helps it feel lighter. Leonard's Field 32 is choked improved cylinder and improved modified and has no rib.

The first day I hunted with this particular Model 32 Remington it was bitter cold, and I didn't get any shooting at our quarry — ruffed grouse. Two days later, the weather moderated, and I got a second chance to put this venerable 32 to the test on ruffs. It took me over an hour to drive to the steep sidehill laden with grapevine tangles, briars galore and multiflora rose in profusion. This is the type of cover

Typified on the Model 3200 Live Pigeon is gold-filled engraving adorning sides and bottom of the receiver.

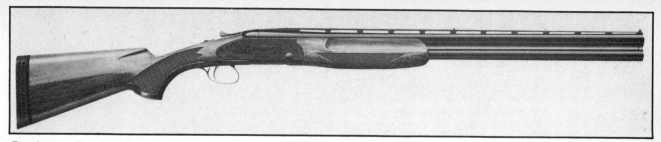

Remington Peerless is available in 26-, 28- and 30-inch barrels with improved cylinder and modified REM choke.

our grouse gravitate to during winter.

My setter, Quill, and I had five flushes in the first three hundred yards. I didn't get a shot until flush number four. It would have been a great shot had I made it, but I didn't. In frustration, I saluted the bird with the second barrel as it disappeared. Then, standing with an empty gun, flush number five occurred within five feet of my toes. Straight-away. In the wide open. I popped open the 32 and heard the empties I had shot at number four go flying, as I watched number five sail away without a shot being fired.

Almost five hours later, I scored with the 32. And my old King, a pointer, made the find. It had been five hours of sweat on steep, snow-covered hills, the crunchy kind where footing is always unstable, so it was a truly rewarding bird

Author enjoys shooting his Remington Model 3200 Live Pigeon. The gun is one of his more prized firearms.

that I hand-carried all the way to the truck, feeling its warmth in one gloved hand, as the other toted the Model 32, a remarkable over-and-under made long ago in the 1930s.

Leonard Reeves' Skeet 32 is heavier in comparison. Well it should be, since skeeters bang away so often and carry the gun at the ready not at all. The Reeves' Skeet 32 weighs seven pounds fifteen ounces with twenty-six-inch barrels. The forearm of the Field is slim, while the Skeet's forearm is thicker and with finger grooves. Both have plastic butt plates.

All of today's skeet guns wear recoil pads, but in the days of the 32, skeet was a low-gun game, and recoil pads of that era hung up too often on clothing during quick mounting. I pulled off the plastic butt plates to see if more wood had been hogged out of the lighter Field 32, compared to the slightly heavier Skeet 32. They were the same. Famed skeeter Alex Kerr shot a 32 a lot, I'm told.

The Trap 32s — called TCs — came in thirty and thirty-two-inch barrel lengths. Reeves has one of these in his collection, too. Weight is eight pounds five ounces with thirty-inch barrels. Other interesting features about the 32 were its mechanical trigger (the Superposed triggers were inertial); its barrel selector, a button in front of the trigger (the Superposed had the sliding top tang safety-shift right or left for barrel selection); its ejectors; and its bore size — the 32 was only made in 12-gauge.

There were only a handful of over-and-under lovers to lament the demise of the 32 when the last one came out of the factory in 1941 or so. Remington didn't see fit to resurrect its over-and-under legacy for over thirty years.

In 1973, they came up with their 3200. The number nomenclature was similar. Ditto for the cosmetics, at least with regard to the separated barrels and top breech lever. Even the engraving of the dogs on the sides of the receiver were identical to that of the old Model 32. But the 3200 was *heavy*! It wasn't even close to being in the classic game gun category, as was the Model 32 Field.

The 3200 had a longer life than the 32, but not much. It died in 1984. Sales figures were much more impressive than for the 32s, with eleven-year sales running at 42,000. Of course, the world had a lot more people in the 1970s, compared to the 1930s. The point is, the 3200 was a great success when matched against the 32's numbers. But Remington's bean counters (probably DuPont's) couldn't be swayed from their decision that the 3200 had to go.

Dead as this gun is in the 1990s, it continues to be a competition favorite. Where shooters bang away by the box, as opposed to counting individual shells, the heavier guns earn their keep with the experienced. Nothing helps reduce

Testing the new Remington Peerless, author found it to be a quick gun for hunting.

felt recoil like added mass, and the 3200s had planty of that.

Like the 32s, the 3200s came in three models, one for the field, one for trap, another for skeet. They all hefted plenty. No hogged-out butt stock wood in any of them. Serious skeeters like to take the Model 3200 twelve bore and fit the barrels up with Briley or Kolar sub-gauge aluminum tubes. These sets of 20, 28 and .410 tubes are hand-fitted to individual 12-gauge guns. The tubes add about fourteen more ounces, but it's out-front weight that tends to keep a gun swinging. This weight also helps alleviate the shotgunner's worst nightmare — stopping the swing.

Serious skeeters who didn't like the extra weight of the sub-gauge tubes could eventually shoot a 3200 four-barrel set, a model introduced in 1979 with .410-, 28-, 20- and 12-gauge barrels, all fit to the same receiver. Skeet 3200s were offered in twenty-six and twenty-eight-inch barrel lengths.

Trap buffs bought plenty of Trap 3200s. Lots continue to be shot today. They were offered in thirty and thirty-two-inch barrel lengths. When Remington discovered competition shooters liked the 3200, but field shooters didn't (they had to carry them too far between shots), Big Green tried to boost sales with a run of "1 of 1000" Trap 3200s and "1 of 1000" Skeet 3200s.

Many of these were scooped up quickly by speculators who hoped the guns would escalate appreciably in value. But these folks would have seen a better return putting their money into U.S. Savings Bonds. Ah, but who wants to fondle a savings bond in October when the leaves are turning?

Interestingly, many "1 of 1000" 3200s never have been fired. They remain ensconced in their original box. There also was a 3200 Special Trap stocked with select American walnut, as well as a 3200 with three-inch chambers.

As much as the 3200 had in common with the 32, the new gun had a number of innovative features. One of the best was the 3200's safety/barrel selector. Without question, the Model 3200 safety was the best ever put on a two-barrel gun. This safety is a lever on the top tang, centered for safe, push left for the under barrel first, right to fire the top barrel first.

One shooter I know asked, "What about two-trigger double guns? Aren't they as fast?" No. Here the shooter still has to select which trigger to move his finger to, while

Doing what he truly enjoys, author hunts grouse with the Remington 32 Field. It's a well-balanced game gun.

My next 3200 came much later in that model's production years, the fall of 1979. It was a new model introduction dubbed the Live Pigeon. It was essentially a skeet gun (stock dimensions), but competition class walnut and a pigeon engraved and gold-filled at the bottom of the receiver, plus gold-filled engraving on the sides of the receiver. All these Live Pigeon models were choked improved modified and full on twenty-eight-inch barrels.

The market Remington attempted to reach was the handful of live pigeon shooters. My guess is the DuPont bean counters were again totally depressed over the sales numbers. Today, the Live Pigeon 3200s are no doubt the most valuable, because there were so few of them made.

I had Jess Briley not only rig my 3200 Live Pigeon with a set of his sub-gauge tubes for serious skeet, but also had him fit the barrels with a set of his thin stainless steel screw-chokes. Traditionalists may claim I devalued the gun by altering it so, but I maintain I improved its worth, at least to me. My heirs can worry about who was right and who was wrong.

Here're a few of the bobwhites the author bagged while hunting with the new Peerless at the Flint Oak Ranch.

with the 3200, it's simply push the safety right or left. No safety ever has matched this one in speed or ease of use. I admit, it's a moot point in most shooting circumstances because barrel selection doesn't come into play. It's get the safety off as you're getting your gun to the shoulder for the quick shot!

Another important design feature of the 3200 was fast lock time. Estimated at 1.2 to 1.8 milliseconds, this gun perhaps had the fastest lock time (release of the sear to firing of the gun) of any shotgun ever!

My first 3200 was a skeet model with twenty-six-inch barrels. Eventually, I had Jess Briley fit it up with a set of his sub-gauge tubes. In the years since, I've shot scores of skeet guns at serious, competitive skeet, but I've never shot one any better than I did that short, tubed Skeet 3200. Maybe I peaked early in my skeet game, or maybe I should have stuck with it through all the intervening years. Further, I took that skeet gun to Colombia's Cauca Valley for doves many times. I never felt I was under-choked with those wide-open bores, and many a Cauca Valley dove toppled to that gun's firepower.

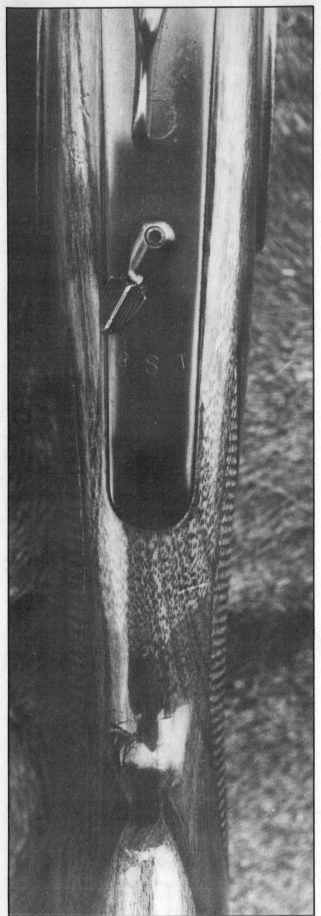

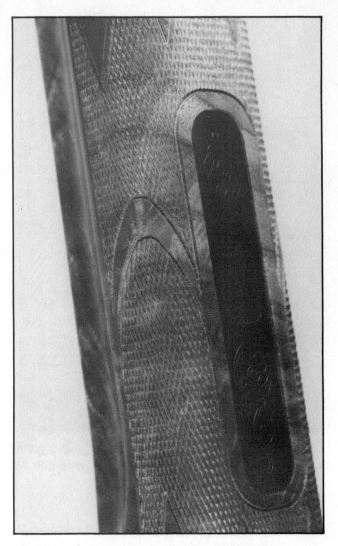

The safety on the 3200 (left) was the best ever for a two-barreled gun. Above, here's a look at the forend engraving and checkering on the 3200 Live Pigeon.

This 3200 Live Pigeon has found a good home on competitive skeet fields, for I've done well with it. I like heavier shotguns for sporting clays, so this special 3200 is one of my favorites for that sport. Live pigeons are my game, but that game is a champagne-taste deal, and I'm on this beer pocketbook, if you get what I mean. That 3200 is a perfect dove gun. Lots of weight — nine pounds — to prevent the stopped swing and suck up recoil on a high-volume shooting day. There is plenty of barrel length, plus a beautiful piece of well-finished walnut for the eyes to marvel over if the birds aren't flying. This gun also is well suited to waterfowling with steel 2¾-inch loads — since I had Briley fit the gun with screw chokes. I use improved cylinder and modified around duck ponds.

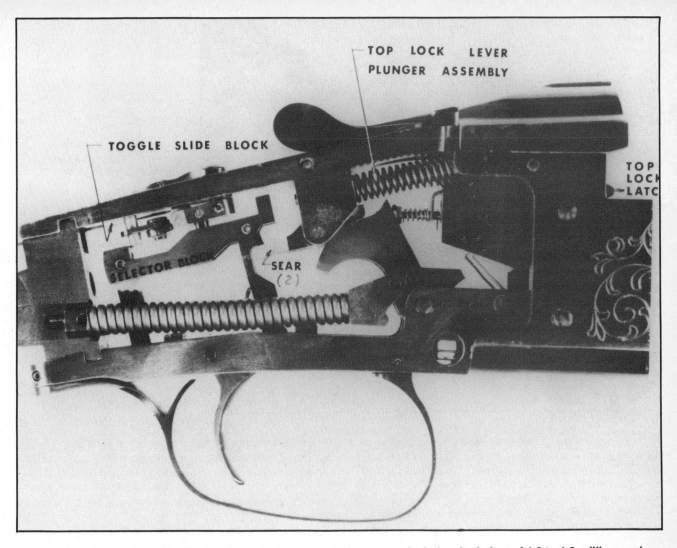

TOP LOCK LEVER
PLUNGER ASSEMBLY

TOGGLE SLIDE BLOCK

TOP
LOCK
LATC

SELECTOR BLOCK

SEAR
(2)

The inner workings of the Remington 3200 shotgun gave it the impressively fast lock time of 1.2 to 1.8 milliseconds.

The 3200 with three-inch chambers, a waterfowl model introduced in 1975, makes a great waterfowl gun, but only if you have the barrels fitted with a good screw-choke system for steel loads. Steel shells were in their infancy when the three-inch 3200 came along, so I'd feel much more comfortable shooting IC and modified screw-in chokes when stuffing the chambers with steel. Don't forget, steel waterfowl loads are big kickers, and the 3200's ample mass helps suck up some of that recoil.

It didn't take Remington three decades to come up with an over-and-under to replace the 3200. In 1993, Remington introduced the world to the maker's third over-and-under. They call it the Peerless, a name borrowed from the company's Custom Shop. Some years back, high-grade guns received the Peerless moniker.

While the 3200 resembled the 32 in so many ways, the Peerless is a complete departure in design and cosmetic appearance. When I suggested to Big Green marketing mogul Bud Fini that the company should have kept the 3200's safety, he came back, "We didn't want the new Peerless to have *anything* on it that could be associated with the 3200." No doubt Fini had felt the heat of DuPont

bean counters in more than one high-level meeting in Wilmington.

For a change, the Peerless is going to make the DuPont bean counters happy. I bet Remington president Bobby Brown he would sell to dealers and distributors one year's production quota the first day of actual sales, and I don't think I was wrong. It's an over-and-under that's going to please both the masses and the competitors.

Colleague Jon Sundra and I shared a new Peerless at the Remington Gun Writer's Seminar at Flint Oak Ranch in November 1992. The company had ten prototype Peerless models rigged for the gun writers to sample at that outing. Sundra and I swapped the Peerless back and forth as we chased bobwhites and pheasants at Flint Oak, and we both began singing the gun's praises at first heft, with the first shot — and with shot after shot thereafter. I believe Sundra ran six or seven roosters straight that clear, blue-sky morning, and I was enjoying similar bobwhite luck when I could wrestle the gun from his hands.

It's not a heavyweight like the 3200, but it's not an extra-lightweight either, as, for example, the venerable Franchi 48/AL. Put the new Peerless on a baby scale and it won't

This checkering pattern is featured on the butt stock of the 3200 Live Pigeon.

impress you. Put the gun in both hands, at the port, then jerk it to your shoulder over and over. Then you're impressed. Remember many paragraphs back when I talked about Leonard Reeves' Field 32? Like it, the Peerless is a shotgun that feels lighter than it is.

There's a game-gun feel to this one, despite its heft. The original recoil pads we used on the prototype guns at Flint Oak were discarded in favor of the recoil pads fit to 11-87 Sporting Clays models, with a thinner profile and beveled top to prevent gun hang-up during quick mounting. Different texture helps get the gun positioned effortlessly, but once in position it stays there, not moving for the second shot.

This is a boxlock-type action, but there are false side

The Remington Standard 3200 features a handsome engraving pattern, familiar to those who hunt with a shotgun.

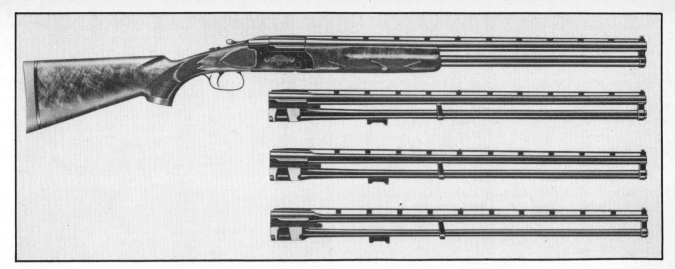

The four-barrel skeet set for the Remington 3200 Competition included .410 bore and 28-, 20- and 12-gauge barrels.

plates where bird dogs are roll engraved on either side. The lock-up is via two rectangular-shaped lugs that protrude from the receiver upon closing to match up with recesses in the monobloc, which are at the midpoint of the bottom barrel.

Barrel length choices are twenty-six, twenty-eight and thirty inches. Lock time is fast — 3.28 milliseconds — but not in the 3200's class. The Peerless comes with the Rem Choke screw-in system. I suggest one skeet, two improved cylinders, one modified, one full, then you'll be set for any shotgunning situation you encounter.

The Peerless stock comes with a new finish the company calls Imron, said to be the best yet when it comes to ruggedness. There's sharp. well-defined cut checkering at the pistol grip and on the forearm. Finger grooves on the latter feel most comfortable. Rolled-on engraving consists of a pointer on the left sideplate, a setter on the right (a la the venerable Model 32), scroll work setting off both. The bottom of the receiver is engraved with the Remington logo and the word, *Peerless*.

Back to Flint Oak. The dog handler had two little Brittany spaniels down, and they scurried back and forth in front of Jon Sundra and me. I had commandeered the new Peerless first. One of the spaniels worked over in front of me. Soon her little tail stub began vibrating in a blur. Her nose waved right and left, scooping up what was obviously fresh scent.

In less time than it takes to tell, the fast-moving little Brit narrowed the distance. The ringneck rooster in front decided it was time to go airborne. With a great flapping of wings,

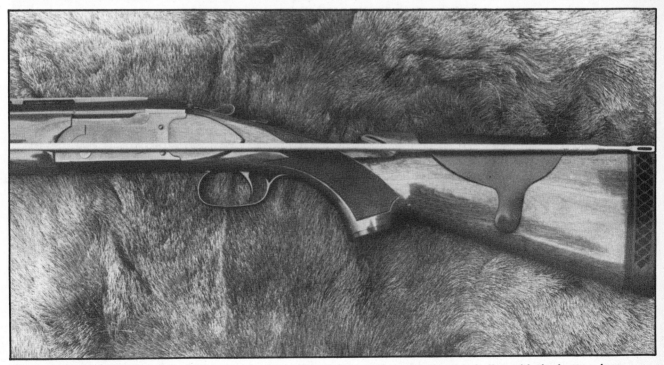

The Remington 3200 featured a higher stock which placed the top of the comb more in line with the bottom bore.

These Remington 32s, the trap (top) and the skeet, while not well received in the 1930s, are highly valued today.

this feathered fellow moved huge gobs of air that sent him helicoptering up with no running start. Too anxious to score with the new Peerless, I scattered only a few tail feathers into the air with my first shot. Gripping the stock closer to my cheek, I also gritted with more determination, got the muzzzles where they needed to be, and the critter that had been so vocal suddenly went silent, dropping like a stone until it hit the stubble field with a hard thud. Three bounces and the little Brittany was trying to get hold of a really big bird in her relatively small jaws. The Peerless had been blooded.

Some preserve quail are frustrating and offer no sport whatever. Sometimes a few need prodding into flight — prodding more than once. When they do fly, it's like their wings are broken, for they might only get three feet off the ground, then land after a fifteen-foot journey.

But not the Flint Oak bobwhite that got up in front of the other Brittany, a white and orange one, a few minutes later. He came up in a whir, boring at a quarter angle from left to right, then he drove hard, at a right angle. I don't know how the Peerless caught up, but this smooth swinger sent this white-masked bob somersaulting end over end with a dead-center hit.

"Jon, you better try this Peerless next," I suggested to my hunting partner. "Tell you what. It works!'

Sundra's first chance was a bobwhite. The bob went out partially behind him, then took a curving flight path directly behind, so my partner had to whirl around a full 180

The Remington 3200 Competition, introduced in 1979, was easily transported with its four barrels in a deluxe case.

A few years ago (note hair style and shooting outfit), author shot .410 barrels of the 3200 four-barrel skeet set.

degrees. He puffed that quail in a pillow-fall of feathers.

"Nick, that's my toughest shot," he told me as he smiled, "when I have to turn around so far with my swing. You're right. This gun really swings beautifully."

The Peerless is not only a superb swinger. It's also quick. The liver and white Brittany skidded to a stop in some low woods. Her nostrils widened as her lungs filled with the sweetest aroma a bird dog can know, then her head and whole body eased up higher. I walked in on the right, fidgeting the Peerless' safety, my nose sniffing to see if I could grasp a whiff of what the dog was so enthralled with.

A zillion blurs rocketed up within ten feet of her mesmerized trance. "Pick one," I chided myself. "Don't flock shoot," I warned once more. My eyes zeroed in on the bird farthest right. He wasn't close, and he was disappearing fast. Cheek squeezed against the stock, I got the muzzles to pass through the bird and hit the trigger.

Seeing the feathers fluff and the bob begin to tumble, I dropped the stock and picked up a later flushing bird. "A white-masked male," I remember thinking as I tried to stare a hole through that buzzer, at the same time trying to get the muzzles of the new Peerless to where they might do some good. When I passed through, I hit the trigger again, and the second bob of the covey tumbled. There had hardly been a second between the two shots. Yep, the Peerless is quick — as well as a top swinger.

Since 1932, Remington has produced only three over-and-unders. This is a most interesting trio. I've long been an admirer of the old Model 32. My 3200s have seen lots of duty on doves, at skeet, at sporting clays. The new Peerless, however, is without question the best all-around Remington over-and-under yet. — *Nick Sisley*

CHAPTER 6

THE ULTIMATE TURKEY GUN

Here's Solid Advice On Gearing Up For Our Biggest Gamebird

THERE WAS a time — not too long ago at that — when turkey hunting was a sport limited to a few areas of the Deep South and was the province of a handful of die-hard hunters. Today, that picture has changed considerably.

Turkey management programs initiated by numerous states stand as a classic example of the benefits of modern wildlife management techniques. Thanks to the restoration of existing populations and the widespread transplanting of birds to establish new ones, it is quite possible there are more wild turkeys roaming America than at any point in our history! And, there's no doubt the bird's ranges have been expanded well beyond those encountered by early colonists.

That's good news for hunters, especially those who enjoy the thrill of stalking, and then calling into close range, one of the sharpest-eyed, and warriest, critters roaming North America. In fact, what used to be strictly a Deep South situation now is readily available to hunters throughout the Midwest, in many areas of the middle Atlantic states and even in the arid West Coast states.

Manufacturers report equipment relating to turkey hunting is among the fastest growing market. That means there are a lot of new turkey hunters prowling the woods, leading many to ask, "What is the best gun for turkeys?"

That's a good question, and to answer it, we'll go right back to the experts in the Deep South where turkey hunting has its roots.

Although regulations vary from state to state, in many areas it is quite legal to hunt turkeys with rifles, handguns, shotguns and bows. In Dixie, however, there is only one turkey gun.

"Most veteran turkey hunters see the sport as more of a woodscraft sport than a shooting sport," states Tennessee turkey expert Gary Sefton. "The real thrill of the sport is in locating the bird, then calling him in close. That, to me, is turkey hunting. Actually taking the bird is secondary.

"For that reason, I don't think one is doing the bird — or the sport — justice if he spots a turkey fifty to 150 yards with a scope-sighted rifle or handgun."

Another consideration is safety. Turkey hunting is a close-range, heavy-cover game that is played best in full camoflauge. With increasing numbers of hunters, the potential for accidents occur anytime an inexperienced hunter gets excited behind the trigger of a flat-shooting centerfire rifle or handgun.

For that reason, most veteran turkey hunters consider a fast-handling shotgun the only real choice for turkey hunters. And men like Sefton, who is known throughout the Southeast for his calling seminars as a representative of Woods Wise Products (P.O. Box 1552 CA, Franklin, TN 37064) have strong opinions on how they should be set up. In no real order of importance, preferences are:

Short, light and handy: "Turkey hunting," Sefton explains, "is a highly mobile sport. You cover a lot of ground in thick cover, and when you do shoot, it's generally in

An interchangeable slug barrel will convert a gun like the Winchester Model 1300 instantly into a turkey gun.

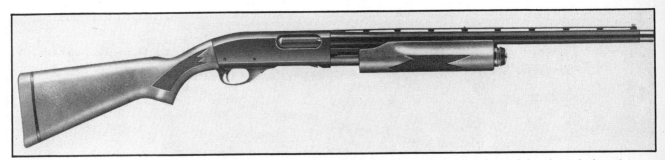

Remington's 870 Express turkey gun has a three-inch chamber, double-bead sight and special turkey choke tube.

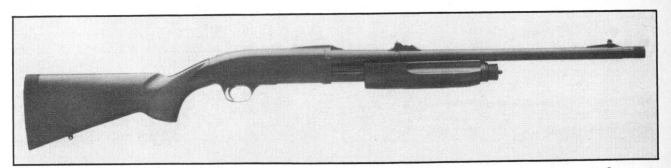

Browning's BPS Turkey Special is designed intelligently. The raised comb permits effective use of iron sights.

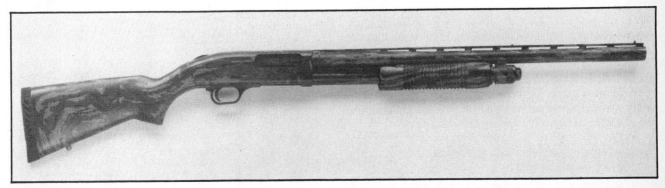

Mossberg's Model 835 Ulti-Mag 12-gauge turkey gun has Realtree camouflage finish over its entire exterior surfaces.

tight quarters. Long, awkward guns are a handicap."

Most experts prefer barrels no longer than twenty-six inches, and many favor them as short as twenty inches. Fitting the gun with detachable sling swivels is considered mandatory, allowing the hunter to have both hands free while on the move, then remove the sling when he settles into a calling position.

Sufficiently powerful: Veterans consider the minimum power level required for clean kills to be a 12-gauge 2¾-inch short magnum throwing 1½ ounces of #4 or #6 shot. That's if the hunter has selected one of the newer plated, buffered loads like the Federal Premium line. The choice of most is the three-inch, 12-gauge with 1⅞ or two ounces of plated, buffered shot in #4 or #6 or, high performance

The popularity of turkey hunting is prompting many gunmakers to produce specialized models for the sport. This Winchester 1300 has everything a turkey hunter could require. Changing choke tubes permits use of slugs or shot.

While many experts prefer pumps, this Remington 11-87 makes a dandy turkey gun for those favoring semi-autos.

reloads in the same three-inch size with 1⅜ to 1½ ounces. Surprisingly, the 3½-inch 12-gauge and the 10-gauge haven't made much ground here.

"A good three-inch load has all the power you need," Sefton claims. "When you see someone toting a 10-gauge, it's usually a new hunter who has not yet learned that extra power is no real substitute for calling skill."

A precise sighting system: Such a system allows the pattern to be centered on a small target (the turkey's head/neck) from any conceivable shooting position. A single bead sight is a poor choice, since it requires that the gun be mounted perfectly every time in order for the eye to act as the rear sight. That's not always possible for turkey hunters, since they often shoot from sitting or prone positions or with bodies turned sideways to the target.

The gun should be choked extra-full: Standard full chokes are intended to produce patterns in the seventy percent range at forty yards. Expert turkey hunters want eighty-five to ninety percent to ensure enough pellets in the head and neck to drop a turkey in its tracks.

Matte, non-reflective finish: Turkeys are masters at spotting anything out of place and nothing stands out in the woods like a shiny shotgun.

Until just a few years ago, purchasing a shotgun meeting the above criteria was about as easy as bobbing for French fries. With today's widespread interest in turkey hunting, however, many of the major makers now include models in their lines that incorporate some, if not all, of the desired features.

Winchester offers the Model 1300 pump gun with a twenty-two-inch barrel threaded for interchangeable choke tubes, with either a bead sight or rifle sight system. A laminated camo pattern stock is fitted with detachable sling swivels. Although the ribbed model sports only a

single front bead, adding a mid-rib bead is a simple procedure for any decent gunsmith.

Browning's BPS pump has a 20½-inch Invecta-choked barrel. Featuring a dull, non-glare finish and rifle sights, detachable sling swivels allow it to be toted easily in the field. The gun is supplied with a new extra-full choke tube claimed to deliver ninety percent patterns at forty yards with premium-grade shot loads.

Remington's extra-full turkey choke reflects the trend for long choke tubes in producing extra-full patterns. It fits the standard Rem Choke thread system nicely.

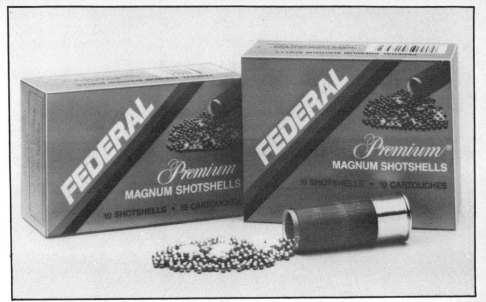

Superior patterns from turkey chokes are produced by copper-plated, premium-grade, buffered shot loads like these from Federal.

Remington has three guns expressly designed for the deep woods. In the pump-action line are the 870 SPS with a synthetic stock, double-bead sight system and a twenty-six-inch barrel, and the 870 Express Turkey gun, with a twenty-one-inch barrel. Both are chambered for three-inch shells and threaded for Remington's Rem Choke system, which includes extra-full turkey choke tubes.

For autoloader fans, the 11-87 three-inch magnum has

been fitted with a twenty-one-inch barrel accepting Rem Chokes, a synthetic stock in a brown camo pattern, and a double-bead sight system. Detachable sling swivels are standard.

Mossberg's contribution to turkey taking is the Model 835 in various configurations, including a twenty-four-inch barrel model with a single-bead sight and synthetic, camo-finished stock. This handles the 3½-inch, 12-gauge shell, in addition to shorter fodder.

Any of these factory guns will require little, if any, modifications to be effective. However, if a new turkey gun is on your wish list, there's no reason you have to begin your search at the local firearms emporium. In fact, chances are the makings for a first class turkey gun are sitting in your gun rack right now!

Any shooter who owns a 12-gauge pump of fairly recent manufacture or a three-inch magnum autoloader should find that turning it into a top notch turkey gun is not only easy, but far less expensive than purchasing a new gun. Such modifications do not have to result in any lessening of its effectiveness for conventional wingshooting chores. Here's how to go about it:

The best candidate for conversion is a late-model pump for which interchangeable barrels are available, or a three-inch magnum autoloader with the same feature. Side-by-sides and over/unders can make acceptable turkey guns, but they suffer one serious drawback: Both barrels may not shoot to precisely the same point of aim. With the tight patterns you'll be achieving in a properly set-up turkey gun, that could cost you a trophy!

If your chosen gun is a pump — the most popular choice among the turkey fraternity due to its inherent reliability under harsh conditions — for which interchangeable barrels are made, your task is easy. Simply obtain a smoothbore slug barrel with rifle sights. Fitting it for interchangeable choke tubes gives you the ability to produce extra-full patterns combined with a precise sighting system, in a short, handy package. If the barrel is chambered only for the 2¾-inch shell, it is a simple matter to rechamber it to take three-inch shells.

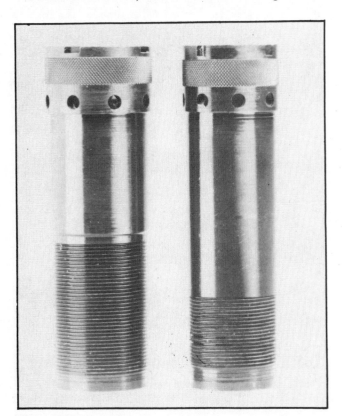

Browning's special turkey chokes feature muzzle ports to reduce recoil. Some experts also believe they allow the charge to release more effectively from the wad.

While the 3 1/2-inch, 12-gauge round hasn't earned a lot of converts among veteran turkey hunters, quality loads are available for those wanting a heavier charge.

If you have a three-inch magnum autoloader for which slug barrels are made, the same applies. If you have a gas gun chambered for the 2¾-inch shell, however, it probably can't be converted to the three-inch version, although some of the newer semi-autos will handle both.

There are a number of 'smiths who have earned excellent reputations in performing this work. They include Hastings Company, P.O. Box 224, 320 Court, Clay Center, KS 67432; Pro-Port Ltd., 41303 Executive Drive, Mt. Clemens, MI 48045; and Nu-Line Guns, 1053 Caulk Hills Road, Harvester, MO 63303.

For the ultimate in performance, however, you might consider sending your gun to Larry Nailon at Clearview Products (3021 N. Portland, Oklahoma City, OK 73107) for a high High Performance package.

Nailon will check and, if necessary, correct chamber dimensions, lengthen the forcing cone, backbore and burnish the bore and install his custom three-inch choke tubes. The resulting barrel will pattern tightly enough that you'll come to appreciate rifle sights!

Setting up an interchangeable barrel for turkey hunting allows the gun to handle traditional chores with the original barrel, creating a really versatile system. In fact, the turkey barrel also will prove highly effective at slug and buckshot chores for big game simply by installing the appropriate choke tube.

If your gun does not have interchangeable barrels available from the maker, you might check with Gander Mountain (Box 248, Highway W, Wilmot, WI 53192). They carry Hastings aftermarket barrels for a number of guns that already are fitted for the Hastings choke tube system.

If you chose to modify the original barrel, the above-mentioned companies can perform the same basic work of shortening the barrel, adding rifle or bead sights and coming up with interchangeable choke tubes.

Fitting a turkey gun for one of the various interchangeable tube systems is critical, because even the tightest fixed choke will not deliver the dense patterns produced by the special extra-full turkey chokes now offered by virtually all choke tube makers.

Once the barrel is set up to handle three-inch shells and extra-full chokes, sights become a concern. Single-bead sights are a poor choice, as stated earlier, even though some factory turkey guns come so-equipped. Any 'smith can add a mid-rib bead to correct that. If your barrel lacks a rib to accept it, one can be installed by Simmon's Gun Specialties (700 S. Rogers Road, Olathe, KS 66062).

Turkey hunting is a highly mobile, close-range sport where few shots actually are fired. For this reason, experts favor light 12-gauge shotguns firing 1 1/2 to two ounce loads from an extra-tight choke.

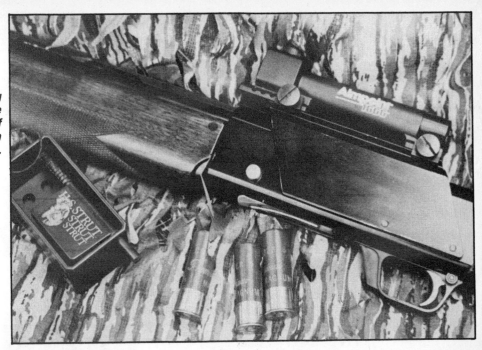

Some hunters favor using red dot sights for the precision placement of extremely tight patterns on the turkey's head/neck area.

The author (below) prefers using a quick-handling gun. Such smoothbores have a major edge in the heavy cover most often associated with the pursuit of turkey.

Another option, if you don't intend to use the gun/barrel for conventional wingshooting chores, is the previously mentioned rifle sights found on slug barrels.

If rifle sights appeal to you, yet one wishes to retain the gun's wingshooting capabilities, you might consider the slip-on rifle sights offered by Innovision Enterprises (728 Skinner Drive, Kalamazoo, MI 49001). They install in minutes with no drilling and tapping or soldering, and can be removed quickly for wingshooting. Models are available for both plain and ribbed barrels.

Another possibility is a red dot sight, like the Aimpoint. B-Square (P.O. Box 11281, Fort Worth, TX 76110) offers an extensive line of mounts, many of which require no drilling and tapping to fit a wide variety of shotguns. They offer precision pattern placement.

The next step is to turn your gun into part of the flora. Turkeys possess exceptional eyesight, and even in hill country they can see an hour down the road.

The easiest and least expensive way to accomplish this is with readily available camouflage tape. It's easy to apply and remove, surprisingly durable and actually can help protect your wood from inevitable scratches and dings.

Many shooters simply strip the glossy finish from their stocks and restain the wood a dark color, then refinish with a low-luster oil finish. Birchwood-Casey offers an extensive line of stock finishing supplies available at most gunshops.

If a shooter has exceptionally good wood on his stock and desires to protect it, a synthetic replacement stock like those available from Bell & Carlson (509 N. Fifth Street, Atwood, KS 67730) might be the answer. Available in a variety of matte finishes, including camouflage, they take the abuse and let the good wood stay at home.

Camo tape also can be used to take the shine off metal action parts, but there are other, better alternatives.

Refinishing the barrel and action in a non-glare matte blue or Parkerized finish is not overly expensive. Neither is having it coated with a self-lubricating teflon finish. This can be had in matte black, olive drab or even camo, and many turkey hunters favor it for its self-lubricating and rust-proof qualities. Either procedure can add value to an older gun. Rebel Gun Works (1203 S.W. Twelfth Street, Ocala, FL 32674) has an excellent reputation for this kind of work, often custom finishing for a number of major manufacturers.

Detachable sling swivels and a padded camo sling are readily available from Uncle Mike's (7305 Glisan Road, Portland, OR 97231) to add the final touches to the ultimate turkey gun.

Regardless of whether you build it or buy it, team the ultimate turkey gun up with today's high performance copper-plated, buffered loads in sizes #4 or #6, and you're well equipped to handle our biggest gamebird. — *Rod Hunter*

CHAPTER 7

SKEET IS EASY!

This Clay Target Game Is Easy To Enjoy, Simple To Master

Skeet is enjoyable, but it's not without its rules of conduct. It is considered proper etiquette to pick up your fired shells as you depart a shooting station. However, it's not acceptable to retrieve the expended shells of other shooters.

It's the shooter's responsibility to know which member of the squad he is to follow and be ready to take the station when the time comes. Note the shooter on the left has locked his semi-auto open so others will know his gun is safe.

THE GAME OF skeet got its start shortly after the turn of the century when three Massachusetts wingshooters got tired of missing game birds in the field.

History tells us that C.E. Davies, his son Henry, and a friend, William Foster, were avid hunters and skilled wing shots. But, as happens to anyone who totes a smoothbore afield, each would have "one of those days" occasionally.

Determined to improve their performance, the elder Davies used a trap machine bolted to a plank to duplicate some of the shots they had been missing in the field. By changing the shooter's position in relation to the trap, and using traps set at high and low positions, they found it possible to duplicate virtually any shot likely to be encountered in the field. They also discovered that not only did this improve their shooting, but turned out to be a lot of fun, as well!

The new game started off slowly, but all who shot it enjoyed it. Trial and error eventually standardized the position of the trap machines and the actual layout of the shooting field, but it wasn't until the mid-1920s that the sport actually was awarded a name.

Today, skeet ranks as one of the most popular clay target games in America. Under the direction of the National Skeet Shooting Association (NSSA), P.O. Box 680007, San Antonio, TX 78268-0007, registered matches are held on a state, regional and national level, and it is a rare shooter who doesn't have a skeet shooting facility located within a reasonable drive of home.

Although skeet originally developed as a hunter's game, it has evolved into a competitive sport in its own right. And while it still is possible — indeed, even desirable — to use a

Guns are never loaded until the shooter steps onto the shooting pad to take his turn. Nothing will result in instant expulsion faster than violating this cardinal rule.

49

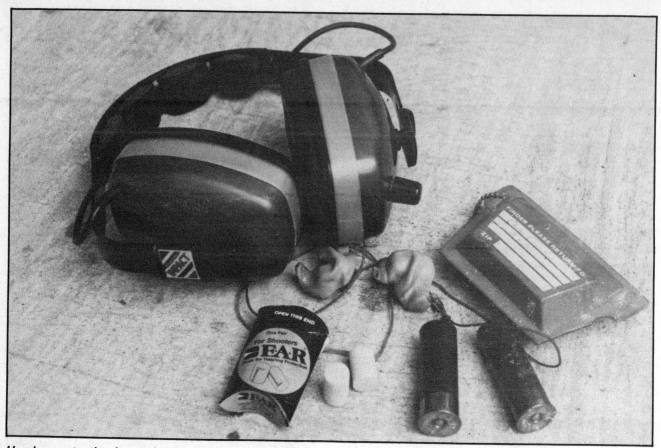

Hearing protection is required at some ranges and is an excellent idea for any type of shooting. Regardless of the type used, ear protection not only guards against long-term hearing loss, but also improves a shooter's performance.

skeet field to tune one's shooting for the fall fields, most competitors are there for the game itself, with improved wingshooting skills only a welcome side benefit.

Competition in skeet has gotten tough. When the first national championship match was held in 1927, the winner missed eight targets out of 125 shot. Today, a top-ranked skeet shooter who misses eight targets out of 1000 might seriously consider suicide! Perfect skeet scores have become so standard at major matches today that anyone expecting to take home the top trophies knows they will have to be won in a shoot-off.

This level of perfection often intimidates new shooters, but it shouldn't.

I certainly don't intend to take anything away from the AAA Class shooters who consider running one hundred straight targets to be nothing more than a "warm-up" exercise. These are true masters of the game whose form and timing approach perfection. But to be perfectly honest, the game does lend itself to that type of performance, because of all the clay target games available today, skeet is by far the easiest! A look at a skeet field will reveal why that is true.

A skeet field is laid out in a semicircle with a trap house located at each end. The left-hand house is called the high house and the bird is launched from a distance of ten feet above the ground. The bird leaves the house at a slight upward angle. The right-hand house is called the low house and launches the bird at a more extreme upward angle from a height of 3½ feet.

The traps are locked into a fixed position and throw the

bird to the same spot every time. When properly calibrated, they launch the bird at eighty-eight feet per second — approximately sixty miles per hour — and the bird must travel fifty-five yards through the air.

Seven shooting stations are set around the outside of the semi-circle and spaced an equal distance — twenty-six feet, eight inches — apart. Station #8 is located in the center of the field midway between the two trap houses.

Ten feet to the outside of Station #8 is a stake, called the Eight Post. The traps are regulated to send the bird directly over the top of this stake every time.

The speed and flight path of the bird is fixed. The shooter knows precisely where it will come from and what path it will take. The shooting positions are fixed. Each position will see the same speed and angle from the bird for each shot from that shooting position.

Different positions will show a shooter a different flight angle, but once a shooter learns the proper lead and technique for each of the eight stations, he has all the information he needs to break that target every time!

Compare this to another popular clay target game: trap. Here, only five stations are used, and while the shooter knows where the bird will come from, once the bird leaves the house, it may take any one of five different angles. Depending upon the station, these range from fast-rising straightways to extreme right or left angles. The shooter must be prepared to respond instantly to any of five different possibilities.

Sporting clays is even tougher!

In this demanding game, shooters are faced with targets

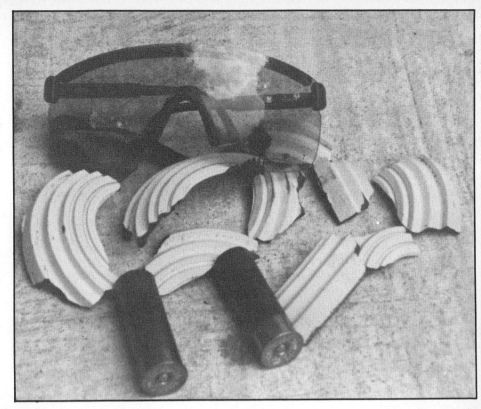

A piece of target flying at 60 mph can cost a shooter an eye. Shooting glasses should be a mandatory piece of skeet equipment.

Many ranges dictate that eye and ear protection be worn by everyone on or near the firing line. New shooters should be ready to comply with these rules when visiting any range.

Guns for skeet: On a competitive level, skeet is fired with four different gauges; 12, 20, 28 and .410. That doesn't mean, however, that new shooters must have four guns. Many scattergunners enter the sport firing in only one gauge class, adding the other gauges as their interest grows. It's quite likely that most shotgunners have a suitable entry-level gun in their battery right now.

Skeet evolved as a game that duplicates field shots, and as such, standard field-grade guns are quite suitable. Any gun that would be at home in a dove field or trailing along behind a pointing dog will handle skeet. In fact, many skeet shooters use their competition guns in the field.

Among the various action types, over/unders are by far the most popular among top-ranked shooters. They balance well, handle quickly and preclude the need to pick up empty hulls from the ground (most skeet shooters are reloaders).

Another factor in the popularity of the over/unders is that, through the use of insert barrels, they allow the shooter to use one gun for all four gauge events. Companies such as Briley (1085 Gessner, No. B, Houston, TX 77055) offer sub-gauge tubes that quickly convert a 12- or 20-gauge over/under to all the smaller gauges. The price for a pair of sub-gauge tubes is considerably less than the cost of another gun.

In years past, most skeet shooters favored twenty-six-inch barrels, but in recent years the twenty-eight-inch lengths have found favor, because the extra weight promotes a smoother swing.

While there are a number of high-priced competition guns in use, moderately priced over/unders like the Ruger Red Label and Browning Citori are more than competitive.

Gas-operated semi-autos rank next in popularity due

that fly faster, farther and from virtually every conceivable angle. Complicating that, many sporting clay stations only give the shooter a brief "window" in which to take the target as it zips through screening vegetation. Even veteran skeet shooters often leave the sporting clays range wondering if they'd remembered to load the shot in their shells!

Yes, compared to other clay target games, skeet is easy. And getting into the sport is equally simple.

Skeet shooters have made some useful accessories. This "skeet cart" makes transporting guns and ammunition an easy task.

largely to their soft-recoil nature. Some competitors opt for a gas gun in the 12-gauge event and use a tubed 20-gauge over/under for the others. The Remington 1100 is a good example of a gas gun that has earned a fine reputation on the skeet field, and this model can be had in all four gauges.

Side-by-sides and pump-actions, although fine field guns, seldom are seen in the hands of a serious competitor. They don't handle the game as well as the over/unders and gas guns, but certainly will serve as entry level guns if that is what the shooter has on hand.

Skeet is essentially a close-range game, the longest shot being little more than twenty-five yards. Since one must

Skeet is one of the most popular, and growing, competitive shotgun events, with registered tournaments held weekly throughout the country. Because of the competitive spirit, the leader board is a popular hangout at the tournaments.

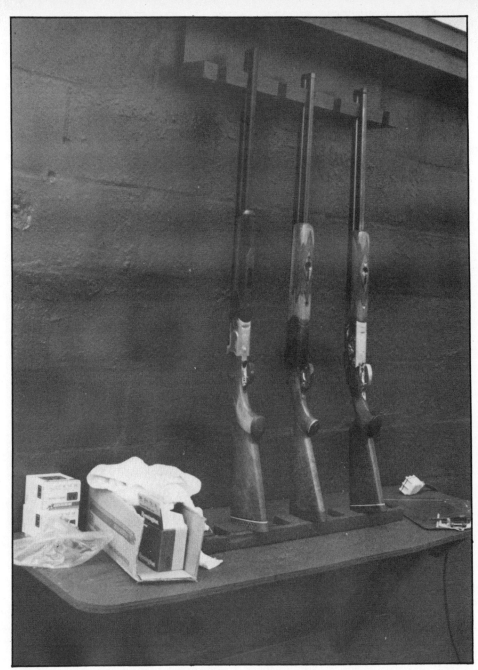

Top skeet shooters pick over/unders as their top choice in competitive guns. There's no need to pick up empty shells and insert-tubes allow the guns to be used for all gauge events.

only knock a "visible piece" off the target to record a hit, #9 shot is favored, and even required. Loads used for registered events are limited in the amount of shot they can carry per gauge to 1⅛-ounce in 12-gauge, seven-eighths-ounce in 20, three-fourths in the 28 and one-half-ounce in .410. All the shotshell makers offer skeet loads.

The proper choke for skeet is one that throws a wide open, evenly distributed pattern. Guns designed for the game feature a "skeet" choke, intended to produce a uniform thirty-inch spread at twenty-five yards. If your gun features interchangeable choke tubes, skeet tubes are readily available. If not, there is nothing wrong with shooting the game with an improved cylinder or straight cylinder choke.

Either will produce the required pattern and anyone who misses a target with them wouldn't have hit it with a skeet choke!

If your over/under has standard field fixed chokes of improved cylinder and modified persuasions, don't despair. It will serve well as an entry level gun. I once had a lightweight little Italian 28-gauge over/under so choked that was sent my way for test and evaluation. After firing a practice round to get used to the lighter weight, I proceeded to run forty-nine out of fifty targets. By selecting the modified barrel for the outgoing targets on doubles, and using the IC barrel for the incoming doubles shots and all singles, I found the gun performed just as well as any skeet-choked 28 I'd ever handled.

The point is that virtually any scattergunner has a suitable skeet gun — or one that can be made suitable through the use of interchangeable choke tubes — in his battery right now. The next items one requires are a few simple accessories.

The shooters on an orderly skeet squad await their turn to shoot during a local tournament. Note that the gun actions are open and those waiting contestants give the shooter plenty of room. This is common and expected skeet etiquette.

Accessories for skeet: Savvy shooters wear eye protection as a matter of course, and on a skeet range that is an excellent idea. A broken bird can send pieces of target zipping along at sixty miles per hour, and it's not uncommon to get pelted with a few during a round. They can cost you an eye, and while you'll see a number of shooters on a field without them, I can't recommend shooting glasses highly enough.

Hearing protection also is a good idea. Not only does it protect against long-term hearing loss, but it also will guard against flinching and recoil fatigue, both of which can be brought on quickly by continued exposure to high noise levels. A jumpy, tired shooter will not perform well. Even the least expensive foam ear plugs are better than nothing.

You also will need some way to carry your shells as you move around the shooting field. Many shooters favor a shooting vest, with pockets to hold fired and unfired shells separately. Some shooters favor a shell pouch that can be worn on a belt. Both work and are infinitely preferable to

lugging a cardboard box of shells around in your hand or stuffing loads in your Levi's pockets.

One last item that can come in handy on occasion is a "shell knocker." It's possible for a shell to hang up in the chamber or for a squib load to leave a wad stuck in the barrel. A cleaning rod will knock either one out, but they are cumbersome to tote.

A simple solution is a piece of brass rod about six inches long with a diameter smaller than the barrel. Pushed forcefully down the barrel, it will dislodge most obstructions and can be carried in a pocket. Nothing is more annoying than for a member of the squad to have a jammed gun or obstructed barrel; everybody else is standing around waiting to shoot, while he searches for something with which to clear the gun. Having a shell knocker handy can make you a most popular fellow!

Etiquette and Procedures: A round of skeet consists of twenty-five shots and is fired in a squad of up to five

Insert tubes are popular with skeet shooters because they allow one gun to be used for all of the four gauge events. This shooter taps out the installed tube, allowing it to be quickly removed so a different gauge tube can be installed.

shooters. You will find skeet shooters, in general, to be among the most friendly and gregarious members of the sport shooting community. I have yet to see a veteran skeet shooter who did not genuinely want to help a novice improve his game and have a good time in the process.

However, there is a certain etiquette involved and it's best to know it in advance.

1. Your shooting order within the squad is determined by the sign-up sheet. It is your responsibility to know which shooter you are to follow, and to be ready to take your shooting station when your turn comes.

2. On a skeet field, guns are never, I repeat, *never* loaded until the shooter has stepped into the three-foot-square shooting pad and is ready to shoot his station. Nothing will turn a friendly, smiling shooter into a rampaging demon faster than finding out another shooter in the squad is wandering around behind him with a loaded gun!

Skeet shooting is one of the safest participant sports there is. In fact, more people are injured bowling, playing tennis or jogging than have been injured on a skeet field. Rigorous adherence to safety rules keeps it this way.

If you're not in the shooting box, keep your gun unloaded and let everybody know it. Over/unders and side-by-sides should have the actions open. Pumps and semi-autos should have the actions racked back and locked open.

3. After you have shot, it is perfectly permissible to take a moment to pick up your fired shells from the ground. It is not considered acceptable to pick up someone else's unless he tells you that you may have them.

4. While awaiting your turn to shoot, do not crowd the shooter presently on the stand. The only person who should be within eight or ten feet of him is the person pulling the targets.

The above rules are simple — in fact, nothing more than common sense and common courtesy. Once a shooter understands them, he is ready to play the game. The only other information he requires is how to break the targets!
— *Chris Christian*

CHAPTER 8

MASTER SKEET'S TOUGHEST SHOTS

Here's A Step-By-Step Look At How To Break Every Target Consistently

This the proper starting position to break one of skeet's toughest targets — high house 2. Note that the muzzle is elevated to the path the bird will take. This allows the shooter to track while keeping his cheek on the stock.

AS STATED in an earlier chapter, skeet is the easiest of the clay target games, because the target flight path is fixed for each station. Once a shooter understands the required lead and body position for each, he has all the information required to break that target every time.

Unfortunately, human beings aren't machines, although some of the top-ranked shooters come close. Despite the fact a shooter knows how to break each target, he still has to execute perfectly to do so.

There are three common ways to miss a skeet target, and at one time or another, each will plague any shooter, whether the rankest novice or a national champion. Understanding them early on will help minimize the effects on your score.

The first problem is lifting your head from the stock. This is most common among newer shooters. In the first few rounds over the skeet field, the targets seem to be the size of aspirin tablets moving at Mach II. It's not uncommon for a new shooter to try to get a "better look at the target" — or just find it. In doing so, the head comes off the stock which will send the shot high every time!

The cure for this is simple and one of my shooting cohorts at the Palatka Skeet & Trap Club sums it up suc-

This wider view of high house 2 provides an appreciation of the challenge this target presents the shooter. Extreme and fast lateral movement is required to break this target which is why the correct starting position is so important.

cinctly: "Love thy wood!"

When the gun is mounted to call for the bird, be certain it is positioned properly and the cheek is in firm contact with the comb. If the gun is moved to the proper position to pick the bird up as it comes from the house, you will have no trouble tracking the bird.

Stopping the swing is the second most common way to miss. And, surprisingly, it often plagues mid-level shooters.

New shooters find the targets moving so fast they have trouble catching them, and as a result, tend to swing quickly. Once a shooter has some experience, however, the targets seem to slow down and grow larger. The shooter knows he has plenty of time, and he becomes more concerned with getting the proper lead than simply catching the target.

The gun is swung through and ahead of the target, the lead is observed and the subconscious mind says, "That's it." The gun is stopped or slowed, as the shot is released, and the charge speeds behind the bird. This can be cured by concentrating on follow-through.

Think of it this way: If a golfer stopped his club when it contacted the ball, a tennis player quit the swing on impact, or a bowler let his arm go limp when he placed the ball on the alley, what would be the results of his efforts? Poor, that's what! To successfully complete those operations one must follow through, and skeet shooting — or wing-shooting in general — is no different.

To hit a fast-moving target consistently with a shotgun, the gun must be moving as the shot breaks. Concentrate on driving the barrel of the gun right through the target. Follow the broken pieces and mentally take a second shot. If you develop the habit of staying with the target pieces after they are broken, you won't have to worry about stopping your swing.

The last bugaboo is simply not being ready when you call for the bird. This usually happens to more experienced shooters who, after all, have broken that target hundreds — even thousands — of times. "What's the fuss?" "This is a piece of cake!" "I can hit this one in my sleep."

What happens is that your mind is wandering somewhere else, and as the bird comes out, you suddenly realize you're late. Your timing goes off and the target sails away unscathed. I watched a world class shooter do just this at a national championship when he took a moment to admire an airplane flying overhead. He called for the bird anyway, and missed the target!

Everyone will develop his own routine when he steps onto the shooting pad: his own way of preparing for the shot. Once you have your routine, don't deviate from it. Once the basics are mastered, the subconscious mind plays a major role in skeet shooting success. Let it prep itself for the shot. Don't interfere. If you normally squiggle around, kick broken target pieces off the pad, straighten your vest or whatever other "quirky" manuevers you deem necessary to prepare to shoot, do them! This is your subconscious mind's way of setting things in order to execute the shot. Let it do its job.

High house 8 is intimidating to new shooters, but it's one of the easier shots. This shooter has broken the bird in the correct position by swinging up and through the bird, triggering as the muzzle reaches the leading edge of the target.

Now, let's shoot a round of skeet!

Station 1: This positions you directly under the high house. That bird will be outgoing, while the low house will be incoming. Four shots will be fired here: a high house single, low house single, and doubles with both houses launching simultaneously, the shooter breaking the outgoing target first, and then swinging back to take the incomer.

The high house target is easy, but deceptive. It appears to be going straightaway, but because it is launched well above the shooter, an angle is involved and the shooter must lead the target by actually shooting below it!

To break this target, take a comfortable shooting position aligning your gun and body on the eight post, since this is where the target will be directed. Bring the barrel upward to about a thirty-degree angle and call for the bird. As soon as you pick up the bird, swing the barrel down and through the bird, breaking the shot when you get six inches below it.

Take this shot as soon as you can. The longer you wait the farther away it gets and the farther it drops. Also, you will need to break this bird quickly during the doubles portion of this station in order not to break the low house along with it.

If you miss this station consistently, try bringing the gun up to a forty-five-degree angle before calling for the bird. This will force you to swing faster to catch the bird.

Whatever you do, don't dawdle with this bird. Get on it quickly and take it as soon as you see your lead.

The low house is just the reverse, and one of the easiest shots on the field.

Again, align your body on the eight post, but swing the gun back toward the low house to a point about three or four feet to the outside of it. On an incoming target, never align the gun directly on the trap house. It will interfere with your ability to pick up the bird quickly — in effect, blotting it out — as it comes from the house.

Once you call for the bird, swing through it from behind, track it smoothly, and don't be in a hurry to break it. Veteran shooters want to break this single in the same place they will take the target as a double, which is on an angle of thirty to forty-five degrees to the left of the shooter as the bird approaches them. If you get into the habit of

Here's the proper starting position for high house 1. The knees are flexed and the barrel is set 30 degrees above horizontal. When the bird comes from above and behind, shooter needs only to swing down and through the bird, triggering when the barrel is six inches below the target.

shooting it there, you will find it an easy matter to pick it up during doubles. The lead for this target in that position is one foot.

If you shoot singles as described, doubles are easy. Align on the eight post, take the high house quickly, then swing smoothly back to take the low house in the same place you were breaking it as a single. The leads are the same.

Station 2: Again, four shots: high and low house singles and doubles, but this one is tougher.

Every skeet shooter has his personal demon, and mine is high house 2. Moving almost nine yards to the right of the house changes the angle to a hard quartering shot that must be taken quickly with a great deal of lateral movement by the gun.

You can shoot station 1 in an upright, knees-locked position, but not station 2 (or 3 through 6, for that matter). Your body must uncoil quickly on this shot and locked knees limit that. Keep the knees slightly flexed, and you'll swing more smoothly on the upcoming stations.

To break the high house, I align on the eight post (sometimes hedging a bit to the right of it). The body is pivoted to bring the gun back about two-thirds of the way between the eight post and the house, at the same elevation as the target will appear.

When the bird is released, the body uncoils rapidly to swing through the bird, and as soon as I see 2½ feet of lead, the shot is triggered. Follow-through is critical on this shot. Like high house 1, this bird must be broken quickly.

Low house 2, however, is easy. Treat it exactly the same as low house 1, but increase the lead to two feet.

Doubles at station 2 are no different than at station 1. Get on the first bird fast, and come back smoothly to take the second.

If a shooter is having problems with high house 2, the best solution is to shoot faster and swing harder. Drive the gun through the bird. It's hard to overlead this station.

Station 3: Singles only here: one high house and one low. The angle on the birds is still a quartering one — high house going away and low house coming in — but they become more "crossing" shots requiring greater lead, but giving the shooter more time. Use the same body position for station 3 high house as for station 2. The shot is similar, but you have more time. The lead is three feet.

Station 3 low house is, again, similar to the 2 low house and can be broken the same way with a lead of 3½ feet.

The shooter should start both stations aligned on the eight post with the gun barrel brought back two-thirds of the way between the post and the house being shot.

Station 4: Singles again, and both houses are direct crossing shots, with the bird passing over the eight post at a distance of twenty-one yards. As should now be becoming familiar, align on the eight post, bring the gun two-thirds of the way back to the house and give the target four feet of lead. Shooters miss this target, because they don't believe a four-foot lead is needed at twenty-one yards — but it is! This is the longest lead you will see on a skeet field.

Until now, shooters have been seeing new angles and leads at each station. For the next three stations, however, things start to get familiar.

Low house 6 is another hard target that requires extreme and fast lateral movement. This shooter missed the bird because his gun was initially positioned too far back. His upright shooting stance with locked knees also prevented needed lateral movement.

Station 5: This is nothing more than station 3 in reverse, with the high house becoming the incoming target and the low house the outgoing. The leads are the same: the high house is shot first using the same positioning and lead of 3½ feet that you used on the incomer (low house 3) at station 3.

The low house outgoing shot requires the same position and three-foot lead as did the outgoing high house at station 3. The only real difference is the low house target takes off at a more abrupt upward angle, requiring the shooter not only to swing through the target, but slightly upwards, as well. This is where one will quickly see the advantage of a flexed-knee shooting stance!

Station 6: This is station 2 in reverse: a pair of singles and doubles. The high house target is shot first in singles and is a dead ringer for the low house 2 target. Take your time and use two feet of lead.

The low house target is shot second in singles, but will be the first target shot in the doubles phase. Again, this is quite similar to the high house 2 in that it is a hard-quartering shot that must be broken quickly with 2½ feet of lead. But it is rising at a more abrupt angle and the shooter must rise with it.

Station 7: This is the easiest station on the field and veteran shooters consider it a reward for surviving the hard, crossing shots.

A pair of singles and doubles will be shot here, with the high house being taken first in singles and the outgoing low house the first bird shot in doubles.

High house 7 is a dead ringer for low house 1: a gentle incomer requiring one foot of lead that is broken at a thirty- to forty-five-degree angle as it approaches the shooter.

Experienced shooters can break this target with no gun movement. Simply align the gun on the eight post, raise the barrel until it is aiming eight feet above it, and call for the bird. If the trap is properly calibrated, the target will appear right over the shotgun's front bead. Just pull the trigger!

The low house is the easiest shot on the field. It looks like a dead straightaway and it is!

Doubles here are incredibly simple. Get the proper gun position to break the low without gun movement, let the recoil move the gun to pick up the incoming target and you've got all day to break it.

Having completed our trip around the outside of the field, it's time to step inside and face the two targets most intimidating to new shooters: high and low house 8. To the uninitiated, one seems to be staring right down the launching tube of a ballistic missile with the targets coming incredibly close and fast.

That's basically an accurate assessment. Except, you have more time than you think, and the shots are far easier than they appear.

Station 8: One shot from each house with the high house taken first. This bird will move toward the shooter at a slight left-to-right angle. The easiest way to break it is to align gun and body on the trap opening, then swing the body to bring the gun three to four feet outside of the house. When the bird is released, the gun is quickly swung up and through the bird. Some shooters trigger the shot as soon as the muzzle blots out the bird, but I prefer to see just a bit of bird behind the muzzle, getting the gun just an inch or so ahead.

The low house is the same. Align on the trap opening, move the gun three feet outside, then swing straight up and through the bird. I fire on this target as soon as the muzzle blots out the bird.

If you've been counting rounds, you'll know we've only fired twenty-four of our twenty-five shots. The last round is called the option round, and it is used to repeat the shot on the first bird you miss on the field. If you get to low house 8 without a miss, it is fired there. For those who never run twenty-five straight, that second low house 8 can be the toughest shot on the field!

"Was I behind that bird?" This is a common question since it is a common reason for missing. The shooter stops or slows his swing. Surprisingly, the trap puller often can "see" where the shot charge goes and advise the shooter.

The above angles and leads provide all the information needed to shoot perfect scores. But it has to be assimilated by the subconscious mind. In other words, the shooter has to see and successfully handle the targets enough to build positive images of them. That means practice and training, and there are good and bad ways to do this.

The worst is simply to fall in with a squad and shoot a round.

Here, each target is a new experience (at least for the new shooter), and by the time he is beginning to understand it, he will move to another one. In addition, he'll also receive a lot of well intentioned, but sometimes confusing, advice. This will do him no good until he gets back to that station on the next round, and only serves to cloud his mind for the upcoming shots. There is a better way.

Each shot on a skeet field is different, but similar to certain others. The best way to learn the basics of skeet quickly and with a minimum of ammunition expended is to start by mastering one shot, and let that positive experience aid you in conquering the next. Here is how one coach I know goes about it:

Start on station 7, shooting only the high house. This is an easy target, giving the shooter plenty of time. Once the shooter can break this consistently — and it doesn't take long — move to station 6 and repeat the high house. The two shots are similar, with only a change of lead required.

Then, move to high house 5. Similar again, with just a slight change of lead.

Each shot builds upon the positive experiences of the last shot. By the time the shooter reaches station 4 high house, he is beginning to see the symmetry and understand the game.

From there, move to station 1 and continue shooting only incoming shots, moving through stations 2, 3 and 4, until the shooter has a firm grasp of the techniques and leads needed to break the incoming targets. This sometimes can be accomplished in as little as two or three boxes of shells!

Now, return to station 7 and start working only on the outgoing targets. These are tougher, but the shooter already has built his confidence and has an understanding of the leads required at varying stations. Learning them this way is much easier than shooting a conventional round.

Once each singles station is understood, the shooter will have little trouble catching onto doubles at stations 1, 2, 6 and 7.

By learning skeet one station at a time, the shooter can save a great deal of time, ammunition and frustration.

And when he steps up to shoot his first full round, there will be no surprises. He's already broken every target on the field and has all the knowledge he needs to master skeet's toughest shots. — *Chris Christian*

CHAPTER 9

SPORTING CLAYS, ANYONE?

First, You'd Better Master Skeet!

In tournament skeet, the gun is fully mounted before the target's release. Hunters say this isn't like field shooting.

The essence of skeet shooting is learning how to apply the fundamentals of the shotgun swing on crossing targets.

REMEMBER WHEN sporting clays first came to the U.S. back in the early 1980s and you were told, "It's a tough game, and you're lucky if you break more than fifty percent!"?

Well, we've got news for you: A lot of guys are breaking more than fifty percent! It isn't unusual for somebody to post a score above ninety percent these days, and more than a few sporting clays buffs average beyond eighty percent for a full year. Indeed, one of the toughest sporting clays courses ever set up in the U.S. was on Okemo Mountain, Vermont, for the 1992 international championship, and George Digweed of Great Britain won that with 192x-200. The boys are getting better!

What sets off these sporting clays champions and top-notch field shots from those who still can't get more than 25x50 on a sporting clays course or bring down more than a half-dozen doves with a full box of shotshells? Most of them have a background in skeet shooting. British and world champion George Digweed, for example, also was a member of England's skeet team, and he broke nineteen perfect scores of one hundred straight. Digweed has written that, "I am certain that shooting skeet has contributed to my success in sporting clays and it has definitely helped my concentration."

Another British and world champion, Mickey Rouse, has won both the English skeet championship and important events in sporting clays. And Dan Carlisle, who was twice U.S. national champion in sporting clays, was first an Olympic skeet and trap shooter, having once set a world record in international skeet of 200x200.

Thus the story goes: Top-scoring sporting clays shooters don't come out of the woods with their field-grade shotguns to set the scattergunning world on its ear. The outstanding clay target and field shots tend to have a meaningful background in skeet.

While the rest of the world still looks favorably on skeet,

Above, the techniques used to take passing ducks is the same as shooting a crossing clay on the skeet field. Left, many hunters who try their skills at sporting clays are frustrated with their scores. A shooter can improve by learning the basics of skeet .

however, many American sportsmen ignore it. This is unfortunate, of course, because skeet is the best game around for teaching one to swing a shotgun. Indeed, sporting clays doesn't teach a swing — it demands one! The hunter or casual shooter who steps onto a sporting clays course without a reasonably developed physical swing is in for a hard time — one that makes sporting clays seem tougher than it really is!

Skeet was developed around the time of WWI for the practical purpose of giving some New England bird hunters practice on crossing, incoming and overhead angles that aren't a part of trapshooting, which throws only shallow-angle, outgoing targets. The originators traced a big circle about forty yards in diameter on an open field, set a trap machine at twelve o'clock to throw clays over the six o'clock point, then they proceeded to shoot from the various hour points on the circle. The trap boy was protected by a sheet of metal, and they all apparently had a good time until a neighbor complained that pellets were falling on her hen house! What to do?

The answer was to place a second trap at the six o'clock point to throw back over the twelve o'clock point, thereby

Some special skeet-grade side-by-sides of yesteryear are now excellent upland bird guns and collector items. This is a Parker GHE. While the side-by-side never made it as a serious skeet gun, it's often used by dedicated bird hunters.

utilizing only that half of the circle which faced away from the hen house. This not only seemed to satisfy the neighbor, but also created the pair of opposed traps we now know as the high house and the low house.

Eventually, this new form of shooting received publicity in that era's foremost outdoor magazines, and the game caught on quickly. Its heyday seems to have been the 1930s and 1940s, when the Hollywood colony was quite active in skeet and the Air Corps used it to train aerial gunners of WWII in deflection firing. Hunters thought it was great practice for everything from rising quail and pheasants to crossing ducks and incoming doves. Indeed, when skeet retained this practical flavor that combined fun with a purpose, it was broadly accepted and enjoyed.

Many skeetmen of that day simply used field-grade guns to practice for hunting. Gradually, though, gunmakers began turning out designs intended primarily for skeet. These featured solid or ventilated ribs, beavertail forearms, the then-newfangled skeet chokes, and generally twenty-six-inch barrels. There were pumps, autoloaders, side-by-sides, and even a few over/unders. Today, the pumps and side-by-sides have pretty much fallen from favor among serious tournament skeet shooters, while autoloaders and over/unders dominate competitions.

But the skeet guns of yesteryear excited shooters then and still appeal to collectors and upland hunters. The 28-gauge Winchester Model 12 skeet gun appeared in 1935, while the Model 42 .410-bore was introduced in 1932.

Remington's Model 32 over/under came out in 1931, as did the same company's slick Model 31 slide-action which became known as "the gun with the ball-bearing action." Winchester's Model 21 side-by-side was on the market in 1930, although it wasn't immediately available in an advanced skeet grade; that came a few years later, but when it was made, it became an outstanding upland bird gun as well as a skeet piece.

Remington's Model 11 and Browning's Auto-5 were extremely popular skeet guns, with the Savage Model 720 series also getting a play. And in 1940, Winchester launched the first semi-autoloading scattergun to be commercially produced with a rounded receiver, the Model 40. All these guns found favor with a bulbous Cutts Compensator soldered to the barrels for overall lengths of twenty-five or twenty-six inches. Such innovations intrigued shooters and attracted them to the sport.

But in the last twenty years or so, skeet has suffered from a decline in interest. The main reason for this slide, it seems, is an overemphasis on tournament shooting.

To simplify the officiating in competitons, skeet rules were changed in the 1950s to permit a fully mounted gun and to do away with the three-second, variable target release. These changes have negated much of skeet's allure for bird hunters and turned it into a groove shooter's contest. Hunters take a look at skeet, feel intimidated by the refined equipment and long lists of perfect scores, then walk away, shaking their heads sadly.

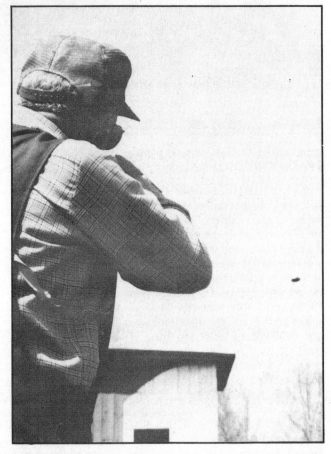

Left, this shooter swings through the target, centers it while continuing into a positive follow-through. Below, taking an overhead incomer on a skeet field is like swinging into a high dove or duck. The range may be slightly closer, but the movement is the same.

This is a shame, of course, because skeet was not devised to be a competitive game. It was a hunter's practice field, a purpose it served beautifully. For the strength of skeet is that it offers all the basic swing angles in one compact layout. The angles of hunting and sporting clays are mainly exaggerations of the shots found in skeet. To be a consistent shooter afield or on sporting clays, then, you've first got to master skeet! Being able to break 23x25 or better in skeet on a regular basis indicates that one has a handle on wingshooting fundamentals.

There is no better place to learn those rudiments than the skeet field, since it's all right there on one semi-circle with about a twenty-yard radius. If one angle bugs you, take a puller and practice it until you've learned the feel of the correct swing. When you're trying to perfect an athletic move (and wingshooting *is* athletic in nature), repetition is the mother of learning.

Another strength of skeet is that its angles aren't extremely difficult nor, as in the case of some sporting clays stands, impossible. A hunter learns nothing by going through a sporting clays course that is beyond his level of achieved skill, unless it is that he finally recognizes his shortcomings and returns to the skeet field to develop a smooth swing.

Finally, skeet gives one substantially more practice for the money than sporting clays. It isn't unusual to pay $15 for fifty sporting clays targets, whereas skeet can be shot for $2.50 to $4 per twenty-five targets, depending upon the club and the location.

If skeet turns off hunters, it is mainly because of the fully mounted gun which is nothing like hunting. But always remember that this high-gun rule (1) only permits a pre-mounted gun, it doesn't require it; and (2) the liberalized skeet rules only apply to registered tournaments.

Thus, if you're interested in hunting rather than competitions — break the rules! Lower your gun for a field-style start and ask the puller to give you variably timed target releases. A good practice method is to drop the gun according to sporting clays rules, which is to a point below the arm pit. Skeet clays do snap out of the houses smartly, but so do ruffed grouse flash in the thicket and sporting clays targets streak between trees. If you can learn to handle skeet clays with a lowered gun, you're on your way to better birds-to-shells ratios afield and higher sporting clays scores.

The point is don't let yourself be intimidated by tournament shooters or tournament rules. Skeet never was intended for that. Use the game as it was developed — as bird shooters practicing for bird shooting. As an adjunct, it's also the best place to start if you get serious about sporting clays.

Skeet is a superb summer game for the bird hunter.

The game of skeet as shot in these United States has eight stations, all of which can be translated into a field-shooting function. The first station is at the base of the high house, which is on the left of the field. The stations then progress around the semi-circle in a counter clockwise manner as illustrated in the accompanying illustration. These stations are set at the hourly intervals. For example, station 2 is where eleven o'clock would be, station 3 is at ten o'clock, station 4 at nine o'clock, et cetera. Station 7 is at the low house.

Station 8 is placed squarely between the high and low house for an overhead shot. The squad starts at station 1 and finishes at station 8. A normal sequence goes like this:

Skeet fields were originally designed to give a shotgunner all the practical angles he would encounter in the field.

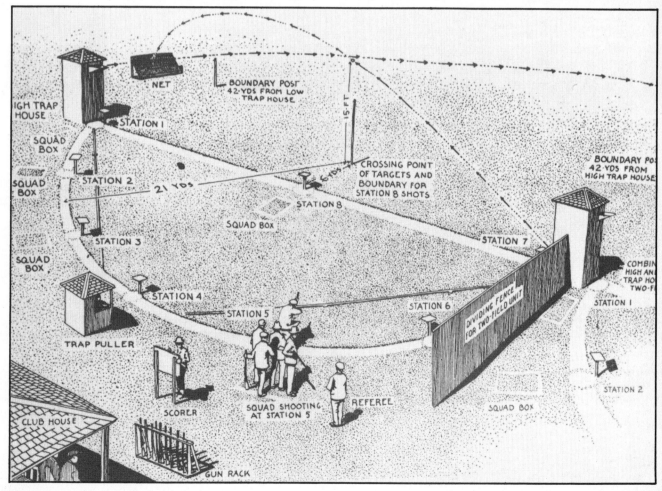

MODEL 720-C
12 and 16 Gauge

WITH CUTTS COMPENSATOR

MODEL 720-C—5 Shot or 3 Shot

...me specifications as Model 720 except as follows: Special ...l with Cutts Compensator attached, furnished with two ...tubes. Over-all barrel length 27″ when fitted with com...or with spreader tube. Over-all barrel length 28″ when ...with compensator with No. 705 full-choke tube. Modified ...tube will be substituted if specified. Compensator regularly

made of blued steel. Can be furnished made of aluminu... on special order.

The Cutts Compensator, when attached to the muzzle ... guns, reduces recoil from 35% to 46% and provides a m... securing various chokes in one barrel by changing the chok... which screw on the end of the compensator.

Price $108.10

EXTRA BARRELS FOR ALL SAVAGE AUTOMATIC SHOTGUNS

In skeet's heyday, one of the the sport's important guns was the Savage Model 720-C (above) which came with a Cutts Compensator. Left, if you can swing on and hit a passing duck, you can be successful at skeet.

Station 1: High and low house singles. Simultaneous doubles.

Station 2: High and low house singles. Simultaneous doubles.

Station 3: High and low house singles.

Station 4: High and low house singles.

Station 5: High and low house singles.

Station 6: High and low house singles. Simultaneous doubles.

Station 7: High and low house doubles. Simultaneous doubles.

Station 8: High and low house singles.

A hunter who first looks at skeet may find it a mechanical game. "You know where they're coming from and where they're going," is the normal observation. And you do.

But it's all different when it's *you* holding the gun and

having to make the shot. Now you have to apply the basics of shotgun handling and swinging in that second or so that the target remains in range, and you quickly recognize that it's easier to watch somebody break skeet targets than it is to do it yourself. Moreover, you'll note the similarities between skeet angles and game shooting afield.

The station 1 high house target, for example, comes out above the shooter's head and flies away with a slight downward bias. It's the shot a grouse hunter can get from a bird flushing out of a pine or a duck hunter can get when a bird sneaks in from behind.

The station 1 low house is a lazy incomer, but it teaches the hunter to keep his head down and gun moving. And it isn't unlike a diver duck coming into the blocks or an upland bird that's been flushed well out by a dog.

Station 2 presents a high house outgoer which also looks like a grouse flushing from a tall tree or a duck or dove slicing in from the left. Station 2 low house is an incomer passing farther out than the first low house clay, and it resembles a flaring duck that took a look at the decoys and thought better of it.

Stations 3, 4 and 5 all are crossing shots not unlike those of doves and waterfowl. The skeet range may be closer than those of actual field shooting, but the swing must be

Left, this is a good low-gun starting position for skeet practice. Below, while the pump gun has fallen from favor among tournament shooters, it's still viable for skeet, especially for hunters.

made the same; consequently, skeet is excellent training, because it forces the same gun handling. The big mistake people often make is believing they can make one kind of swing on skeet, then use another on game. It doesn't work that way. Apply the swing that scores on skeet crossers, and you'll do well afield and/or on longer sporting clays shots.

Station 6 has a high house incomer that looks like a dove, while the low 6 outgoer is a tough target that moves like a low-flushed quail with its tail feather aflame. Catch this one consistently, and no quail or close-in ruffed grouse will ever confuse you again.

Station 7 has an easy incomer riding high; it again tests one's fundamentals to make certain of a head-down pivot and a positive follow-through. The low house from station 7 is a straight-away, but you'd be surprised how many beginners miss it by applying faulty technique. In fact,

some important skeet matches have been lost at low 7 when the shooter nonchalantly thought he or she had it in the bag. It's good practice for those shots taken over a pointer.

Station 8 has a pair of overhead clays that teach a quick pivot. Beginners view this as a trick shot, but it isn't; it requires a coordinated swing and well-timed shot. Afield, it jibes with quick overhead shots on wood ducks weaving through the tree crowns.

And there you have a round of skeet — something that emulates practically every shot a hunter can expect. The angles of skeet are realistic, whereas those of sporting clays are often exaggerated. Indeed, the wonder of the last double decade is why hunters gave up on skeet when it is really the best and most economical training set-up for learning, improving and refining the fundamentals of wing-shooting. — *Don Zutz*

CHAPTER 10

IS SPORTING CLAYS A FAD?

The Sport Seems Here To Stay — If In-Fighting Doesn't Kill It!

John Cloherty, director of sporting clays development for the National Rifle Association, says sporting clays is here to stay. The NRA sees the game as a way to interest people in shooting and to get established shooters to shoot more.

Shooting sporting clays is a lot like taking game birds. Here, Carl Cupp sits in a boat to shoot clays that imitate ducks.

BY VIRTUALLY any measure, sporting clays is everything but a fad. It not only is here to stay, but the game continues to grow and embrace more and more casual recreational shooters rather than simply those who wish to compete.

Top shooters, range operators and representatives from the shooting sports industry all insist that, with each passing year, the game in the United States is evolving and expanding.

Precisely how much the game is expanding is a matter for interpretation. For example, even though the number of registered shooters is well established at between 13,000 and 14,000, the number of actual shooters is a guess. Guesstimates of how many people have shot the game range from 200,000 to three million.

Robert Davis, recognized as the founder of organized sporting clays in the United States, is amazed at how the game has grown since he first helped organize it in the last decade.

"At first, everybody thought it was just another fad," he chuckled as he recalled the early days. "But it isn't a fad. It is the closest thing to hunting you can get. And it's just plain fun."

Although sporting clays has been a factor in England since the 1920s, it was not an organized activity in the United States until 1985.

The way it started in the U.S., Davis explains, was as a spin-off of the Orvis Cup Classic which was held in Houston, Texas, in 1983. There, a basic form of the game was played.

Then, in 1984, Orvis started a shooting school in Houston which furthered interest in the clay target procedure. In May, 1985, the United States Sporting Clays Association was formed. At the 1986 Shooting, Hunting and Outdoor Trade (SHOT) Show which was held in Houston, the game of sporting clays was officially introduced to the shooting sports industry — and it has been a big hit since.

Davis estimates that there about five hundred sporting clays clubs in the country today, and that of them, 250 are affiliated with his USSCA, which has a membership of about 5000 tournament shooters.

During 1992, the USSCA hosted both the nationals and the world shoots, held consecutively at the same area. The world shoot was first, and five hundred shooters from around the globe participated. There were 612 shooters at the nationals.

Jimmie Hughes operates the Peppermill/Arvada Gun Club in Mesquite, Nevada, and because of the unique nature of his facility, Hughes is able to gauge the overall acceptance and enthusiasm for sporting clays from among hosts of people who never knew anything about the game before they tried his range.

The gun club is part of the sprawling Peppermill Hotel and Casino complex which is located where Nevada, Arizona and Utah come together — up the road about 1½ hours from Las Vegas. In fact, the casino and hotel are located in Nevada, and the shooting grounds are in Arizona, even though both are located on opposite ends of the small community of Mesquite.

"For outdoorsmen and the guys who like shotguns,

Shooting clays means doing a lot of shooting and that means having a lot of fun. Range operators keep busy.

major competitions each year, ranging from state championship shoots to the Tournament of Champions event which is put on by *Western Outdoors*.

That tournament is the culmination of an entire season of qualification rounds at ranges throughout California, and the event sees about three hundred top shooters from all over the country each year. In fact, it has become the third largest event of its kind in the country, smaller by only a bit than the nationals and the U.S. Open.

So Hughes sees not only the reactions of first-timers to sporting clays, but also the nation's best shooters at least once a year at the club.

Carolyn Morse operates the sporting clays course at the Mike Raahauge operation in Southern California — not only one of the first full-time sporting clays facilities in the nation, but one of the busiest.

"The sport is here to stay," Mrs. Morse insists. "It offers a shooter something, whether that shooter hunts or not. Everyone can participate in the sport."

Not only is Mrs. Morse a sporting clays course operator, but she is a shooter, as well, and sees a major movement within sporting clays which involves women and girls, as well as the guys.

Assisting Carolyn Morse in operating the facility is

sporting clays is a breath of fresh air," Hughes says. "I think sporting clays is a way of life."

He explains that shooting on his sporting course — which has expanded this past year from ten to seventeen stations — skyrocketed upward between fifty and sixty percent during 1991-92, and that was just the third year it was in operation.

"We see a tremendous number of hotel guests shoot here," Hughes says. "These are people who we introduce to sporting clays for the first time. Many of them are husbands and wives, or even entire families."

According to Hughes, the gun club sees about three hundred shooters a week on average, and more than half of them never have shot sporting clays before. Yet, once most of them try it, they really like it.

Interestingly, the sporting clays operation there competes directly with many other activities for the attention of guests in the 750-room complex. Major league golf courses are among the other activities.

Yet, sporting clays continues to be one of the more popular activities for hotel guests — many of whom become active shotgun shooters and sporting clays enthusiasts due solely to their exposure to the sport at the gun club.

Although the bulk of the shooters at the gun club are recreational participants only, this facility also is the site of

Actors Robert Miranda (left) and John DiSanti clearly are enjoying a day at the range shooting sporting clays.

Estie Qualey of California is one of the women who have discovered the fun of shooting sporting clays.

Estie Qualey, another of the top women shooters in the sport. Both also stress that there is a family connection to sporting clays.

"We have our kids out here everyday," Estie Qualey explains.

"All of a sudden, it occurred to us: A kid could do this," Carolyn Morse says. "It's a family sport." And she should know. Her son, Zachary, age 12, is the sub-junior national champion in sporting clays.

John Gillette runs the Tampa Bay Sporting Clays facility in Florida, the range which happens to be the "home course" for General Norman Schwarzkopf.

Although Gillette agrees with most people involved in sporting clays that it is not a fad, he does see some potential problems looming which, if left unattended, could turn the sport into more of a flash in the pan than a long-term, total success.

"It's our last big chance," Gillette says of sporting clays, posing one of the most pivotal questions ever to face the game. "Are we going to have fun, or are we going to have registered shoots?"

Gillette's words constitute a double-edged sword which has cut to the quick in sporting clays since the first day it was shot on this side of the Atlantic Ocean.

For all kinds of reasons, sporting clays is the kind of activity which could easily evolve into an elitist endeavor, and there are folks within the sporting clays superstructure who have gone far out of their way to assure that does not happen.

Even more potentially devastating, however, is the tendency for sporting clays — like any other game based on skill — to become relevant only for the top shooters, leaving everyone else in the dust.

Gillette is concerned that the sport remain viable for any interested shooter, and that it serve as a conduit to help introduce new gunners to the shooting sports in general.

Bob Edwards operates the super-posh sporting complex in Virginia known as The Homestead. In addition to other claims to fame, this course is home to the annual U.S. Open Sporting Clays Championships.

"Sporting clays is well established in Europe," Edwards says. "It is the second most popular participation sport — second only to fishing — in Europe."

Edwards notes that it was the increasing scarcity of game in England and Europe which helped spur sporting clays to its position there as a major shotgun sport. He sees parallels here in the United States.

"Sporting clays is doing that in this country now," Edwards insists. "We're following that trend. It's appealing to the sixteen to eighteen million hunters in the United States. Sporting clays is their game."

John DiSanti, of TV's "Homefront," gets into the swing of things on the sporting clays range with an over/under.

Numerous shooting angles and target presentations of sporting clays capture, hold the interest of shooters.

Although Edwards is involved in some of the most keen competition in sporting clays via the U.S. Open each year, for most of the shooters who visit his course each year, competition is not even part of the equation.

"The fun side is what is important," he notes. "We don't even encourage the use of score cards for casual shooters."

And he contends sporting clays is getting bigger all the time. "The growth is phenomenal," he explains. "Courses are popping up all over."

Meanwhile, Edwards keeps busy planning for the U.S. Open each year. In 1992, a total of 437 shooters competed, he says, noting that for 1993 he expects to see between five to six hundred. Eventually, that is a shoot which could see more than 1000 shooters compete — as is the case with certain key competitions in England.

George Vann operates the Grinders Switch sporting clays facilities near Nashville, Tennessee. This is among the most prestigious courses in the nation.

"We're involved in course design," Vann says, noting that in that role he sees exactly how much the game is gaining in popularity. "There is an increasing interest in private courses rather than public ones. There is a grass roots interest."

Vann insists one need only look at the numbers to see how steadily sporting clays is growing. For example, in its first decade in the United States, it went from a single course to several hundred registered courses, to say nothing of the many strictly private facilities.

And, Vann says, he is seeing sporting clays in the United States become more and more a part of the international scene.

"It's an international movement," he insists. "We're seeing more and more Europeans coming here. A lot of people get hooked on it very quickly."

Phil Murray of Beretta USA keeps abreast of all developments in the shooting sports in the United States, including sporting clays. And, Murray, one of the nation's leading skeet shooters for years, is excited about sporting clays and its future.

"Sporting clays is one of the best things that's come along," he says. "It has opened up a market for hunters and recreational shooters."

Murray explains that many shooters view trap and skeet as being too structured, noting that, to a large degree, sporting clays offers an environment similar to that of hunting.

"It's here to stay," he says of sporting clays. "It's going to get bigger and bigger. It has introduced a whole new kind of person to competition."

Beretta has been a major supplier of guns for sporting clays since the game first emerged in the United States. Murray explains that his company's involvement in the sport in England over the years made the presence in the United States in the sport a natural progression.

Jon Kruger of St. Ansgar, Iowa, is one of the leading sporting clays shooters in the United States. The list of his accomplishments is lengthy, including his having been a sporting clays All-America contestant every year there has been such a title. He also holds championship titles in virtually every level of competition short of the world.

"A fad?" he asks himself. "I don't think so. It's a clay target game that can keep hunters' interest going, and there are about 19½ million licensed hunters in the United States."

Kruger said he felt one of the better ways to judge the acceptance of sporting clays nationally is the fact that the game is now being reported in all kinds of non-shooting-related publications like *USA Today* and the *New York Times*.

"Sporting clays keeps getting bigger by the month," he says, explaining that variations like five-stand sporting are helping expose more and more shooters to the sport.

He feels such games are good for a lot of clubs around the country where there is not enough room to establish a full-scale sporting clays layout.

John Cloherty is director of sporting clays development for the National Rifle Association of America, as well as a world record holder for having broken more clay targets in an hour than anyone else on earth.

Cloherty has been shooting sporting clays since that

game's early days in the United States, and was a AA level competitor before taking on his current job — promoting sporting clays nationwide.

Cloherty insists the sport is certainly no fad, and so long as normal folks can shoot it, it never will fade.

"If it becomes so costly that the average guy can't do it, then the possibility exists that sporting clays could become a fad," Cloherty explains. "But so long as a guy — or gal — can take out a gun and shoot the game, it will continue to grow."

Cloherty explains that the NRA is interested in having sporting clays help promote the concept of recreational shooting around the country, insisting that the organization has no plans to become a sanctioning body for competitions or other shoots.

In a relatively small recent survey, the NRA found that more than 300,000 of its members showed a strong interest in sporting clays — and that is a long way from the kinds of numbers generated by any kind of a fad.

"The NRA is looking into various programs, including things like sporting clays leagues," Cloherty explains, noting that the NRA also is interested in "taking sporting clays to areas where there are no specific courses for the game, but where other shotgun shooting facilities do exist."

The many challenging shooting stations keep sporting clays an exciting game that is enjoyed by young and old.

It's a delight to take targets at odd angles, as this shooter is doing. He must shoot down and away to hit the target.

Rick "KK" Kennerknecht of Lomita, California, is a sporting clays pioneer in the United States, having shot the game here since its official beginnings in the 1980s.

"At that time, I think there were about twelve to fifteen sporting clays courses in the United States, and only one in California which was owned and operated by Dan Carlisle (Olympic shotgunner) at the Raahauge Shooting Sports facility," he explains.

"I have been actively involved in the sport on a national and international level since 1988 as both a competitor and a businessman in the shooting sports." (He owns KK

Not all shots in sporting clays are overhead. Here, a shooter takes a clay target that is dropping and quartering away.

Awards Manufacturing which provides medals and trophies for shooting events.)

"I have seen this new discipline grow from fifteen locations to over six hundred locations nationwide to date, not to mention the uncounted private courses," he says. "The industry has invested millions of dollars developing sporting clays guns and gadgets. The industry has written a dozen sporting clays books and made two dozen sporting clays video tapes.

"We now hear about sporting clays stories and happenings in non-related periodicals such as *Business Week, Forbes* and *USA Today*," KK stresses. "I've heard that over 1.5 million people have shot some form of sporting clays since 1985. Sporting clays has been popular in England and Europe since the 1920s, so if this is a fad, I'll bet it's one of those seventy-five-year fads!"

Doug Fuller of Oklahoma City, Oklahoma, feels sporting clays is here to stay. "I don't think it's a fad," he says, noting that he feels economics are probably the biggest inhibiting factor to an even faster expansion of the sport.

"Cost is a big deterrent," he contends, noting that in his part of the country, ranges routinely charge $15 for fifty targets, and that doesn't include many "specialty" targets like rabbits, battues, minis or midis. By comparison, trap and skeet facilities in the same area routinely charge $10 to $12 for the same number of targets.

Another problem facing sporting clays in some areas, Fuller notes, is that many of the ardent trap and skeet shooters are reluctant to get involved in sporting clays. Perhaps that is because they are a bit timid, even maybe a

bit afraid of a game in which perfect scores almost never happen.

And Fuller feels that some courses are boring their clientele to death. "A lot of courses are getting into a rut, because they don't change their layouts." He notes that all it would take would be a few different target presentations every now and then to keep particular courses interesting and to keep shooters coming back for more.

"Five-stand (sporting) seems to be picking up pretty good out here," he says, noting that the five-stand layouts allow more and more people to experience some of the kinds of target presentations encountered in sporting clays. Meanwhile, Fuller says it is the variety of targets and presentations which keep his interest keen in the game.

"Specialty targets," he sighs. "To me, that's what sporting clays is all about."

As much as sporting clays continues to grow and gain in popularity, it does have its darker side — an element which, if left unattended, could not only retard growth in the future, but which could upset the entire apple cart.

To understand this facet of the game, it is necessary to appreciate that there is a difference between the sport itself, as a game, and the "organized" entity of sporting clays.

The game, itself, is relatively simple. It is composed of a host of different types of clay target presentations which generally imitate rather closely the kinds of shots made at game animals and birds. Hence, it has become known as the "bloodless" game.

Like golf, no two sporting clays facilities are exactly

Getting together for clays can be an enjoyable social event. This group gathers at Raahauge's Sporting Clays range in California.

alike, nor are they ever intended to be. Hence, there is an inherent individuality about the sport itself, with target presentations and surroundings changing from one facility to another.

Unlike the more traditional trap and skeet layouts, sporting clays lends itself more to reflecting the natural surroundings of the area of the country, or world, where it happens to be. For example, along the East Coast, there are facilities which are located in various kinds of wooded areas. In the West, there are desert motifs.

Yet, on the organizational front, there have been a number of efforts to strip the sport of its inherent individuality in favor of a dictated uniformity. The roots of this reality are based in the fact that for a number of years there have been two separate sanctioning organizations nationwide.

The United States Sporting Clays Association, founded by Bob Davis, was the original sporting clays sanctioning organization in this country.

However, within the first few years that the game was being shot in the United States, another national sanctioning group emerged. This is the National Sporting Clays Association which is tied to the National Skeet Shooting Association.

Both sporting clays sanctioning groups are headquartered in Texas — the state which played a major part in the evolution of the sport in the United States.

Disagreements within the inner circles of sporting clays were at the crux of the formation of the NSCA in the first place, and there has been no love lost between the two groups since.

For several years, individual courses around the country would hold shoots, sometimes sanctioned by one group, and other times by the other group. However, in 1992, the NSCA began enforcing a rule it had which set in motion a divisive strain on the entire game. Simply put, that organi-

zation dictated to ranges that if the range wanted to throw NSCA-sanctioned events and targets, they could not also host USSCA events.

This level of in-fighting caused some facilites to take a close look, not only at each of the organizations, but at themselves, as well. Range operators, most of them independent business people, did not uniformly lock step and go in either direction.

Some ranges even put the question to a vote among local shooters. At Raahauge's in Southern California, the shooters voted that they wanted to be able to shoot both kinds of tournaments. However, the shooters' desires were ignored, and the NSCA dictated that since Raahauge's had USSCA events, it could not have NSCA events.

This rift is far from over as this chapter is being written. Suffice to say that any such unilateral moves are definitional divisive and that there is a measurable degree of fallout from those activities. Such activities are exclusive in nature at a time when the sport needs things to be inclusive, instead.

Sporting clays is not a fad. However, until there is some sort of peace within the ranks, sporting clays will not be able to enjoy the success it otherwise could. And, depending upon how far such internal political matters are taken, the sport could actually be measurably harmed.

Some among the sport are pushing for a single, uniform sanctioning organization, but at last check, there was no consensus on what that organization might be — or even if it might eventually be neither of the first two.

Regardless, it will become necessary, if the sport is to thrive in the future, for there to be a more united front within the game. And, if the sport is to realize its full potential, that unification must be immediately apparent to newcomers when they first become excited about shooting clays. — *Steve Comus*

CHAPTER 11

BASICS OF SPORTING CLAYS

Here Are The Targets You'll Face — And What To Do About Them!

As a means of protection, cages such as this are built on many sporting clays ranges to limit swing of the gun.

TRAPPER READY. Pull! Dead Bird.

Sporting clays — golf with a shotgun — is the fastest growing shooting sport today, and the best and most exciting way to sharpen your hunting skills. Even the station names emulate the thrill of the hunt: rising teal, driven pheasant, darting dove, bolting rabbit, running fox, whistlin' woodies, flushing grouse, wily woodcock, to name a few.

Just as golf courses vary, each sporting clay range is unique. In fact, the courses are changed frequently to keep them new and challenging — just like hunting. Targets confound the sporting clays shooter from every conceivable direction: right to left, left to right, coming and going, in singles and multiples — or in any combination thereof. They spring, fly, dive, roll, hop, even multiply.

Each sporting clays range is designed and matched to the terrain and consists of various stations that simulate hunting situations. For example, in the ducks-over-water station, clay pigeons sail above the surface of a pond with the shooter positioned in a boat or blind. It's up to the hunter to shatter the clay pigeons before they hit the water. No pigeons — no score.

On a sporting clays course, each station simulates a certain species of game animal as the shooter shoots from a boat, blind, open field or wooded area. The stations can vary in number from course to course, but they all imitate hunting situations such as quail flying over brush, doves

The size of the claybirds differs for the various facets of sporting clays. The differences are explained in the text.

rocketing through trees or running rabbits. As simple as it sounds, even the most expert shotgunners have to get the feel of sporting clays. A challenging course can humble you.

So is this sporting clays game all it's cracked up to be? This seems to be a question many shotgunners ask after they've tried this wingshooting game — sometimes even before they've finished their first round. It is, if you keep the right perspective so you get out of the sport what you're looking for. Not keeping score and shooting the gun with which you're used to bird hunting are but two secrets that will help avoid the first-round, shattered-ego blues.

So how do you shoot a sporting clays course without frustration; so it's fun like it's supposed to be?

First, and most important, be consistent. Pick a gun you like and stick with it. Then pick a load you like and stick with it. Then you'll be able to concentrate on the finer details of how to shoot each station.

While each course and station will be a little different, some rules of shooting remain the same. You can compare clay shooting to shooting baskets. A good basketball player may fake a shot when he is off balance to get a defensive player out of position, but when he actually shoots a jump shot, he always will try to be squared off to the basket. In clay shooting, it's the same thing.

What a lot of inexperienced shotgunners will tend to do, if say the bird is going from right to left, is face where the bird is coming from. But if the bird travels to his left, by the time he gets ready to engage the target, he's run out of swing. What the experienced target shooter has to do — just like the basketball player — is square himself up to the target. What he does is place his foot position where he's actually going to shoot at the bird, then wrap himself back to where the bird is coming from. This is also true if you're shooting from a blind sitting down. Square yourself with the spot where you want to break the target, then swing back to where you believe the birds will come from. That way, you'll always have good fluid movement — an important point for any shooter to remember.

The other thing a shooter needs to remember is the rear sight of a shotgun. If you move your head off the stock or to the right or left, that really changes the strike of the pattern. If you move your head a quarter-inch off the stock, to the right or left, it will change the strike of the pattern ten inches at forty yards. So it's really important to concentrate on keeping your head on the stock as you pull the trigger. This is especially important when the targets are high, for you may have an unconscious tendency to lift your head and take a look. Once you get these basic rules down, you will be ready to approach each station.

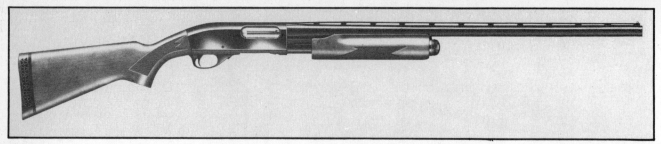

Pump-action shotguns such as the Remington Sportsman 12 can be used in sporting clays, as can the autoloaders.

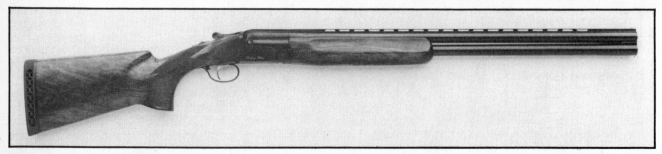

Perazzi was one of the first to climb on the sporting clays bandwagon, producing a special model for sport.

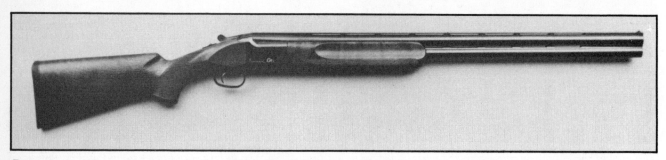

Browning's GTI also has been produced in a sporting clays version. Interchangeable choke tubes are a help.

DARTING DOVES

This testy target can be presented either as an incoming or going-away shot that may vary from directly overhead to a slight quartering shot. But regardless of how it is thrown, count on the birds being high.

With going-away targets, most experienced shooters tilt their heads backward to peer at or just in front of the trap house so they will be able to pick up the path of the bird as soon as possible. Feet should be pointed toward the spot where the shooter anticipates he will break the bird. Begin swinging the muzzle to track the bird as soon as it's spotted, firing as soon as the sight picture is correct and the gun's butt is shouldered. Shoot quickly, since the longer you wait, the farther the target will be.

On incoming doves, you usually have a bit more time to shoot, because the target gets closer the longer you wait. Sounds easy? Well, there are actually two common pitfalls to this type of shot. The first is that many shooters "ride" incoming doves by tracking them too long with a fully shouldered gun instead of snapshooting them instinctively. The second mistake is in waiting until the clay is directly overhead or past and dropping, when the shooter is off balance and longer leads are needed.

For overhead clays, #8 shot works fine with the choke depending on the height of the tower and the angle of the

bird. For really long-range tower shots, some favor #7½s. But don't make the common mistake of choking too tight for tower birds. Improved cylinder will reach a lot farther than many shooters believe.

DECOYING DUCKS

The problem with these web-footed wonders is that they are usually *dropping* the entire time they are in range. Mix in the distinct possibility they will be battues — wafer-thin clays that resemble flying razor blades — and the station seems to be "for the birds." Before you concede these deadly droppers are equally deadly to your scorecard, consider a few tips the pros use to up their scores.

These duck targets usually are thrown from in front or to the side of the shooter. As the clay zooms toward the decoy spread, it planes to present an edge on view to the shooter. Wait it out — without "riding" it out — and the clay will turn to reveal its full top or underside surface just as it begins to descend. This is the time to take your best shot — before the bird begins to fall rapidly toward the water.

This timing is particularly crucial when shooting battues, because this specialty target is a mere three-eighths-inch thick. In addition to timing, you've got to know where to send your shot. Experimentation will show just how far under the target you have to point. But don't forget to allow

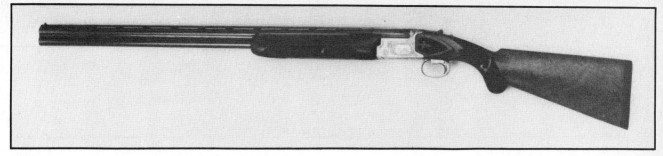

While other shotguns serve well, the over/under seems to be taking over the sport as the instrument of choice.

for the forward lead necessary to dust a crossing duck. This need to shoot both under and in front of a clay is what catches most shooters off-guard when dealing with dropping crossers. But that's what makes sporting clays a challenge.

Like all stations, you've got to get the timing and leads down pat. Then it's practice, practice — and more practice.

WILY WOODCOCK

This might be the name given your local course's close-range incomer — a well-earned title due to the timber-doodle's disarming habit of flushing close and flying back toward the shooter. These shots may be true incomers or slightly quartering, with many courses throwing a combination of both, either as singles or pairs.

Best to wait out these incomers until they're close, but not too close. Even cylinder-choke patterns are deceptively small at ranges under ten or fifteen yards, leaving extremely little margin of error in your gun point. Rendering clays to mere puffs of smoke at such ranges, however, is satisfying if not spectacular. Try #9 shot here, and you'll likely never use anything else.

The object is to block out the bird and shoot. Simple

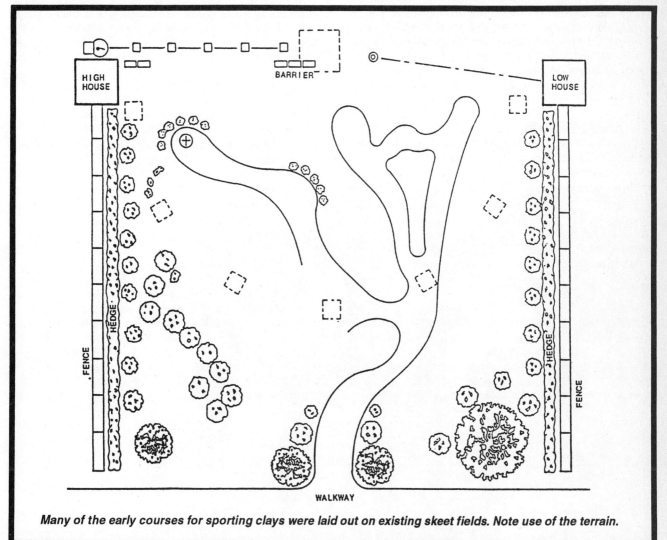

Many of the early courses for sporting clays were laid out on existing skeet fields. Note use of the terrain.

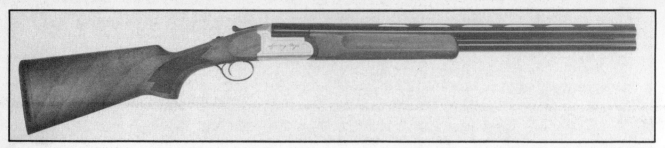

Savage Arms has reworked their popular Model 312 over/under for use in sporting clays. The price has helped sales.

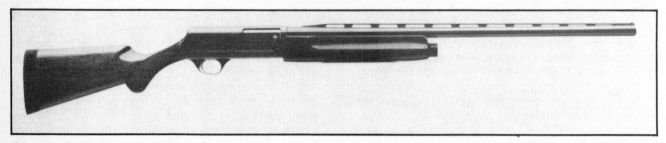

Among gas-operated semi-autos, Browning's A-500G has a following. Low recoil factor is a plus for some shooters.

enough until you introduce brushy tangles, downed treetops and lots of shadows to the recipe. Decide where you're going to kill the bird and shoot without hesitation. Wait and the clay will be lost behind a screen of vegetation — sometimes to never present another shot. Doubles thrown under these conditions are guaranteed to cure any shooter from "riding" birds. There simply isn't enough time to take anything more leisurely than a truly instinctive snapshot.

FUR AND FEATHER

Here's a one-two combination delivered to see how well the mixed-bag gunner can handle bunnies and birds — often in quick succession!

The rabbit, a thick-edged target rolled on its side, bounds along the ground with the sole intention of bouncing out of the path of shot charges. So the savvy shooter takes his shot just after the rabbit has headed skyward, when its trajectory is predictable — at least, until it hits the ground again.

Those gunners who insist on shooting this clay while it is rolling on the ground find it helpful to shoot just *under* it, taking any advantage the flying debris and ricocheting pellets can muster to render the rabbit to pieces. In any case, #8s or even #9s work well on this typically close-range target, despite its thick appearance.

Most shooters who miss the rabbit shoot in front of it.

Sporting clays courses take advantage of the flora to make it difficult to spot the various types of claybirds.

By putting the shooter in a pit-type blind for one of the sequences, the low shooting angle can add realism.

Even when led too far, the dirt kicked up from the shot charge will often appear behind the bird. This causes shooters to think they have shot behind the target while the clay actually rolled past the impact point after the shot hit the ground.

The other half of this act, the feather, is an aerial target. Call it a pheasant or grouse or quail or whatever — but don't call it easy!

The bird, usually a crossing or quartering target, isn't usually tough by itself. But when thrown after the slower rabbit as a report or following pair, it's a real fastball that can throw even experienced shooters off kilter.

To handle this dynamic duo, remember the basics. Take the rabbit where it presents itself the best — usually in mid-air for the least surprises. Make sure you don't cut off your follow-through prematurely in an effort to find and track the bird target. Simply wind back to where the bird will come from, pick it up with the muzzle, swing on it and fire when the gun's butt has been gently shouldered — all in one smooth motion.

BOUNCING BUNNIES

This one looks so easy, just two targets which simulate rabbits bouncing along the ground. But these targets might bounce anywhere. They're completely unpredictable and can cause more frustration than any other station. The most important factors here are stance and gun position. Once you have squared yourself to the point where you hope to break the target, your body should be wound back toward the trap, with the gun just off of the shoulder and the muzzles just under the line the target will be taking.

Shoot below the target. Don't start your gun too high or too low. Find that smooth plane so you can move your gun through the target and break it. You pick your spot out there, square your stance, and when you come to that spot, your gun will be moving smoothly and you can break the targets. It's best to break the back target first, keep the gun moving, then move through the front target; you already have that fluid movement for pulling the trigger. Also, keep the target on top of your gun, because sometimes shot can ricochet up and break the target. It's especially easy to over-shoot these targets so don't raise your head; almost all new sporting clays shooters fire high on rabbits their first time. Remember, shoot low and swing through. Concentration is especially important here; don't let the two targets confuse you. If you're really lucky, you can break both with one shot. If the targets are really hard, such as rocket-type rabbits, a few nickel shells for extra shot hardness and pattern density may help.

ROUGH GROUSE

You might know them as ruffed grouse, but this partridge is "rough," a real challenge on the sporting clays range. You can expect a quartering shot, usually away from you in thick cover. You'll have to shoot through openings in the brushy timber, and you'll have to shoot quick. True pairs usually are not seen here, because the singles are tough enough. But following or report pairs will test the reflexes and shooting eyes of the best shots.

This devilish quartering shot demands that your footwork and gun swing technique be exact. Pick the spot where you plan to break the bird and square up your feet to that mark. Wind your upper body back toward where you'll first see the bird, your gun muzzle placed where it will be in line between your eye and the bird when it first appears. Swing smartly to catch the bird quickly as you gently bring the butt to your shoulder. Whisk the barrel past the bird as the gun's butt meets your shoulder and pull the trigger.

With enough practice, your lead will meet clay more often than trees and brush. This is short-range work calling for open chokes and small shot. Depending on the distance, many shooters opt for #8s or #9s from a skeet or even cylinder bore.

CRAZY QUAIL

If there is a "gimme" station on your local sporting clays course, chances are it's the quail shot. These birds usually zip directly or almost directly away from the shooter, so determining the amount of lead isn't too difficult. But take a tip from the trap shooter and learn to read the angle of slight variance from the true straightaway bird. Even a slight left or right angle calls for more lead than some gunners realize.

Don't wait too long, because the target is dropping; in fact, you should shoot quickly at the first and then move to the other. There's a tendency to shoot over the second target. Since it's dropping, you've got to get under it. You've got to speed the first shot in there fast.

One change-up the range manager can throw at you, however, is a "covey" of targets. Four is the typical number, just enough to unsettle all but the die-hard quail hunter. The secret is to pick just one target, shoot it, then repeat the sequence quickly before the birds are out of range. A lot of shooters will pick out one bird and just before they get ready to shoot, they will change birds. That breaks your concentration. So pick a bird and stay with it. If you miss the first shot, don't change birds, shoot at the same bird with a second shot. Most right-handed shooters pick the right target then swing to the left for the next. It's the natural thing to do. Reverse the procedure if you are a southpaw. Sounds simple? It really is, with practice.

Speed is essential at this station — or while chasing real quail behind a brace of fine bird dogs — since the targets

Sporting clays practice can be accomplished with portable trap in proper surroundings, changing angles frequently.

This set-up would be more challenging if the trap operator was hidden and the shooters didn't know from which angle the claybird would be launched.

are going away from you and doubles are common. You should get a rhythm going...you've got to have that rhythm. Take a tip from experienced quail hunters and get on the first one quick. That way, the second bird still will be well within range of an improved cylinder choke. For this target, #8 shot is just the ticket, though some opt for the more-dense patterns afforded by #9s, especially when the trapper decides to spice things up a bit by throwing 90mm midis or even the diminutive 60mm minis.

SPRINGING TEAL

Taming the teal is not as tricky as most novice shooters believe. While it is no secret that success is mostly in the timing, the secret is getting that timing down pat. The rest, including the lead, will usually take care of itself.

When single birds are presented, many pros take their shot just before the target peaks, pointing a bit under the bird, which will have begun descending by the time the shot charge arrives.

This station often presents true doubles, however, and that's where the real fun begins. If you wait out the pair and take your first shot just as the targets peak or nearly peak, your second shot will be at a rapidly falling clay. Good luck. You're going to need it!

Some course operators try to bring realism to their scenario, offering shots duplicated in real hunts.

At the better courses, the sporting clays layouts are changed frequently so that a new challenge is there.

Women shooters have found they can compete in this exciting new sport.

Better to take the first bird on the rise and the second just before it peaks. Here's how. Quickly track one bird of the pair and shoot as soon as the muzzle blocks out the bird. The correct lead should be built in from the fast swing needed to catch and pass the bird. Then, simply continue your upward swing to find and track the remaining bird and shoot as if it were a single bird as described above. For this target, #8 shot from an open choke works well on most teal stations.

These are a sampling of the stations you'll likely find on a sporting clays course. The variety of stations is nearly endless and limited only by the imagination of the course manager. One thing is certain: A bouncing bunny or a wily woodcock or a springing teal in Oklahoma or Georgia or Missouri will be different than a bouncing bunny or a wily woodcock or a springing teal in Minnesota or Virginia or California. But that's what makes sporting clays so much fun. It mimics the challenge of real hunting, the foundation of this sport.

Crossing. Quartering. Incoming. Outgoing. Overhead. You'll encounter them all on a sporting clays course. A sporting clays course will test you and require that you return to the basics of good wingshooting. But remember that with sporting clays you can use your misses to your advantage. Take the opportunity to shoot a perplexing station again — and again and again — until you've figured

Developing a challenging course in the dry, low-brush areas of the Western mountains requires a lot of thought.

out how to make the shot. That's a benefit hunting simply can't offer. Besides, there is a new gun and a smart-looking vest to buy, new loads and that pair of colored shooting glasses...

TIPS FOR HIGHER SPORTING CLAYS SCORES

Safety — In sporting clays, you always keep your gun broke unless you're shooting. Keep the chamber open on a pump or automatic. That way, everyone knows your gun is safe. Always follow the safety rules and regulations of the NSCA and your local club. They are there for your protection and the safety of others. Eye and ear protection is a must at all times when on a sporting clays course.

Sportsmanship — Always help your fellow shooters, lending advice and shooting tips where appropriate.

Preparation — Find a gun that fits and shoots well for you and stick with it. Fellow shooters at your local course are a good source of guns to try before buying the one that's right for you.

The shotgun should be fitted with a smooth recoil pad without a sharp, pointed heel, so it won't hang up on your clothing when shouldered. A quality shooting vest with a long pad extending from the shoulder to your waist will aid smooth, consistent gun mounting.

Try different shotshell loads to determine which ones pattern well in your gun and perform best on different targets and stations. Most shooters find #8 shot in medium to light loads works best for most situations.

Effectiveness — Know where to attempt to break a target before you call for it. Before shooting a station, watch the shooter before you to observe the flight of the target and to determine where during its flight to break it. Of course, pay attention to where the shooter attempts the target only if the shooter is an accomplished one with a shooting style similar to yours.

Position your feet and body facing toward where you intend to break the target. Then, swing your body back toward where you will first see the target before calling for it.

Hold the gun with the butt against your side just low enough to be visible under the arm from behind. Keep the muzzle elevated to a point where it will be in line with the target's flight path. As you lift the gun's butt to your shoulder while swinging on the target, the muzzle will already be pointed at the clay.

Always swing the shotgun smoothly through the bird, firing as soon as the sight picture is correct and the butt is placed firmly but gently in your shoulder pocket.

Keep your head down on the stock while firing and even after the shot is taken. A smooth follow-through is integral to helping keep the shotgun "cheeked." — *David Couch*

SPORTING CLAYS & THE LADIES

This Sport Has Become A Means Of Financing Efforts Against Domestic Violence

These were the participants in the inaugural Ladies Charity Classic. Turners Outdoorsman was a major sponsor.

Left, top shooter Cindy Raahauge-Shenberger (right), is recognized as the HOA Champion by Carolyn Morse. Shenberger led the competition by two clays.

Below, Jane Vujovich takes aim on a quick left-to-right pair. The bamboo window was just one of the event's many challenging stations.

LADY SHOOTERS are making names for themselves in sporting clays and battling domestic violence at the same time. The Ladies Charity Classic is an evolving tour throughout the country that eventually could become the first female circuit in the game.

Two years ago, the Classic was born in Houston, Texas, through the efforts of Sue King and the National Shooting Sports Foundation. King, in addition to being an ardent sporting clays shooter and high level shooting instructor, is also on the board of directors of the National Rifle Association.

Since the initial "mother" shoot in Houston, there have been five classics, including the most recent event on the West Coast. The inaugural California edition of the Ladies Classic was held at Mike Raahauge Shooting Enterprises in Southern California, in September, 1992.

In all, fifty-eight women participated in the event that was held to raise money to help combat domestic violence. The turnout for the classic varies from location to location, and the number of shooters increases each time the event is held in the same region for a second or successive time. For example, when the first shoot was held in Houston, nearly 150 women competed. The next year, there were more than 250.

Cindy Raahauge-Shenberger of Fayetteville, North Carolina, was top gun at the California shoot, breaking forty-two targets out of a possible fifty. Cindy has been a world level international skeet shooter for the past five years. She competed around the world as a member of the U.S. Army team and had this to say about her experience with the classic:

"This was my first Ladies Charity Classic. I would like to see it become an annual event and let people know women are involved in shooting for a good cause." Cindy Shenberger notes further, "This event shows that women as a team can raise money for a charity they strongly believe in."

Whether it might be considered a handicap or not, she competed in a way no man has ever done: Cindy Shenberger was five months pregnant at the time. Actually, it might be said she did it with a little help from within.

"All of these events are viewed as annual events — not one-time happenings," says Sue King of the Ladies Charity Classics being held around the country. "These events accomplish the following: increase the number of women actively shooting; promote women's shooting; provide

Shooters have lunch as they await the results of the morning's shooting. Nearly 70 women from six states competed.

highly favorable publicity for shooting; promote the shooting industry generally; and make it harder for the anti-gun/anti-hunter forces to portray the shooting sports as evil."

King stressed that shooting is a great activity for women. "It's the perfect sport for women," she said of sporting clays. "Only average strength is required, you don't have to run fast, jump high, catch things that are thrown at you, or chase balls around."

She also said she sees the sport as a great social activity. "It's also a social game, so many truly nice men and women play the game and you enjoy each other's company at the same time."

Actress Leslie Easterbrook of California is also an ardent shooter who participated in the classic.

"Such shoots accomplish many things, but mainly they have the potential to keep sport shooting in the public eye and in a positive light," Easterbrook feels. "It also encourages women to learn to shoot and ultimately arm themselves against possible attack."

Easterbrook encourages other women to join in the shooting sports. "I would tell any woman to try it. No one shoots a perfect score, so the heat is off. The power you feel and the satisfaction you get from blasting a clay target is unbelievable.

"As women, we don't get encouraged to compete — we need it and can use it to break through obstacles we face while living in a man's world. You're outside in the fresh air, you get exercise and you can eventually beat the socks off men. You can even meet nice people — and it's a lot safer than the personal ads."

Bonnie Fogel-Huddleston, also a Californian, and a high ranking sporting clays competitor, sees the game as a positive activity in many ways for women.

"This shoot was my first experience with the Ladies Charity Classic," she says. "I had a wonderful time and look forward to it becoming an annual event. Anytime I can be part of the solution to a good cause such as combatting domestic violence, you can count me in. I believe awareness that these charity events will bring through the positive aspect of women shooting will really make the difference."

Shari LeGate traveled from Phoenix to shoot the event.

Ladies Sporting Champion
Jan Vujovich awaits a clay.

Not only does she invite other women to join in the fun, but she encourages them to accompany the guys they know who are already shooting. "If your boyfriend or husband shoots, ask him to take you along next time and make a day out of it," Fogel-Huddleston explains. "It will be worth the experience, and it's quality time spent together."

Sharon and Kim Rhode of Southern California competed in the mother-and-daughter segment of the classic, as well as individuals. They both have some relevant things to say from their different perspectives.

"I would like to see a lot more kids participating in the shooting sports," said Kim, who recently turned 13 years old. "People can shoot at any level they want and have fun."

Kim Rhode should know about different levels of shooting because she is a champion in her own right.

"I have broken six world records, and I'm the youngest woman ever to break one hundred straight in skeet," she explains, noting that she also likes to hunt. "I have been hunting since I was 8 years old, and shooting skeet for the last 1½ years."

Young Kim Rhode is also familiar with setting and achieving her goals. "Two of my biggest shooting goals have been to shoot for the United States in the Olympics and to take a record-book kudu on an African safari," the teenager grins and says, "I've already taken my record-book kudu."

Kim's mother says, "The Ladies Charity Classic shows that shooting is not just a man's sport, but women can have fun shooting also," she explains. "It's a fun and challenging sport that women can enjoy with their husbands and/or whole family."

Sue King (right) shoots an incoming clay as actress Leslie Easterbrook and Kimberly Rhode observe.

Sheila Link is prepared for the presentation of targets.

Sheila Link, another Californian, has shot in two of the classics, and is a staunch supporter of the concept, and of women participating in the shooting sports. This, she said, is even after she received anything but encouragement to be a shooter when she was growing up.

"Despite parental objection, disapproval and even punishment, I've been shooting since I was about 10 or 11, and I have seen a dramatic increase in the number of women who shoot," Link says.

"My most memorable achievement in sporting clays was to have my daughter fly to Houston to shoot in that Ladies Charity Classic event and spend Mother's Day there together," Link explains, noting that clay target shooting is not her primary shooting sport.

"The shooting sport I engage in regularly is hunting, not competition. I'll go anywhere, anytime to hunt any game that's legal and in season — from waterfowl to varmints, and from ground squirrels to African big game."

Katy Skahill of Wilmington, Delaware, is a veteran of several of the initial ladies classics, and sees them as outstanding opportunities for women to compete, enjoy themselves during the events and make a social statement, all at the same time.

Skahill seems to know about the game, because she is one of the leading women sporting clays shooters in the United States, and holds numerous championship titles, including that of the 1992 U.S. Open Ladies Champion.

"I would love to see these events grow into regional

A competitor swings on a low-flying target that is moving just above the river.

Thea Hubbard of Corona, California takes aim at a pair of Battues as her coach Don Ewing gives encouragement.

shoots which would comprise the first ladies' tour,'' she explains. ''I think the most important things for people to know about these events is that they are fun and not intimidating, even for women who do not feel proficient with a shotgun.

''Also, the poetic justice employed when women take up arms to help victims of domestic violence is quite appealing,'' she stresses.

''What these shoots accomplish is greater awareness of the sport, a message to the normally non-shooting public that legitimate reasons do exist for owning and enjoying shotguns, and, most importantly, they raise the desperately needed cash to save lives by providing shelter for victims of domestic violence.''

Although the fund-raisers are serious business, Skahill does not hesitate to explain what it is about sporting clays itself which first grabbed her interest — and held it since. Asked, she replies bluntly: ''Instant gratification when one of those orange targets breaks in front of me.''

Chauvinist perceptions of the past would have women shooting only dainty guns, if they shot at all. In sporting clays, most women shoot 12-gauge shotguns, just as their male counterparts have always done.

A competitor tests her shooting skill on a bouncing target at the challenging Rabbit Stand. The target was launched from the traphouse in the background.

The team of Sharon and Kimberly Rhode posted the best score to take the Mother/Daughter honors.

The majority of the women interviewed had a lot in common, and had much to say about the shotgun gauge they favor. Skahill uses a 12-gauge, and advises other women not worry about the gauge of the gun. However, she, like many new shooters, originally started with a 20-gauge.

"Women should not worry one way or another about the gauge or which gun make they're shooting," she explains. "Most misses that occur in clay target games are due to a lack of lead or some other technical reason other than equipment. They should find a gun that fits, period."

Fogel-Huddleston states, "I started shooting skeet with a Browning 12-gauge pump. I have a slender physique and I might surprise some people by shooting an over/under 12-gauge for sporting clays," she further explains. "I found that by getting proper coaching, learning proper gun mount, and using a fitted gun, I feel virtually no recoil at all. With all these ingredients intact there is no reason a woman shouldn't use a 12-gauge.

When LCC director Sue King was asked about gauge preference, she replied, "Good instruction, a properly fitted gun, and a light recoiling load puts the 12-gauge in any woman's hand. It's not seen as a women's gauge, because so many husbands, boyfriends and would-be instructors, who don't know what they're doing, have caused a woman's first introduction to a 12-gauge to be an unpleasant experience."

The combined shooting experience of the ladies involved in these classics spans over several decades. The authors were curious to find out if there has been an increase in women shooters to date.

Zach Ewing (left) checks these shooters' score cards. All the event's coaches and score keepers were men.

From left are Sue King, NRA board member and founder of the Ladies Charity Classic; Carolyn Morse, organizer of the California Chapter competition and Johnny Cloherty, director of sporting clays development for the NRA.

Sue King of Houston, Texas, is proud to say, "I have been shooting sporting clays since its introduction in this country, and skeet before that. There is an enormous increase in the number of women shooting today.

"I have introduced thousands of women to the shotgun sports through the LCC events and through my work as a full-time instructor."

U.S. Open ladies champion Katy Skahill, one of the top competitors at the event, shoots the river station.

NRA-certified instructor Sheila Link states, "I have seen a dramatic increase in the number of women who shoot and I have personally introduced and taught many women to shoot."

Although the perception by some of the women interviewed on whether or not more ladies are shooting nowadays varies, we know the classics, taken as a whole, have managed to attract more and more women each year. "We're also seeing a lot of familiar faces and lots of absolute novices," they note.

Sponsors of the classic series have included the National Shooting Sports Foundation (NSSF), Browning Arms Company, Outdoor Life Magazine, B-Square, Rhino Gun Cases, Lorcin, United States Sporting Clays Association, Mike Raahauge Shooting Enterprises, Inland Beverage, National Rifle Association, White Flyer Targets, Olin-Winchester and Stan Fitzgerald of Sporting Clays Specialists. Also providing products for the California event were Turner's Outdoorsman, Sportsman's Emporium, Rancho Guns and Miller's Outpost.

Even though the shoot was for women only, a lot of men were on hand, helping where needed. Most of the volunteer help was provided by the local Raahauge club members and by Quail Unlimited, a national group of conservationists who conduct upland habitat projects around the country. For more information on your club conducting a Ladies Charity Classic, you may contact Sue King c/o The National Shooting Sports Foundation, 555 Danbury Road, Wilton, CT 06897 or call 203/762-1320. — *Steve Comus & Rick Kennerknecht*

CHAPTER 13

TOUGHEST SPORTING CLAYS SHOTS

Here's How Top Shooters Combat Problem Birds

Carolyn Morse has trouble with the rising teal presentation. Experts say shooters must beat the intimidation factor.

For young shooters, guns that don't fit can make just about any target a tough one. This youngster has a gun that fits.

WHAT IS the most difficult shot in all of sporting clays? The answer to that question depends upon who is answering. Each shooter has his — or her — own most challenging presentation. What is an easy target for some shooters is the most difficult for others.

A quick look at the score cards from any shoot verifies this reality. Some shooters will score all targets at a given station, while others, shooting the same station, have dismal scores there.

There is no single factor which makes this situation a reality. Some shooters simply see some target presentations better than they see others. Or an individual's personal coordination makes a particular type of shot easier than others.

The difference between a good shooter and a great shooter is that a great shooter not only recognizes which types of shots are most difficult for him or her, but also takes steps to minimize the negative results of that difficulty.

In fact, really great shooters advance to the level where they can opt to use more than one shooting technique on most presentations. This means they can use whatever technique happens to make a particular presentation easier for them.

For example, some target presentations might be easier if a sustained lead is used, while others are candidates for the come-from-behind approach. Still other target presentations might be nothing more or less than spot-shooting propositions.

Even armed with such advanced knowledge, every shooter encounters presentations which are easier or harder than others. Following are some observations by a number of the country's top shooters and what they do to achieve re-

spectable scores, even with the presentations which give them the most problems.

It is important to keep in mind, however, that sporting clays in the United States remains in its infancy, and that shooters around the country still have a lot of learning and practice before they will be totally competitive on a world level.

Among the many leading shooters in the United States, the longer shot presentations often are the ones which present the highest level of difficulty. There is a good reason for this. In the United States, there has been no long-standing tradition of shooting long target presentations.

About the closest most American shotgunners have come to long shots in the past has been when pot shooting trap. This, however, is hardly a good measure of one's ability to hit long targets since all of the targets in such pot shoots always are going away, rising at first, then falling. There are no long crosses, or long shots which see the target quartering or coming into the shooter.

Jon Kruger of St. Ansgar, Iowa, has been one of the nation's top sporting clays shooters, almost since the game began in the United States. Among other things, Kruger won the U.S. Open in 1992 and placed third at the National Sporting Clays Association Nationals the same year. He also won a number of state and zone shoots during the same season — as he does each season.

Yet, there are some shot presentations which are more difficult for him than others. Certainly, this is not to suggest anyone would want to bet that a shooter of Kruger's ability is going to miss many shots, no matter what the presentation, but there are some which do give him headaches from time to time.

Chuck Stapel, a noted knifemaker, is a solid clays shooter, but he sometimes finds battue presentations challenging.

All-American Mike Finger is all smiles after winning another tournament. His difficult shots are long ones.

"My hardest target is the long quartering-away shot — past thirty-five or forty yards," Kruger explains, noting that the secret to hitting those difficult targets is "just not to be intimidated by it."

Among the key words in Kruger's statement is "intimi-

dated." It cannot be stressed too strongly that shooters have to do whatever is necessary not to be intimidated by a target presentation, regardless of what it is.

The moment a shooter becomes intimidated by a particular presentation, that shooter will fail to do well in overall shooting. When a target presentation begins to intimidate a shooter, the best thing for a shooter to do is to practice that presentation until it is understood and is more shootable. Only then can the scores begin to rise.

John Cloherty, director of sporting clays development for the National Rifle Association of America, said his toughest target is one which is both quartering-away and dropping at the same time. To hit those tough presentations, he says he consciously makes an effort to keep the gun moving in line with the target.

"Don't end up crossing the path of the target with the gun," he insists, "or you'll miss it."

Cloherty knows all about crossing paths with targets and that sort of thing because, in addition to his official job with the NRA, he also is a trick shooter who performs for audiences around the country. His signature shot is one in which he holds the shotgun upside-down and above his head. From that position, he can hit targets better than most shooters can when they hold the gun in the traditional way on their shoulders.

It is not unusual for Cloherty to run straight scores on skeet fields, holding the gun upside-down and over his head. In fact, he can shoot AA scores on sporting clays ranges by holding the gun that way.

Further, he is an accomplished aerial target shooter with handguns and rifles. Although he uses shot loads for exhibitions, when he is in areas where such shots are safe, Cloherty can hit flying targets just as well with rifles and handguns using regular bullets.

When the shots call for such precision, it is critical for the shooter to understand the total dynamics of the exercise, and Cloherty does. He passes on this knowledge in his "spare" time as an instructor.

Sporting clays pioneer and world-level competitor Rick "KK" Kennerknecht of Lomita, California, insists the toughest targets are those which deceive the shooter.

"I would have to say that my toughest target is one that I can't read well," he says. "Target flights are sometimes deceptive. They look like they are flying one way when they're really flying another way.

"Some targets actually are falling when they look like they are rising or vice versa. So what I'm saying is that, if I don't really know what flight pattern the target is taking, I have to experiment. When you experiment in competition, you lose targets. You lose confidence on that particular stand, and it can have an effect on stands later on in the course if you don't recover mentally.

"You can help combat this problem by practicing as many different presentations as possible. This is done by shooting as many different courses as you can. In a competition, watch the unfamiliar presentation as closely as possible.

"Watch it from behind the station cage, watch it from down the path or from another stand," Kennerknecht insists. "You'll be surprised what you can learn. Also, be familiar with target types and their flight characteristics — what happens to that particular kind of target in its flight.

"Ask the trapper what kind of target he's throwing if you are not sure — 110, 90 or 60mm. These techniques will help your game more than you would expect."

Doug Fuller of Oklahoma City, Oklahoma, who has placed second and fourth at sporting clays nationals, and who has won the Oklahoma State Sporting Clays championship every year it has been held, said his hardest shot is the long, rising teal.

"You have to learn to drive the gun through both targets,"

Jon Kruger is one of the United States' top sporting clays shooters, however, the sports' long shots challenge him.

Fuller says, in describing the long, rising teal targets as those in the thirty-five to forty-yard class.

"I shoot sustained lead," Fuller explains. "When the target has to disappear under the barrel, it is tough."

Actually, Fuller says he runs a bit hot and cold on the

Dan Carlisle (left) is not only a former Olympian, but he is also one of the pioneers of sporting clays in the U.S. He doesn't have a lot of trouble with any presentation. Key to his success is concentration.

Celia Milius of California doesn't miss many targets. Yet, long presentations give her trouble on occasion.

J. Cloherty, NRA director of sporting clays development, is a record holder who has difficulty with some targets.

long, rising teal presentations. Sometimes he does well, but other times the presentation gives him the most trouble.

Like many other things in sporting clays, he feels hitting these difficult targets requires concentration, concentration and concentration.

Fuller is among the nation's most accomplished all-around shotgunners. He is one of those people who happens to be a good shot with just about any kind of gun and at just about any kind of game.

Fellow shooters have said he is one of those guys who only needs to pick up a gun, shoot it once or twice to determine where it is shooting, then go out there and shoot any game well. So, when such a shooter says that concentration is important, take note. He knows of what he speaks.

John Boyle of Cerritos, California, is evolving as one of the United States' leading sporting clays shooters. Although Boyle has been shooting shotguns since he was a youngster and has been competing in one form or another for decades, he has been shooting sporting clays for only a couple of years.

For Boyle, one of the most difficult targets is the long, looping presentation one gets with battues and midis.

"These are presentations where the target is constantly changing," Boyle explains, noting that, to combat the problems presented by such a presentation, he makes certain to establish the flight line of the target, stay on it and establish lead at the same time.

He placed third at last year's USSCA Nationals and already has placed well in international competition here and in England.

For Boyle, it is important for American shooters to begin to shoot the kinds of presentations found in other parts of the world so shooters from this country can become truly competitive at the international level.

To that end, he and some of the other top shooters in Southern California have begun to establish courses which are designed to challenge shooters with these longer, more complicated presentations.

Carolyn Morse focuses on mastering her one difficult presentation: the rising teal.

Even Junior All-Americans (below) occasionally miss clays. They are (from left) Zach Ewing, Mike Finger and Tommy Bukovensky.

Eventually, Boyle said he sees a professional form of sporting clays competition evolving in the United States. When that happens, he predicts, some of the top shooters in the world will be Americans.

But probably a few years will pass until that point. After all, the shooters in some other parts of the world have been seeing and hitting such presentations for decades.

This is where some of the younger shooters come to the fore. If they are able to shoot some of the more difficult presentations, beginning now, by the time they are adults and competing in the various events around the world, they will be in a position to be in the winner's circle more and more frequently.

Zachary Ewing is a top shooter in the junior ranks of sporting clays. The 15-year-old from Upland, California, has been a serious competitor since 1988, when he won his first shoot. Most recently, in 1992, he placed second in the Junior B Division at both the world and USSCA nationals, and is currently rated at eighteenth in the world.

His most difficult shot is the long, quartering and dropping target.

Ewing says he looks at these targets closely, trying to determine the angle of the target while estimating the target speed. Then, when he shoots it, he deliberately uses a lot of gun speed, noting that when he misses such a target, he usually is shooting behind it.

To practice for such presentations, Ewing goes to a skeet field where he stands back about forty yards and shoots at the targets from different angles.

Another top-level junior shooter is Mike Finger of Corona, California. For Finger, the most difficult target presentation is the long right-to-left crosser.

Finger says that, to practice the shot presentation, he heads to a skeet field and shoots right-to-left crossers from all kinds of angles and distances. The longer the yardage, the better for practice, he explains.

Among women shooters, Carolyn Morse of Norco, California, is one of the high-profile people in the game, due in large part to the fact that she also operates one of the nation's busiest sporting clays facilities — the one at Raahauge's near her home.

For Mrs. Morse, the most difficult presentation is the rising teal.

"I can always hit the targets on the way down," she explains, noting that for her, it is quite difficult to hit them on the way up, or when they are at the peak of their flight.

This is not a major problem with some teal presentations, because the targets are visible for a long time on their way down. However, on some courses, where the targets disappear quickly after starting downward, she has problems.

What does she do to combat this problem? "I practice, practice, practice," she chuckles.

Estie Qualey helps operate the Raahauge's range and is a shooter, as well. Her most difficult presentation is one in which the targets are low, dropping crossers.

Like Carolyn Morse, her suggestion for combatting the problem is "Practice, practice and more practice. — *Steve Comus*

CHAPTER 14

SLOWPOKE SHOTGUNNING

If You Want To Slow the Competitive Pace, Try A Black Powder Muzzleloading Scattergun

Firing the percussion shotgun is similar to firing a modern shotgun, except that it is difficult to see what you have or have not hit. The bellowing cloud of smoke from the black powder muzzleloader shotgun often obscures the target.

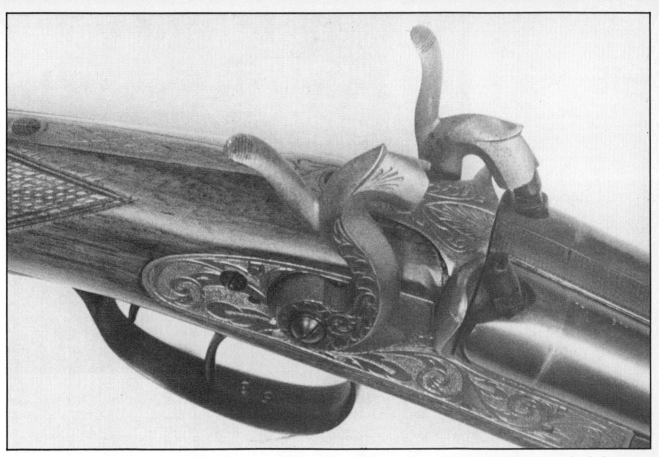

This double shotgun is from Dixie Gun Works. It has scroll engraving on the tang, standing breech and twin hammers.

MOST SHOTGUNNING moves rapidly. Skeet shooters burn hundreds of shells in an afternoon, and bird hunters think nothing of expending several boxes of shells. In general, shotgunners live in a hurry-up world and pace themselves accordingly.

If you would like to slow your shooting to a more leisurely rate, try swapping your shotgun for a front-loader. Loose powder and shot, ignited by flint or cap system, can do wonders to ease your tensions.

Shooters who haven't tried muzzleloading shotguns will be surprised at the efficiency of the old designs. A good front-stuffer can drop birds or clay targets almost as well as a modern cartridge gun; it just takes a bit longer to ready it for firing.

Since the value of old muzzleloading shotguns hasn't grown nearly as much as that of black powder rifles or handguns, chances of picking up a bargain-priced original are pretty good. If you prefer the convenience of purchasing a newly manufactured shotgun, good quality replicas abound at competitive prices.

A few earnest muzzleloading fanciers select a smooth-bored, single-barreled gun for slinging shot. Most will opt for a double barrel. The weight and balance of today's double guns are almost identical to those of the middle 1800s. Serious shooters who hope to become competent wingshots should avoid the musket-like handling of many of the smoothbore, single-barrels.

For those who can afford such things, custom-built doubles are available. Custom guns permit you to choose barrel length, length of pull, cast-off or cast-on, comb height, pitch and drop. Of course, you also may select any degree of decor and finish that appeals.

Unfortunately, a newly made, custom muzzleloading shotgun costs almost exactly the same as a custom-made cartridge gun. It's no problem to invest thousands of dollars in a custom gun. Luckily, for those of us with more pedestrian tastes and pocketbooks, there are plenty of replica shotguns around at realistic prices.

Connecticut Valley Arms, Dixie Gun Works, Navy Arms and Sile offer double shotguns in kit or finished form from as little as $150 to a touch more than $400. Most replica guns are 12-gauge, but a few may be seen in 20-gauge. The 12-gauge is probably a better choice for effective patterning.

Unlike modern shotguns, muzzleloaders can't be grabbed off the shelf and a box of shells purchased at the corner grocery store enroute to the hunting field. Guns that fire loose powder and shot require more accessories and a bit of knowledge before they can be expected to perform. In addition to the gun, you will need a powder flask or horn, a shot bag or flask, flints or caps, a ramrod with an assortment of tips, plus over-powder and over-shot wads.

Other items usually found in the shooter's bag include a powder measure — not the one built into the flask — several screwdrivers, a spring vise, spare nipples and a

Note the contouring of the wood around the lock plate of Pate's flintlock shotgun.

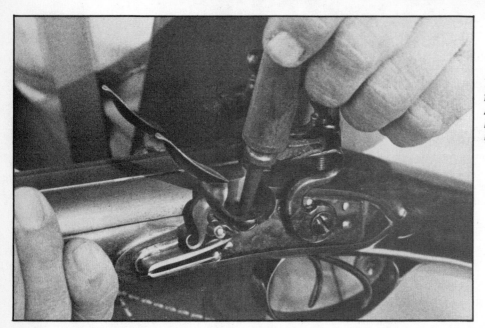

The final step in loading a flintlock is priming the pan. A fine grade black powder is needed. Most shooters use FFFFg grade powder.

variety of cleaning equipment.

Instead of trying to stuff all the above into your pockets, it's a good idea to figure on carrying a "possibles bag" slung over your shoulder. Favored by the old-time shotgunner, this bag may be made of leather or heavy fabric and usually is compartmented and stuffed with anything you may "possibly" need.

Before hunting with a muzzleloading shotgun, it's a good idea to break in the gun — and yourself — on clay targets. A few shots at a pattern target certainly won't hurt and should give you a good idea of the effective range of your shotgun/load combination.

Three shotguns were chosen for use in preparation for this article. My favorite of the lot is a slender 12-gauge manufactured by Davide Pedersoli of Brescia, Italy, and sold by Dixie Gun Works. Another is made in Spain and sold by Connecticut Valley Arms. The third is also Spanish and was sold some years ago by Century Arms Company.

The Dixie gun is a sleek, English-style percussion shotgun weighing a bit over six pounds. It is fitted with white steel sidelocks and hammers, engraved with a floral scroll pattern, and the barrels and steel buttplate are browned rather than blued. There are touches of engraving on the

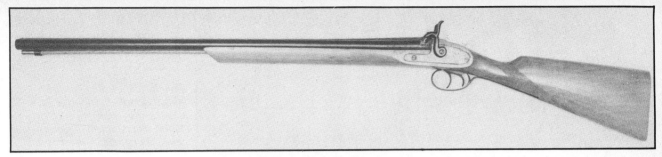

This percussion-lock double from Century Arms was made in Spain. Instead of a buttplate, it has a checkered butt.

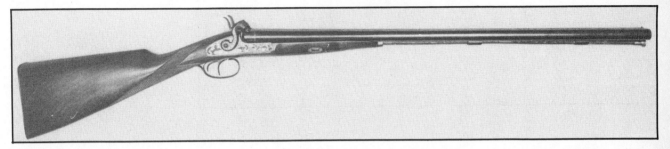

This Dixie Gun Works English-style percussion shotgun weighs just over six pounds. It has sidelock action.

tang and trigger guard as well as on the rod thimble. Checkering along the wrist is about eighteen lines per inch and is bordered with a single-line cut. Like most quality front-loading double guns, it has a hooked or patent breech.

CVA's caplock offering is somewhat heavier than the Dixie gun, tipping my scale at about 7.25 pounds. It has white metal lock plates, hammers and trigger guard, and well polished, blued barrels. The stock is checkered at both the wrist and forearm and has a glossy finish. Lock plates are engraved with a duck in flight, and light scroll work appears on the hammers and trigger guard. Like some early guns, the butt of the stock is checkered, and the gun has no buttplate. This gun also has a hooked breech.

The third gun in this group was manufactured in Spain for Century Arms and is a 20-gauge, percussion-lock double weighing just under seven pounds. All metal parts are blued and the stock is of European walnut.

Finish on the stock reminds one of the Mauser rifles of World War II. The wood has a definite yellowish cast and a smooth but not glossy surface. Checkered panels are along both sides of the wrist, cut about sixteen lines per inch. A small cap box with a shell-like design is inlaid into the right side of the buttstock. This gun also has a checkered butt with no buttplate. Unlike the other two shotguns, this one does not have a patent breech. To detach the barrels, it is necessary to remove a screw from the underside of the forearm and another from the tang.

Traditionalists will insist on using black powder for shooting muzzleloaders. Most shooters will choose either Fg or FFg granulations. Pyrodex also is used successfully in muzzleloading shotguns and grade RS is usually appropriate. Whether you choose black powder or Pyrodex, thorough cleaning after firing always is required.

To load any black powder shotgun, dry the bores with a clean patch before starting. Next, fire a couple of caps on

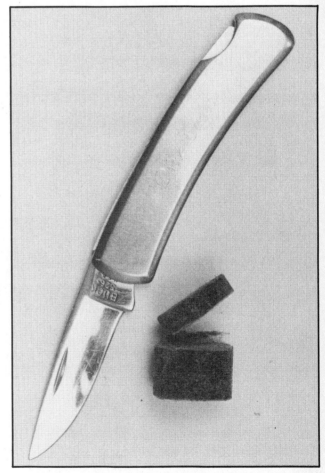

A Lujtic Mono Wad can be sliced to provide several top or over-shot wads for muzzlerloaders. Depending on the bore diameter, they also may serve as over-powder wads.

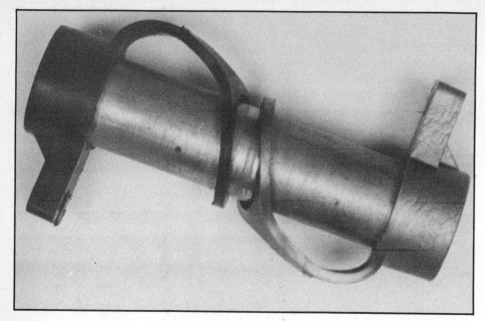

This is a speedloader for muzzleloaders. Powder is kept in one end, shot in the other. Percussion caps are carried in slots in the caps.

Powder flask and measure are used for shotguns. A separate measure is used. It would be dangerous to expose the entire flask to a lingering spark in barrel.

each nipple to be sure they are dry and open before loading. Flintlock shooters may want to burn a pan of powder and check the touch hole before proceeding. Vents or nipples *must* be clear for the gun to work.

After checking for clean, dry bores and nipples, pour a charge of powder into *one* bore. For a 12-gauge, a 3¼-dram equivalent load may be created by using 85 to 90 grains of powder. Follow the powder with an over-powder wad. Wad diameter varies greatly, depending on who manufactured the gun. I have seen well-fitted over-powder wads as small as .680-inch and as large as .760-inch. A wide variety of wads is available from Blue & Gray Products. Measure your choke or bore and select one that fits tightly. Some shooters still build up a wad column using filler wads after the over-powder wad, but modern materials permit use of a single wad to serve as both over-powder and filler.

Shot is measured next and poured into the barrel. For a starting load, 1⅛ ounces of shot is appropriate. There's no need to weigh the shot charge, simply use the markings on your shot measure. After the shot is settled, place an over-shot card and ram tightly enough so that the rod will bounce if dropped down the bore.

After repeating the above procedure in the second barrel, place a percussion cap on each nipple or a priming charge in each pan. You now are ready to fire! See what I mean about a front-loading shotgun slowing your pace? If you are in a hurry to shoot, forget the muzzleloaders and stay with your cartridge gun.

Most original muzzleloading shotguns had no choke at all, and were true cylinder bore. A few degrees of choke were worked into some originals, but they are the exception. Replica guns run from no choke to what measures full choke.

Think about this for a minute. If you can load a wad through a full choke muzzle, how much gas sealing will it do when it gets into the bore? Some shooters overcome this problem by using newspaper for wadding. That will work,

Black powder in FFg granulation or Pyrodex in RS do well in percussion shotguns. Pyrodex isn't usually used in flintlocks. Its ignition is slower than black powder.

The Remington and CCI percussion caps are shown with two basic black powder tools, a nipple wrench and pick.

This fringed possibles bag holds all the odds and ends needed by a shotgunner. Old bags were frequently tooled with designs similar to this one from Dixie Gun Works.

but I never have seen truly consistent patterns thrown by a gun loaded with newspaper wadding. The best bet is to obtain wads that can be seated only with effort and stay with that diameter for both over-powder and over-shot use.

According to most specifications, a full choke will produce a pattern of about seventy percent at forty yards. Modified chokes will throw a pattern of about fifty percent at the same range while a cylinder bore will print about thirty percent of its pellets in a 30-inch circle at forty yards. Most muzzleloading guns that I have experienced do well to hold thirty-five to forty percent pattern density at forty yards.

In use, you probably will fire your muzzleloading shotgun at game more than thirty yards only rarely and frequently will find game is taken at twenty-five yards or less.

In the telling, of course, ranges usually increase markedly.

Velocities from properly loaded front-stuffers are astonishing. My pet double churns out 1⅛ ounces of shot at 1200 feet per second (fps) regularly. Check your modern, factory-loaded shotshell velocity. A field load that betters 1200 fps is a rarity, indeed. Although muzzleloading patterns tend to become a bit sketchy at relatively short ranges, there's more than enough energy to take feathered game cleanly with a decent hit.

A friend who lacks a chronograph tests his loads by firing #8 shot at an ordinary soup can. If the shot penetrates both sides of the can, he figures it will do in a rabbit, squirrel, quail or dove. This may not be scientific, but I can't argue with his hunting success.

Although it's decidedly untraditional, recently I've been using some modern plastic shotshell wads in my muzzleloaders. Inclusion of a shot protector seems to improve patterns slightly. Not all modern shotshell wads lend themselves to use in muzzleloaders, however. Many are too small in diameter to provide sufficient gas seal and some

seem to be larger at the heel — bottom — than on the main body of the wad. If you can find a modern wad that fits your bore properly, try it.

After breaking enough clay targets to convince yourself of the adequacy of your front-loader, take it bird or rabbit hunting. You may not get as many birds as usual, and you almost certainly won't fire as many shots. You will find yourself turning down marginal shots, waiting for a closer bird or a better angle.

Chances are good your percentage of hits will go up. At the same time, your blood pressure should come down. If you hunt just to display the quantity of game taken, forget using a front-loader. If you hunt for the pleasure of watching game and the feeling of success when you make a good shot, by all means try your hand with a muzzleloading shotgun.

It'll make a slowpoke of you alright, but it can also bring the fun back into your hunting or shooting. — *Dick Eades*

THE .410 IS FOR HUNTING

The Author Finds Bigger Isn't Always Better

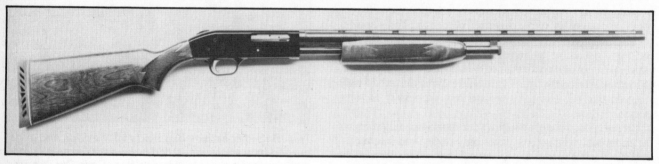

This Mossberg 500 pump is typical of a number of inexpensive yet serviceable .410 shotguns available today.

T WAS ONE of those chilly winter mornings that most north Florida bird hunters wish would come more often, but seldom do. The air temperature hovered in the mid-thirties and the frigid wind that had howled off the Canadian prairies for the previous three days finally had subsided.

The calm dawn air was broken only by the scrabbling feet and plaintive whining of two Brittany spaniels eager to be free of the confines of the dog box, and the hushed tones of three men readying their gear for the morning's hunt.

There's an excellent reason why such bracing weather is favored by Southern bird hunters: poisonous snakes. Given crisp conditions, any venomous critters sharing the tangled creek bottoms with quail and woodcock would be too sluggish to pose a threat to the dogs, allowing prime coverts — effectively off limits for much of the year — to be hunted in safety.

That's what Jim Gant, Bob Morgan and I, along with Bob's Brittanys Dusty and Dixie, were doing at the end of an obscure North Florida dirt road as the sun slowly eased its way over the horizon.

This was to be the first time I hunted with Gant and Morgan, and when the phone invitation to join them came, Bob Morgan had advised me that we would be in some really thick cover. Most shots would be close and fast.

With that in mind, I had brought along a 20-gauge over/under with its twenty-six-inch barrels choked skeet and skeet. At about 6½ pounds, I considered it to be the epitome of a fast-handling, heavy-cover bird gun. Knowing my two cohorts had been prowling the thickets for almost fifteen years each, I assumed they would have something similar. What they pulled from their gun cases, however, was surprising!

Jim Gant produced an inexpensive little .410 side-by-

108

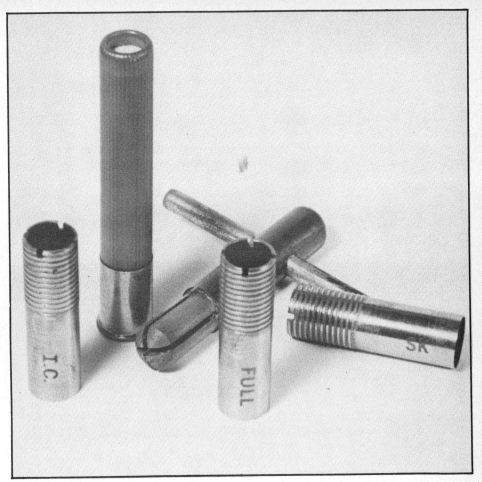

Interchangeable choke tubes like these from Briley greatly extend the versatility of the .410 and make it a far more practical field gun than the standard full-choke models.

side with barrels that couldn't have stretched much beyond twenty inches. Bob Morgan's choice I recognized instantly as a Mossberg 500 .410 pump. But, it bore little resemblance to the one I had reposing in the gun rack at home. In contrast to the twenty-six-inch ribbed barrel mine sported, his featured a petite little 18½-inch tube. It looked for all the world like the world's smallest riot gun, though I tactfully resisted the urge to point that out.

Even more surprising, both guns were choked straight cylinder! I couldn't resist asking about their choice of shootin' irons.

What they told me made sense.

"When I said the cover was thick," Bob Morgan stated, "I wasn't kidding. In most places you'll be lucky to even see twenty yards, let alone get a shot at that range. And on a cold, still morning like this, the birds — there'll be quail and woodcock in there — are going to hold real tight for the dogs. What that means is that most shots will be at about fifteen yards, and a lot will be less.

"At that range," he continued, "you don't need a big load of shot to drop a bird. In fact, the more shot in the shell, the more you're going to tear the bird up when you hit him. Jim and I enjoy eating quail as much as we enjoy hunting them, and there isn't much point in shooting something you can't eat. At the range we'll be shooting, these little .410s have plenty of shot to do the job. It only takes two or three 7½s to put a quail down, but the patterns aren't so dense that they hamburger the bird."

"Another thing we've found," Jim Gant chimed in, "is that the .410, especially with the three-inch shells we're using, tends to open patterns quicker than the larger gauges. We've patterned a lot of loads in different gauges and chokes and found the cylinder-bore .410s we use will produce wider usable patterns at fifteen yards than any other gauge and choke combination.

"That," he noted, "is real important when you're shooting close in heavy cover, because you can pretty much forget any kind of sustained lead shooting. You won't have time. Even a fast swing-through technique isn't always possible.

"What usually happens is that you have just enough time to lock your eyes on the bird, poke the gun at it and pull the trigger. A short, light gun throwing a wide pattern is an ideal tool for poking. These guns aren't worth a damn beyond twenty yards, but I don't expect we'll get any shots at that range in here."

As it turned out, he was right.

I can't recall spending a day cussing a gun as much as I did that little 20. What had seemed so light and handy in the open soon became an unwieldy burden as I struggled through the tangle of vines and brush. There were plenty of birds, but every time one got up, there was invariably a vine or tree trunk waiting to leap out and grab the barrel as I tried to get the bead on the bird.

Through luck — or maybe just the law of averages — I did manage to connect with a few quail and one woodcock.

When gunning is close and fast, many wingshooters have found the cylinder-choked .410 is an ideal shotgun. Offering quicker-opening patterns than larger, more popular gauges, the little shell still has plenty of shot.

Upon retrieving the birds, however, I almost wished I hadn't.

I like hamburger. Whether it's packed into a savory meatloaf, sizzling on the grill as neatly shaped patties or simmering in chili, it ranks high on my list of favorites. I don't particularly care for it, though, when it began life as a quail. Unfortunately, that's about all that was left after the one-ounce load of shot got finished with them at ten and twelve yards! I'm certain there are some Iraqi tanks rusting in the desert that don't look as bad as some of those birds did.

My companions, on the other hand, were faring quite well. Their little sawed-off .410s, which couldn't have tipped the scales at more than five pounds apiece, were as easy to tote as a handgun. And when a bird got up, they wasted no time in sending a load of shot its way.

More often than not, they connected. And even casual examination revealed their birds were going to look a lot better on the table than the few I'd managed to bag.

It was an eye-opening experience. I would have bet the farm that no .410 would beat an open-choked 20-gauge on birds. I would have lost, and when we finally worked our

Author found by experimenting with choke tubes that a modified-choked .410 offers the same pattern at 25 yards as do 12- and 20-gauges with skeet chokes. While the pattern density is less, there is still enough shot.

way back to the vehicles, Bob Morgan showed me why.

Digging into the back of his Bronco, Jim Gant produced a partial role of thirty-inch craft paper. Ripping off a good size piece, he found two convenient trees to string it between, where we had a safe backstop by shooting down into the creek bottom. Marking a small X in the center with a felt tip pen, Morgan backed off fifteen paces and fired a round. Putting up a second piece, Jim Gant instructed me to do the same. When we compared the two patterns, I could see instantly what they had been talking about before the hunt.

The pattern from the skeet-choked 20-gauge was a dense, uniform circle of holes about twenty inches in diameter. No bird was going to slip through that without taking a lot of hits, too many hits, if the birds I shot that morning were any indication.

The pattern from Bob Morgan's short .410 barrel was not nearly as dense as could be expected, when comparing a one-ounce shot charge to the .410's meager 11/16-ounce. But, it was uniform, and try as I might, I couldn't see anywhere a bird could hide without running into a half-dozen pellets.

The biggest difference, however, was the size of the usable pattern. The little .410 offered an area almost twenty-six-by-twenty-five inches!

Combine that with the short, lightning-fast little guns they were using and it's not hard to see why they scored so well: They had found the ideal tool for that hunting situation. They also had changed the way I thought about the .410!

Mention the diminutive .410 to most scattergunners and you'll get a number of varying opinions. Most of them aren't particularly flattering.

Skeet shooters will moan about the little shell's lack of ability to deliver good patterns with skeet chokes and invariably blame their misses on the targets sailing right through the pattern unscathed.

Hunters will admit that, in the hands of a steely-eyed shooter, a full-choked .410 can harvest game, but only if the shooter can point with rifle-like precision. Most will agree it makes a fair meat gun for rabbits and squirrels, but beyond that it is pretty much a novelty.

There is some truth to all of the above, but I'm convinced also is a good deal of misconception. The .410 has a lot more going for it in the hunting fields than many give it credit for having. In fact, when the range is less than twenty-five yards or so, the little .410 is not only an acceptable choice, but a pretty good one!

One reason is that most .410s truly are lightweight guns. When the shooting is close and quick, they'll get on the birds fast. Carrying less weight also tends to keep a hunter fresher and more alert. The same, of course, could also be said for the 28-gauge, and admittedly, if the dandy little 28 was more readily available in affordable models, the .410 might fade from the scene. But it's not, and the .410 is.

You can pick up a decent .410 for less than $400, and

The 18-1/2-inch barrel on author's Mossberg 500 makes the shotgun an incredibly light, quick-handling package in cover. The 26-inch barrel is better for open terrain.

fifteen yards, yet not so much that they are rendered useless for the table.

A call to Mossberg revealed that the little 18½-inch cylinder-bore barrel Morgan was using is a standard catalog item and I quickly obtained one for my 500 pump.

Once I came to accept the fact that the .410 could be effective in something other than a full-choke gun, I shipped my twenty-six-inch ribbed barrel to Hastings Co. (Box 224, Clay Center, KS 67432) and had the barrel threaded for the Briley choke tube system.

With interchangeable tubes available in chokes running from cylinder through full, I felt this would allow me to fully explore the potential of the little .410. After a lengthy session of pattern testing, what I found surprised me.

One of the major criticisms of the .410 as a field gun is its inability to deliver uniformly distributed patterns. Most shooters who take the time to pattern the .410 find it offers

The author finds the .410 an enjoyable and effective tool anytime a skeet-choked 12- or 20-gauge is called for. Author's springer doesn't care what gauge is used.

sometimes notably less. Any 28-gauge that even functions is going to run considerably more in price.

You also can find a good selection of .410 shells at any country store than handles even the barest ammo selection. Locating 28-gauge shells generally involves a trip to the Big City, and even then the shot size selection might be quite slim.

If you're a hunter — as opposed to someone who just wants to hang around the local gun club and look sporty — the .410 becomes a much more viable choice when a small-gauge gun is indicated or desired.

As Jim Gant and Bob Morgan demonstrated to me those many years ago, it often can be the best choice when the shots are close and fast, as happens when gunning thick woodcock and quail coverts. From a straight cylinder choke, the three-inch shells (with their overly long shot column and partially unprotected charge) open patterns more quickly than does any other gauge and choke combination — providing enough pattern density to drop birds at

One advantage the .410 has over the 28-gauge is in the availability of shells. Most popular brands of .410 can be found easily. However, hunters often have a difficult time locating 28-gauge shells.

more than adequate center density, but suffers from patchy outer-ring pellet hits and throws a high percentage of its charge in the form of flyers well away from the main pattern.

There is truth in this, and the reason is that virtually every .410 intended for field use comes equipped with a full choke. For whatever reason, gunmakers have become convinced that the little .410 must be choked tighter than a banker's heart to be effective. Combine that tighter constriction with a long shot column, plus shot deformation, and flyer pellets are inevitable.

Prior to having my gun tubed, its full-choke barrel threw precisely that type of pattern, and once tubed, the full-choke tube continued the tradition.

Installing the modified tube, however, was like shooting a different gun! At twenty-five yards, the modified tube delivered patterns exhibiting good center density, ragged edges, and a usable pattern spread of about twenty-five-by-twenty-four inches!

In terms of real world performance, the pellet spread and the uniformity of pellet distribution compared quite favorably to the patterns thrown by my 12- and 20-gauge skeet guns!

Interestingly enough, a number of top skeet shooters and gunsmiths specializing in competition shotgun work have come to the conclusion that the .410 performs best on the skeet field with a choke constriction of .008 to .009 inches. The American standard bore and choke dimensions list .008 as a modified choke in the .410!

Have .410 shooters been handicapped for years by too much choke constriction? Maybe.

While pellet spread and distribution weren't far behind skeet-choked patterns from the larger gauges, pattern density, obviously, didn't measure up. But, a few test patterns using the Hornady pattern targets showed me that there was more than enough density to drop game birds cleanly.

Dead is dead; there are no different degrees of dead. And if it only takes a half-dozen pellets to achieve that effect, there is little point in nailing a game bird with twenty or more shot pellets. Those extra pellets serve no purpose beyond giving you something hard to chomp down on at the dinner table.

What my pattern testing told me was simple: At twenty-five yards and less, the modified-choked .410 was delivering the same "practical" field performance as my skeet-choked 12- and 20-gauge guns. And I can think of a lot of wingshooting situations where the latter two guns had been my first choice!

Quail and woodcock obviously come to mind. But so too do doves dipping into an evening waterhole. Such shots seldom exceed twenty-five yards, and it makes little difference whether your load of #8 shot comes from a 12-gauge or a .410.

The same holds true when visiting a preserve for pheasant. With good dogs, the birds tend to hold tight and I can remember few shots past twenty-five yards. In fact, on some occasions, I've had to slow up my shot to avoid hamburgering the bird with even a skeet-choked 12-gauge and

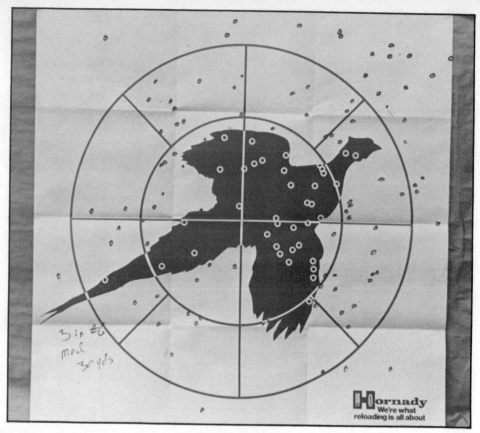

This Hornady patterning target shows one dead pheasant at 30 yards. White rings mark pellet hits from a three-inch load of #6 shot at 30 yards using a modified choke. This bird wouldn't be any "deader" if it was hit with a 10-gauge.

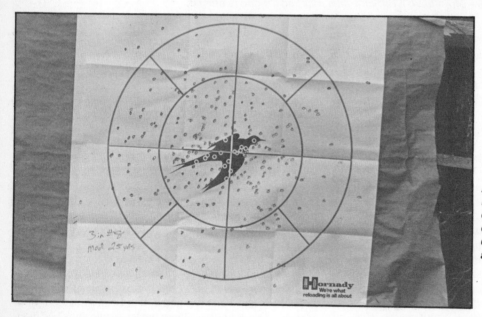

Author finds three-inch #8 loads extremely effective on dove and quail-sized birds out to 30 yards with a modified choke installed. The .410 is attractive for these situations.

a 1⅛-ounce field load of #6s!

The same size shot from a three-inch .410 shell offers the shooter no handicap here.

Reaming out the full choke on a .410 to the .008- or .009-inch range is a simple matter for most gunsmiths. So too is having the gun fitted for the Briley system, which allows the shooter to slip in a cylinder tube and achieve maximum pattern spread when the going gets real close and fast.

Another advantage to interchangeable choke tubes is in restoring the .410 to traditional duty. Full-choked .410s

rank high in popularity in my neck of the southern woods. Among those who pursue rabbits with beagles, it is considered the best compromise between efficient bunny busting and safety to dogs and hunters.

Squirrel hunters, especially those hunting in semi-developed areas, where homesteads may dot the landscape at five hundred-yard intervals, find the .410 an ideal solution. Sending a .22 rimfire bullet skyward is highly irresponsible under these conditions, but the short fallout range of #8 shot poses no hazard.

As houses continue to march into the wilderness, many

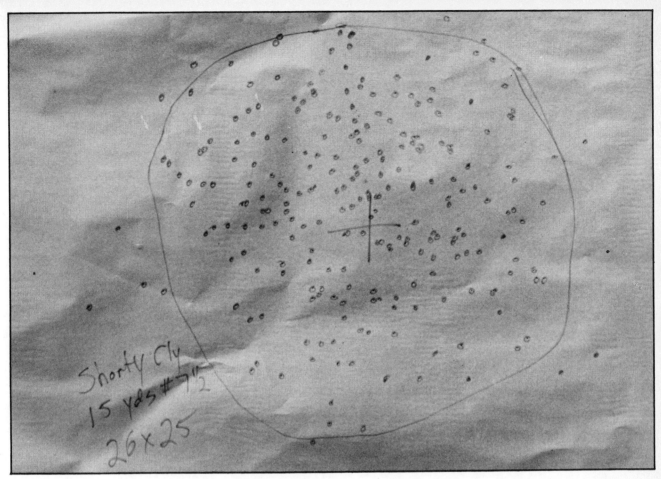

A cylinder-choked .410 with a three-inch load of #7-1/2 shot has a pattern five inches larger than a skeet-choked 20-gauge at 15 yards! Open-choked .410 is a favorite for heavy cover hunters who like eating what they shoot.

small-game hunters find themselves forced to utilize small-gauge shotguns, and few would argue with the effectiveness of a full-choked .410 under these conditions.

Having a .410 fitted for the Briley interchangeable tube system allows the gunner to achieve maximum versatility from this highly underrated smoothbore!

Shotshell selection for the .410 is a simple affair. Both Federal and Winchester offer excellent factory three-inch shells in sizes 4, 5, 6, 7½ and 8. From the twenty-six-inch barrel of my Mossberg 500, the 11/16-ounce shot charge reaches about 1120 fps.

Given the twenty-five-yard performance envelope of the .410, I find little use for shot sizes 4 and 5. Size 6 is more than ample for my occasional use on pheasant-size birds, and has proven the most effective size on beagle-run rabbits. Close-range gunning in heavy cover generally sees 7½s stuffed into the gun. I find that it only takes a few of these to drop a quail or woodcock decisively, and I seldom lose a bird in even the thickest cover.

In more open areas — and especially when gunning the waterholes for doves — I find the denser patterns achieved with #8 shot an asset.

The .410 shell also is available in 2½-inch length launching one-half-ounce of shot at about 1180 to 1200 fps. Some gun scribes in the past have opined that they achieve more uniform patterns with the shorter shell. That is some-times the case at the patterning board. But in the field, where the .410 belongs, the nod definitely goes to the three-inch load.

The downside to that is that I have yet to develop a hand-load that will equal the performance of the factory load in the longer shell. The upside to that is the Federal and Winchester shells are readily available virtually anywhere ammo is sold, which frees me from the arduous task of con-verting my MEC 600 Jr. press from the 2½-inch setting to the longer shell: a task that no doubt requires an engineering degree from MIT!

In the shorter shell, 14.5 grains of Hodgdon's H-110, combined with the Federal hull and .410 shotcup — using hard, black shot like the Lawrence Brand Magnum shot — will equal the performance of the factory .410 load with a velocity of about 1200 feet per second. Given the mini-scule amounts of powder and shot used, reloading the 2½-inch shell is highly economical. That allows plenty of inexpensive practice, which pays serious dividends in the field.

Of course, the .410 never will replace the larger gauges. Regardless of how it is choked or loaded, it still is a .410. But when the shooting is close and quick, it certainly doesn't take a back seat to any of them. As far as I am concerned, this is more than ample reason to keep a .410 in my hunting battery. — *Chris Christian*

IF STEEL SHOT COMES TO THE UPLANDS

Here's What To Do Instead Of Shoving Your Head In The Sand!

Target practice will help upland hunters adjust to the higher velocities and huskier recoil of steel shot in light guns.

No. 7 steel is best restricted to close-range shooting and small upland game like the woodcock in thickets.

WHEN STEEL shot first became part of American shotgunning, it was intended to eliminate the lead poisoning losses among waterfowl that otherwise would have ingested lead shot. Steel isn't the toxic metal that lead is.

Then it was learned that some eagles had died from ingesting the lead rifle bullets which were in big game that had died after having been wounded and lost by hunters. And thereupon the environmentalists began to question whether *any* lead should be used for sport shooting, regardless of whether it was used in a rifle, handgun or scattergun, or in the uplands as well as the marshes and swamps.

To date, the pro-hunting and pro-lead forces have managed to hold off the anti-lead faction. In most areas, lead shot still can be used for upland game hunting and target shooting.

But what if things go against hunters and lead shot is outlawed for the uplands? Do we throw up our hands in despair and quit, as did some duck and goose hunters? You remember the cop-out: "I'm not going to shoot that steel stuff through my guns!" some hunters protested, and with that they gave up the sport.

Perhaps we should be grateful, because waterfowling was cleansed of people who weren't real hunters, anyway. Folks who truly love the sport won't let a little matter like steel shot deprive them of their pleasures. As recent history has shown, steel shot can indeed get the job done, *if* one takes a scientific approach to load selection rather than thinking he can follow traditional pellet-size recommendations from lead-shot days.

As waterfowlers have learned, steel shot is about thirty percent lighter than lead shot in any given size. A steel No.

For squirrels, heavy steel shot is needed to penetrate their tough hides. No. 1s are recommended for starters with, perhaps, BBs needed for long-range squirrels.

2, for example, weighs less than a lead No. 2; the ramification is that the lighter steel No. 2 will be slowed quicker by air drag than will the heavier lead No. 2.

The standard rule of thumb in steel shot selection has become known as "the rule of two," which means that, to get downrange energy equivalent of any size of lead shot, one must pick a steel pellet that is at least two sizes larger. These added sizes give the pellet more weight with which to overcome the force of air drag.

In waterfowling, the steel T-shot (0.20-inch diameter) gives about the downrange performance of a lead BB (0.18-inch diameter). To get approximately the energy of a lead No. 4, the hunter must shoot steel No. 2s or 1s. And if one reads the exterior ballistics of the steel No. 4, he finds it gives nothing more than the energy level of a lead No. 6. Thus, the downrange energy values of lead and steel shot do not equal each other when the pellet sizes are equal. We must go to larger shot sizes if we wish to duplicate the retained striking energy of lead shot.

The same factors are at work when it comes to selecting steel shot sizes for upland hunting. We'll have to go at least two shot sizes larger than those in our former lead loads.

Let's say, for instance, that your favorite lead pellet size

for long-range pheasants or sharptails was the No. 5. It was a fine choice, splitting the difference between the pattern density of No. 6s and the energy of No. 4s. But where do you go for the same approximate ballistics in steel loads? Try the No. 3 steel pellet. It's two sizes larger than No. 5s, and in cursory experimental shooting, I've found it to be quite lethal on ringnecks inside forty-five yards. But if the birds are jumping well out, steel No. 2s may be in order for even more retained energy. As stated, steel No. 2s have about the energy of lead No. 4s, and nobody has ever questioned lead 4s on pheasants!

Turkey hunting also would present a load-selection problem, if steel shot were mandated for upland hunting. The old traditional lead shot loads used No. 6 shot to saturate the ol' gobbler's head/neck area, but in more recent times, some hunters have gone to lead 4s or 5s to ensure bone breakage. Some failures have been reported with lead 6s. How do we duplicate the former load of lead 6s? That would be with steel 4s, which are obviously two sizes larger. But those who question the performance of steel shot might wisely go to steel No. 3s for that added energy. Moreover, a magnum load would be in order for optimum pattern density. And if a hunter wanted the rough equivalent of lead 4s, he would shoot steel No. 2s, again in magnum packaging for maximum full-choke density.

Turkey hunters who consider full body hits undoubtedly

For dove hunting, steel No. 4 shot will deliver about the energy of lead No. 7s and 7 1/2s to about 35-40 yards.

Steel No. 4s, which give about the energy of lead No. 6s, are about the minimal pellet needed for pheasants.

On close-flushing upland game, steel No. 6s will deliver about the same energy of lead No. 7 1/2s at close range. They then drop off to that of No. 8s as the range moves beyond 20-25 yards. Steel No. 6s are best on small game.

would be frustrated by steel No. 4s. Indeed, a major reason why waterfowlers experienced some crippling in the early days of going with steel is because they continued to use their old favorite number, the No. 4, which is a relatively weak-hitter on heavily boned and feathered birds. A far better bet for body hits on turkey is the steel BB.

The ruffed grouse is an in-between bird, not as large or as tough as a pheasant, but certainly not in the category of quail. The oft-suggested lead No. 8s are, in many instances, rather light for grouse, and the lead No. 7½ is perhaps a better selection with lead No. 7s being ideal.

Unfortunately, there is no perfect equivalent for lead No. 7½s, but steel No. 5s come close, emulating the performance of No. 7 lead shot. This writer has used steel No. 5s for two seasons on ruffed grouse in both the one-ounce 20-gauge magnum load and the 1⅛-ounce 12-gauge load with exceptional results.

These steel 5s cut cleaner than lead 7½s or 7s, both of which tended to drag clumps of feather into the bird, and all hits held birds where they fell. An extremely high percentage of clean kills was noted, but the birds weren't mutilated by shot. The same results were observed on hunting preserve chukars and pheasants inside twenty to twenty-five yards.

There are currently No. 6 and No. 7 steel shot loads on the market. At this writing, the major shotshell manufacturers all offer steel No. 6s, while Fiocchi of America makes some twenty-four-gram (370-grains) 12-gauge loads of No. 7 steel shot. Initially, bird hunters would opt for them, because their sizes equate more closely with those of the traditional lead 7½s and 8s. However, these steel 6s and 7s lose their energy/velocity values quickly in the teeth

of air resistance, and the steel 6s drop to the energy level of lead 8½s and 9s.

Hunters who use doubles for woodcock and ruffed grouse might try a first barrel of steel 6s for the first open-choked shot followed by a load of steel 5s in the tighter tube when the foliage hangs dense in the early season. Bobwhite hunters might try the same combo, if their birds hold snug for a pointer. When the birds begin flushing farther out, however, steel No. 5s are advocated for both barrels. And if the ruffed grouse are skittish, a load of steel No. 4s in the tighter-choked second tube is in order.

For canyon-dwelling chukars and the running, far-flushing species of desert quail, the steel No. 5 also may prove to be a good, all-around choice, although spooky chukars may require steel No. 4s or even No. 3s for clean kills, if they insist on running wildly.

When doves fly high, the steel No. 6 is the smallest size that can be recommended. It will arrive at long range — meaning between thirty and forty yards — with about the lethality of a lead No. 8. But if steel No. 6s don't bring them down cleanly, the hunter's only alternative is again to switch to steel No. 5s.

Those who hunt cottontails, snowshoe hares and tree squirrels also will have to make adjustments in their shot-size selections. The steel No. 3 or 4 should prove adequate on rabbits and hares, delivering about the energies of lead 5s and 6s. For gray and fox squirrels, however, more per-pellet energy will be needed to penetrate their ultra-tough hides.

Thus far, actual hunting has indicated to me that steel No. 1s do a credible job from a gun that slings a solid full-choke pattern. This will give about the pellet energy of lead No. 3s and 4s with a tad of built-in extra energy for insurance. For those gauges where steel No. 1s aren't yet avail-

Steel No. 7s are needed to produce the downrange energy of No. 9 lead.

To receive the downrange energy supplied by lead No. 8s, an upland bird hunter would select steel No. 6s.

Lead No. 5s are tremendous upland pellets for turkey hunting and for long-range shots at pheasants and sharptails. For same impact with steel, a hunter should use No. 3s.

able, the steel No. 2 is a *must* for tree squirrels. And we may learn that steel BBs are needed for long-range squirrel sniping!

There is no doubt upland hunters will grimace at these larger pellet sizes for upland gunning. Traditions have ingrained us with the idea that anything larger than No. 7½s will ruin the aesthetics of an upland hunt. This can be especially true for sportsmen who like to wave the smaller gauges and/or lightweight guns, including the finer doubles.

If steel shot ever becomes law in the uplands, the .410 bore and 28-gauge can be considered collector's items, because neither can hold enough of the larger steel shot sizes to make it a humane fowling piece.

But from the 20-gauge through the 16 and 12, steel shot loads generally can handle adequate steel shot charges for the majority of upland bird hunting. The exception may be turkey and long-range hunting, in which case the 12-gauge would be the only sensible all-around selection with the 10 bore coming into its own as a turkey gun.

From the standpoint of sheer aesthetics, however, I always have thought it more important to make a clean kill than to commiserate over another 0.01- to 0.03-inch of pellet diameter. Indeed, if we were to put a mixture of pellet sizes into a typical hunter's palm and ask him to separate them according to exact sizes, he probably couldn't come close. So why haggle over the shot size number printed on a box of bird loads? A game bird cleanly dropped and retrieved is more important than lingering traditions in shot size selection.

If steel shot has any shortcoming in upland guns, it will be in recoil. Steel loads are normally pushed faster than lead ones to generate the energy/velocity level that will overcome air drag for the best possible exterior ballistics. Common lead-shot loads have published starting velocities around 1185 to 1330 feet per second, whereas many steel-shot loads range from 1350 fps for standard 12-gauge, 1⅛-

ouncers to nearly 1500 fps for the twenty-four-gram charges.

The added velocity of steel loads simply adds to the reaction factor of the action-reaction equation which generates recoil. This is especially so in featherweight, fixed-breech bird guns. The gas-operated autoloaders stretch out the recoil impulse and aren't as upsetting. I have taken ruffed grouse, pheasants and game preserve chukars with the Remington M1100 and both 1⅛- and 1¼-ounce loads of steel 5s and 4s without being upset by recoil. Not so with the lighter doubles and pumps.

Currently, the three-inch, 20-gauge magnum chambering is a better upland piece than the 16-gauge, because the former offers full one-ounce loads of steel as compared to just ⅞- or 15/16-ounce in the latter. However, steel loads pattern quite efficiently, and the 16 does quite well with No. 4, 5 and 6 steel. If some venturesome company bothered to create a three-inch, 16-gauge hull, though, it could become a stellar upland smallbore easily because of its better bore expansion ratio over that of the 20.

The three-inch, 20-gauge magnum steel loads fired in a gas-operated autoloader like the Remington M1100 or Beretta Model A303 are about as mild as they come, while still delivering a published starting velocity of around 1300 to 1330 feet per second. The standard-length 20's steel load also is light on recoil and has a published velocity of 1425 fps. But it is only a three-fourth-ouncer and doesn't fill out patterns too well if long-range gunning is part of the hunt. At this writing, there are no 28-gauge or .410-bore steel shot loads.

Patterning is another aspect of steel shot usage. There is currently a popular belief that steel loads invariably pattern like a rifle through the open degrees of choke such as improved cylinder and modified. If one tells a big enough lie and tells it often enough, people will start to believe it—which is what has happened relative to open chokes and

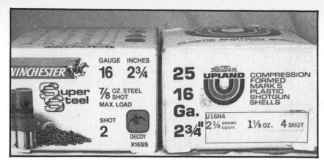

In 16-gauge, steel No. 2s are needed to provided about the same energy and killing power as lead No. 4 shot.

Bismuth is best known for medical uses, but it now is used in shot; some qualities are similar to those of lead.

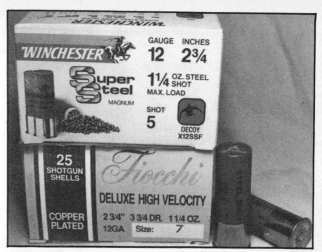

Steel No. 5s may seem coarse for upland hunting, but they deliver about the same energy as No. 7 lead shot.

steel shot. The truth is that skeet, improved cylinder and modified chokes still will deliver variously more open patterns with the finer sizes of steel birdshot than they will from the tighter choke constrictions like improved modified and full choke. It is mainly the larger sizes of steel shot — the BBs, BBBs, Ts, TTs and Fs — that tend to tighten up when shot through the skeet, IC and modified chokes.

Experimental patterning indicates that skeet and improved cylinder chokes will indeed give spreads akin to those they'd print with lead shot using steel 4s, 5s, 6s and 7s. Number 3s frequently will follow suit, as will steel No. 2s, but steel No. 1s can *sometimes* lean toward tighter clusters. Each gun/load tandem is a physical law unto itself, so it must be tested individually, if a hunter wants to know exactly what he's getting out at working ranges.

One point that should be made is that, despite spreading out from open-choked barels, steel loads will tend to hammer a reasonably dense center. This is because steel shot doesn't deform under the pressures of firing setback and bore travel; pellets which retain their spherical shapes will fly straighter than those which are misshapen. As a result, the open patterns will find a broad overall pellet distribution, albeit with some irregular "patchy" areas in the outer ring. Steel No. 5s seem to do the best job of distributing themselves evenly from a skeet choke, but, again, there's nothing written in stone, as each combo can differ.

In general, open-choked bores with constrictions of less than 0.015-inch in 12-gauge were prone to throwing erratic patterns at distances beyond fifteen to twenty yards with the smaller shot sizes. While this would suffice for most upland game inside twenty yards, there is a potential for crippling, if the pattern is stretched. For truly close-range shooting with steel No. 5s or 6s, a cylinder bore or reverse

flare seems to prove the best examples of even distribution.

A choke that eventually may do yoeman service with steel loads in the uplands is skeet No. 2 or light modified, which has a contriction of about 0.015-inch in 12-gauge. When fired through the fifteen-point choke, steel loads begin to retain their symmetry beyond twenty yards and function effectively to at least thirty-five yards.

For the tighter upland patterns, chokes of 0.020- and 0.025-inch are excellent in 12-gauge. These are known as modified and improved modified, respectively. The improved modified constriction might well team up with skeet No. 2 to give an effective upland pairing in a double barrel. Although some gunmakers do not provide skeet No. 2 or improved modified choke tubes for their production-grade shotguns, independent choke tube manufacturers like Hastings will supply them, as will Briley, Colonial and Nu-Line.

A final point is that we cannot take anything for granted about steel shot patterning. Armchair and barstool "experts" may expound on the subject, but it is too complicated for vague generalizations. As stated, there are indications and tendencies, but each outfit should be tested individually, because there can be exceptions to rules of thumb. Moreover, hunters must learn to score with smooth swings to center the pattern, not by relying on a few extra inches of pattern width to make them look good.

The speed of high-velocity steel shot loads may alter the forward allowance distance somewhat at close range compared to the leads needed for light field loads of lead shot. This differential sometimes can be noticed on the skeet field. However, the difference often is measured in mere inches that can be absorbed by the pattern's width.

If the velocity factor bothers a hunter, his best bet is to spend an afternoon shooting skeet with his steel loads to adjust his timing and picture. The biggest mistake a hunter can make with steel loads in the uplands is to be overly conscious of a departure from lead shot. Ignore the change and make a good point and swing. With the right shot size aboard, steel shot will score as heavily in the uplands as lead.

The important thing is hunter education, followed by the hunter's application of what he learned. — *Don Zutz*

CHAPTER 17

3 WAYS TO BETTER WINGSHOOTING

Following This Trio Of Tips Should Mean More Birds This Fall

Author's Mossberg .410 shot high, but a bit of sanding on the comb and a recoil pad spacer brought the gun into line.

Author demonstrates his version of the Satterwhite Ready Position. He says hunters should practice the position during the pre-season, ignoring the mounted positions used in skeet and trap matches.

WINGSHOOTING HAS been called an art. It also has been called a science. In truth, effective smoothbore handling requires a good bit of both.

There is little doubt that watching a shotgun master's precise, fluid moves — as he snaps his gun to his shoulder, swings through his target, subconsciously computes the myriad leads and angles that only wild birds can present, then folds the bird in a puff of feathers — is artistry in action. Such skill may take many years to develop and may be, in large part, due as much to the shooter's knowledge of what the birds will do as it is to his gun-handling ability.

However, even the most gifted virtuoso will find his performance suffering if he neglects the scientific side of scatter-gunning. Is the choke appropriate for the range and species being gunned? Are the loads delivering uniform patterns with sufficient density? Does the gun even shoot where you are looking?

If the answer to any of these questions is no or, worse, "I don't know," field shooting will suffer and the shooter will not even understand why he missed nor be in a position to correct his error on subsequent shots!

The key to effective wingshooting is to achieve that blend of art and science that allows the shooter to be certain his gun is delivering his patterns where he is looking, that those patterns are the best choice for the range and species, and that the gunner understands, and practices, the types of shots he will see in the field. Here's a three-step program that should do just that and boost those scores on birds this fall.

FIT THE GUN

European and English shooters pay a great deal of attention to fitting the gun to the individual shooter. Americans, on the other hand, generally purchase a smoothbore off the rack, then attempt to fit the shooter to the gun.

Traditional clay target games may not adequately prepare the shooter for the field. However, the games can be modified to place emphasis on the type of shots the hunter is apt to encounter in the field.

That system works for some. If a shooter is naturally talented, and has sufficient time and practice to learn how to 'snuggle' up to the gun just right, it may not be a significant handicap.

For most shooters, however, a properly fitted gun will result in an immediate improvement in shooting ability.

What makes a fitted gun so important? Consider this: On an iron-sighted rifle or handgun, impact of the bullet is regulated by a set of sights — a fixed front sight and a rear sight adjustable to move the impact point up, down, right and left. Although we don't consider shotguns to have the same type of sighting arrangement, they actually do.

The front bead becomes the front sight and the shooter's eye becomes the adjustable rear sight which can, by changing its position, move the pattern up, down, right or left.

For the shotgun to shoot where the gunner looks, the eye must be in the proper position and, more importantly, it must return to that exact same position each time the gun is mounted.

This is accomplished most easily with a shotgun stock that is fitted to the shooter's dimensions and allows the gun to come quickly to the shoulder with the head naturally and comfortably against the stock without further adjustment by the shooter.

Since humans vary considerably in size, and most mass-produced shotguns are made to "standard" dimensions, the chances of getting a properly fitted gun off the rack are not great.

Such a gun may perform quite well when the shooter has the time to slowly mount the gun, then crawl around on the stock to get everything lined up. But, how often do you have that luxury in the field?

A better bet is to check gun fit under actual hunting conditions, and that's not hard to do.

To determine how well your gun fits you for the field, put up a large sheet of craft or butcher paper, draw an aiming point on it that is about the size of a quail, and back off to twenty-five yards, wearing your normal hunting garb. Then bring the gun quickly but smoothly to your shoulder, and fire as soon as the bead is on the target. Do not aim. Do not take your time. And do not crawl around on the stock after the gun is mounted.

Fire three or four rounds in this fashion before you check your target.

If there is a large hole where the aiming point used to be, your gun fits well enough for the field. If not, it may need a few simple adjustments to the stock.

If the pattern is high, you need to lower your eye on the

Corky Robarts, a Florida hunting guide, had his Ruger Red Label custom-fitted for use with the lightweight hunting garb worn in sunshine states.

stock. This can be accomplished by lengthening the stock slightly (which will slide your eye farther back and down on the comb) or by reshaping the comb to lower it.

Lengthening the stock with a new recoil pad or spacer is the easiest route as long as the additional length does not interfere with your ability to mount the gun. If that is the case, a slight bit of wood may have to be removed from the comb to lower it, but do this in small steps.

My Mossberg 500 .410 pump gun placed most of its pattern above the point of aim as it came from the factory. I needed to sand the comb down less than one-sixteenth-inch to make it shoot dead on. Even slight adjustments in comb height can alter the impact point noticeably.

If the pattern is low, the eye must be raised on the comb, and this can be easily and inexpensively accomplished with a Meadow Industries Convert-A-Stock pad (P.O. Box 450, Marlton, NJ 08053). This soft cheek piece attaches to the stock via velcro and allows the comb to be raised to varying heights with removable inserts. The pad can be removed instantly or installed just as rapidly.

The eye also can be raised by shortening the stock.

Slight adjustments in elevation also can be achieved simply by changing the front bead height: the higher the bead, the lower the gun will shoot and vice versa.

Guns that shoot to the left or right can be a bit more difficult to correct. Extreme right or left dispersion could indicate a bent barrel or other problem that may require the services of a gunsmith, although slightly off-center patterns generally indicate a comb that is too narrow or too wide.

A gun that shoots slightly to the left indicates a comb that is too thick and removing a bit of wood from the side of the comb can correct that. If the gun shoots to the right, adding a bit of moleskin to build up the comb will help.

If the gun has exceptionally good wood and the shooter

is reluctant to hack it up, changing comb height and thickness can be done by many stockmakers simply by bending the stock. This is done routinely, using hot oil to soften the wood temporarily to allow the stock to be bent to the desired position.

Regardless of how the stock is altered, if the gun does not shoot where you look, alterations are in order. Only when the shooter and the gun are looking at the same spot will consistent results be realized.

Checking your gun's point of impact in the described manner also will point out any problems you will face in mounting the gun smoothly. Thick and cushiony recoil pads often tend to catch on clothing and ruin the mounting process. Rounding the heel of the pad can help prevent that, as can the application of PVC tape to the sides. Another solution is to replace the recoil pad with one of the the newer models designed for sporting clays use. These feature rounded edges and slick surfaces that mount quickly.

An additional problem that can surface when fitting a gun centers around clothing. If the gun is fitted to lightweight summer garb, the additional bulk presented by thicker winter garments can change the stock dimension fit, creating problems with point of impact and mounting the gun. Some shooters who use the same gun for warm and cold weather wingshooting find it advantageous to fit the gun to the winter garb and use a slip-on recoil pad to lengthen it for lighter, summer outfits.

KNOW YOUR CHOKES AND LOADS

Once the gun and shooter are singing from the same sheet of music, the next step is to make certain the gun is delivering effective patterns with the loads used in the field and, most importantly, at the shooting ranges.

Choosing effective chokes and loads is a task made far

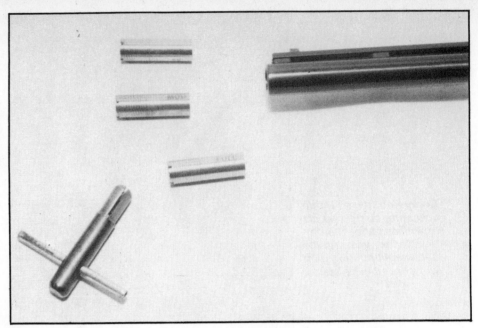

Adjustable choke tubes, like this Briley set for the author's Mossberg .410, allow hunters to change the pattern size to match the conditions and quarry.

easier with the widespread use of interchangeable choke tubes that allow the gunner to alter his pattern spread quickly. Unfortunately, too many shooters simply accept the markings on the tubes and never actually test them out to see what they are really delivering with different loads. That's a mistake you may pay for in the field.

Choke tubes generally are made to pretty precise tolerances and do meet the specified inside diameter for the marked choke. Unfortunately, shotgun barrels are not quite as precise, and since it is the relationship in constriction between barrel and choke tube that largely determines the pattern it will produce, a barrel that is larger or smaller than specified cylinder diameter for the gauge in use can change the patterning performance of the tube. It is quite possible — and not uncommon — for a tube marked "modified" to deliver full or improved cylinder patterns, depending upon the barrel's inside diameter.

Savvy shooters will check each choke tube with their favorite loads to find out what they really are throwing. The super-savvy shooter also will take the time to check those loads at the ranges he is most likely to use them.

For example, a southern quail hunter isn't likely to get a shot past twenty-five yards. So, why test the loads at the standard forty-yard range? The same holds true for those pursuing preserve pheasants, grouse, woodcock and other close-flushing species. On the other hand, those gunning chukars, desert quail and cornfield pheasants may find most of their shots in the thirty- to forty-yard range. It makes sense to test your tubes at that range.

Once a shooter understands what his tubes are doing at various ranges, it becomes a simple matter to select the right tube for the task at hand.

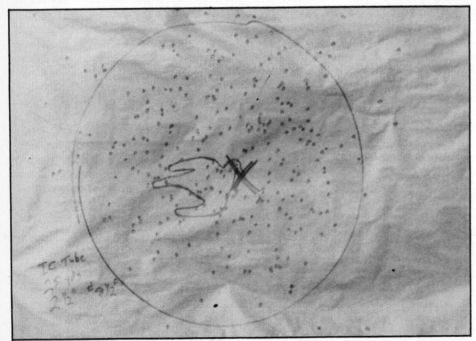

How effective is your load in the field? This load and choke would prove deadly on waterhole doves since most of them are taken at a range of 25 yards or less.

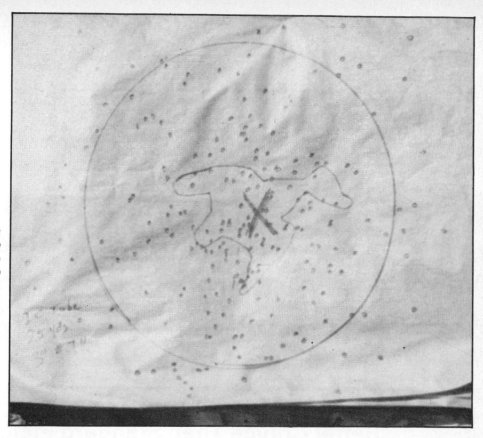

Tested at 25 yards, this steel shot load would give good density well out to 35 yards, making it a top choice for decoyed ducks.

When pattern testing, avoid using a small aiming point on the paper. Instead, stencil in a life-size replica of the game birds you'll be hunting. This will give one a far better idea of the load and choke's actual killing effectiveness than will simply counting holes in a thirty-inch circle.

PRACTICE INTELLIGENTLY

It's a common pre-season tactic for many shooters to head out to the local skeet or trap range, shoot a couple of rounds, then pronounce themselves "ready." Most of the time, they are not.

Simply shooting a shotgun will not make one an appreciably better field shot. Different gamebird species characteristically present certain types of angles (ducks crossing, quail straight or quartering away, doves incoming, etc.), and until a gunner sees enough of those angles, his or her subconscious computer will not have the input required to successfully execute the shot.

Constructive practice involves working on those angles you're likely to see in the field, and many hunters go awry here.

For example, a dove hunter shooting a round of trap may be having fun, but he's not doing his own internal computer any good since he could spend many a year in a dove field and never see any of those angles presented on a trap field. Those hunting chukars or cornfield pheasants, on the other hand, will be gaining valuable practice, because they will see those angles in the field.

Dove, duck and pigeon shooters will find skeet, especially the high house stations, excellent practice. So too is sporting clays. The angles are there. Quail hunters can get no better practice than skeet station low #7, #6 and #5.

Duck hunters will find skeet stations #3, #4 and #5 equally rewarding, especially if they belong to a small informal club that allows some leeway. At my club — the Palataka Skeet & Trap Club in Palatka, Florida — we routinely sharpen up for duck season by moving fifteen yards behind those stations before calling for the birds. Crossing ducks are easy after that!

Those chasing fast-flushing birds might try starting at the sixteen-yard line on a trap field and walking toward the house, just as you would approach a dog on point, while a buddy pulls the target at some undetermined point enroute. If trap facilities allowing that are not available, a portable target thrower (with an additional forty feet of line added to the release) allows a great deal of creative practice.

One pitfall to avoid while practicing on clays is to emulate other target shooters and call for the bird with the gun mounted. You won't have that luxury in the field, so why do it in practice?

Instead, call for the bird from a field-ready position. Here, the gun butt is held below the forearm, with the muzzle pointing straight ahead and upward at a forty-five-degree angle. The muzzle end should be in the field of vision, just below the eyes.

This is one of the best field-ready positions since it keeps the muzzle in a position to be acquired visually as soon as the bird is seen, and allows the gun to be mounted smoothly while following the bird.

Becoming a good field shooter isn't that difficult, but it does require a different training regime than that needed to master any of the clay target games. Once one understands those differences and incorporates them into his pre-season practice, he'll be well on his way to more birds this fall. — *Chris Christian*

TAKE TARGET LOADS AFIELD

These Clay Busters Often Are A Better Choice Than Standard Field Loads!

Author's many patterning tests show that target loads offer denser, more uniform patterns than virtually any field load.

Reloaders using the basic target load recipe of hard shot and moderate velocity will gain the advantages of target loads at a low cost.

REGARDLESS OF where you hail from, there are few wingshooting experiences more enjoyable than a good, old Southern dove shoot. Not only can the shooting be superb, but the prehunt barbeque is guaranteed to please even the most jaded palate. As I pulled into Jim Hammock's place that mid-October afternoon, I already could smell the pig on the spit.

Jim Hammock's eldest son, Jason, was there to direct traffic and pointed out a parking spot for my pickup, while informing me they were "fixin' to start servin' in about twenty minutes."

With time to kill, I let my springer spaniel, Lucy, out of the dog box for a stretch after the two-hour drive. With typical spaniel-like efficiency, she immediately set about becoming fast friends with the milling shooters, knowing full well such would pay dividends when they started heaping the plates!

Digging into the back of the truck, I popped open the Doskocil gun case and made certain the improved cylinder and modified tubes were installed firmly in the twin barrels of my Ruger Red Label, and that a pair of skeet tubes and a full tube — plus the tube wrench — were tucked away in a pocket on my shooting vest.

This being my first invitation to shoot the Hammock place, I knew the regulars already would have the best spots on the field taken (they did) and that I would be assigned (I was) to whatever less than desirable spot (it was) that remained. Not knowing how the birds flew on this field, I wanted to be ready for anything from forty-yard-plus passing shots to birds barreling in right down the gun barrel.

With that in mind, I set about loading my camo tote bag with shells. First in were two boxes of Federal's Flyer load, followed by a couple boxes of their International copper-plated load, and topped off by a pair of their Sporting Clays, all in size 7½. I'd just about completed that operation when one of the onlooking shooters noticed the word "target" on one of the boxes.

"Son," he grinned good naturedly, "the skeet range is about twenty-five miles down the road. Did you just pick up the wrong shells, or did you forget where you were going?"

I'd heard it before. In fact, it's quite common. If there isn't a picture of a critter on the shell box, "it ain't a hunting shell."

In years past, I might have taken the time to explain my choice of shells. Nowdays, I don't. I take the easy way out and just play stupid (something my close friends feel I do on an Emmy-winning level).

Since the amicable gentleman was in his 60s — and in the South, it is considered poor form not to show respect for one's elders — I just put on my best "humble young fellow" look and allowed as how they were the only shells I could find at the store. I hoped that would end the matter, and let me start sinking my teeth into the pig which was presently being sliced, but I wasn't going to get off that easily.

Digging into the back of his truck, he produced three boxes of a popular dove and quail load and said, "Take these, so you'll have something to shoot. Whatever you use you can swap out with some of those skeet shells you got there."

It took a bit more tact than I normally possess, but I did find a way to graciously refuse his offer. By the time the last bird had flown for the day, I was glad I had.

My assigned spot wasn't the best one on the field, but there were certainly plenty of birds, and, for once, I had arrived properly prepared.

The first wave of birds arrived with the nonchalance typical of a dove that hasn't yet had to dodge lead. With the

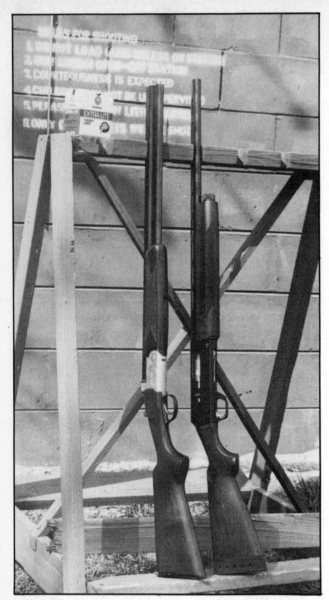

A significant benefit of target loads is reduced recoil, especially for those using lightweight 12-gauge guns.

see nothing more than the word, "target," on a box of shells in order to completely dismiss them for field use. Put a picture of a critter on the box and add the words "High Velocity" or "High Brass" and everything is okay. In reality, I frequently find the situation reversed.

When it comes to actual performance on game, not only will many target loads handle the task in exemplary fashion, but they'll often do a better job than all but the most expensive copper-plated/buffered premium grade field loads.

If that sounds surprising, it shouldn't. In fact, it's quite logical. A shotload's effectiveness on game birds starts with a pellet size and weight sufficient to penetrate the bird's vitals. Once that is achieved, the determining factor then becomes how well that load is capable of placing those pellets into a dense, yet evenly distributed pattern that leaves no gaps or open patches that a bird — or its vital organs — can slip through unscathed.

It's the pellets that kill the bird, but it is the pattern that puts the pellets there to do the job. Given two loads using the same appropriate shot size, it will be the one that consistently delivers the most evenly distributed pattern that fills the game bag the quickest.

Velocity is not really an important factor in killing power with lead pellets, although it does play a real role with steel shot. In fact, excessive lead shot velocity often can be detrimental.

The single most important patterning factor is round, undeformed shot. Shot pellets that have become slightly flattened and deformed will not maintain the same velocity and direction as undeformed pellets. Often they become fringe flyers outside of the main pattern, and may not even arrive on target with the undeformed pellets.

The velocity loss by deformed pellets frequently causes them to lag — or string out — behind the main shot charge, not arriving in time to be part of the pattern when it intersects a moving target. Pattern tests on a stationary patterning board will not show this. But patterning tests on a moving patterning board have repeatedly shown that it occurs. In some extreme cases, as much as twenty to thirty percent of the pellets in a load may arrive too late to do any good and, in effect, have been removed from the pattern.

A shotshell that deforms a significant percentage of its shot upon firing invariably will produce patterns lacking uniform density, and often feature one or more open areas a bird can slip through. The shooter may execute a perfect shot, but if a patchy pattern lets the bird slip through without a vital area hit, a cripple is usually the result.

Producing a load that consistently delivers uniform patterns doesn't require the services of an alchemist. The basic recipe is proven: hard shot + low to moderate velocities = uniform patterns.

The softer the shot, the more easily it is deformed by set-back pressures upon firing, and the higher the velocity and pressure, the more set-back pressure and deformation occur.

High-velocity loads can be made to pattern quite well, but are more complex and expensive in their construction. The shot must be extremely hard (preferably plated with copper or nickel), the shot cup must be tough and it also helps to buffer the shot.

The key to all of this is hard shot, and hardening shot sufficiently to prevent deformation in even low-velocity rounds requires antimony, a substance that noted shotgun writer

quick-opening Sporting Clays load, I was almost halfway to my limit fairly quickly, with what were relatively easy shots. Once the guns starting booming in earnest, however, the doves wised up fast! By shifting to the full and modified tubes, loading up with the potent 1¼-ounce Flyer load, I managed to tally a limit, dropping the twelfth bird on a forty-five-yard-plus quartering shot that surprised even my springer.

As we packed our gear and said our goodbyes, I made it a point to find out how the elderly gentleman had done. To put it in polite terms, he had not seriously impacted the dove population, although he had made one ammo maker quite happy! I wasn't surprised. Not only was he handicapped by his choice of shells, but by his belief in one of those wingshooting myths that refuses to die.

It always has amazed me that most wingshooters need to

Rabbit hunters finally have learned that target loads in shot size 7-1/2 used in fast-handling, open-choked guns make a fine combination.

Bob Brister once observed as "the most expensive stuff since alimony."

Ammo makers are caught in the same cost crunch as the rest of us, and they know full well that when it comes to weekend shooters and field loads, price sells! To keep prices competitive, they are forced to cut back on something and that generally is antimony.

One area where they do not scrimp on antimony, however, is in their target loads.

Competitive shotgunners, especially trap shooters, are quick to notice any difference in the way their shells are breaking the targets, and they won't hesitate to switch shells if they feel the ones they are using aren't up to snuff. Target loads may not be the biggest moneymaker in the product line, but they are the most prestigious. Ammo makers know sales increase throughout the line when one of their target loads is used to win a major championship. As a result, they go to great pains to assure their target loads are made with the best quality control, top quality components and the hardest shot. That's exactly the type

The low velocity of most target loads isn't a handicap in most upland settings where birds are taken under 30 yards.

of shell I want to use in the field!

The only drawback to utilizing target loads afield is (with one exception, which will be discussed later) that only the 12-gauge loads are suitable. Smaller gauges are available only in skeet loads with #9 shot, which I feel is a poor choice for the field under any circumstance because it lacks adequate penetration.

Another drawback is that these loads are offered only (with the exception of size 9) in sizes 7½, 8, and 8½. That does limit their use on larger birds. Still, shooters selecting target loads in sizes 7½ and 8 will find them suitable for a number of popular game birds.

Doves obviously spring to mind, as do quail and woodcock, but one also can add bandtail pigeons, rails and snipe, grouse and, in many situations, #7½ shot can be an excellent choice for pheasants, chukar and similar-size birds. Add rabbits, squirrels and airborne varmits like crows, and it becomes evident target loads can handle a wide range of hunting chores.

There also is an equally wide variety of target loads from which to choose. Shooters have the option of selecting loads carrying 1, 1⅛, or 1¼ ounces of shot, operating at velocities ranging from about 1100 feet per second right on up to almost 1300 fps. Here's how to make the most effective use of these in the field.

Light Loads: Carrying 1 or 1⅛ ounces of shot, these 2¾-dram equivalent loads operate in the 1100 to 1140 fps range and are among the lightest recoiling 12-gauge loads

Light 2-3/4 dram target loads in 1- or 1 1/8-ounce are superb for doves. They're easier on the shooter than field loads.

Copper-plated shot in Federal's Target Load produces dense, uniform patterns for better field performance.

available. Some of the more popular offerings are the Federal H-114 (1⅛-ounce Extra-Lite), Federal H-117 (1⅛-ounce Champion Target load) and the same company's F-113 (1-ounce Gold Medal). Winchester offers similar loads that perform equally well.

These loads are a joy to use in lightweight 12-gauge guns and, despite their modest velocity, quite deadly out to thirty-five yards. For quail, woodcock and waterhole doves, they are hard to beat in size #8.

Reloaders can duplicate the velocity, recoil, and game-killing performance of these loads with a Federal Gold Medal hull, Federal 12SO (one ounce) or 12S3 (1⅛ ounce) wad, 21.5 grains of PB powder and top quality hard black shot like Lawrence Brand Magnum shot. Over my Oehler chronograph, velocities with either shot charge run about 1120 fps, with perfect functioning in my gas-operated semi-auto shotguns.

Medium Loads: For years, one of the best kept secrets among expert dove shooters was the 3-dram, 1⅛-ounce, #7½ trap load. With a velocity of about 1160 to 1180 fps, they have all the power needed to "reach out and touch" a forty-yard dove, and do it with mild manners. Federal markets them as the H-118 (paper-hulled Champion) and the F-116 (plastic-hulled Gold Medal), while Winchester denotes them as the AA Trap Load (3 dram). They are a superb shell any time 1⅛ ounces of #7½ is called for.

My reloading recipe for this is a Federal Gold Medal hull, 12S3 wad, 23.3 grains of PB, and Lawrence Brand Magnum shot for an average velocity of 1168 fps.

These shells have such an enviable and well-established record that one would think it would be difficult for any other target load to equal. But, there are two new offerings that might just do it.

The first is the new Federal Sporting Clays load. This 1⅛-ounce load moves out at about 1200 fps and, instead of the standard plastic wad, features a biodegradable fiber wad system with an uprotected shot charge. This lets the pattern open a bit quicker for close targets, but the hard

shot still maintains good pattern density for those thirty-five-yard kills.

This load also is available in a seven-eighths-ounce 20-gauge load (the exception noted earlier) that should offer outstanding performance in the smaller gauge.

As a general purpose 1⅛-ounce "under thirty-five yards" load, it offers a lot of promise. I have yet to come up with a reload duplicating its velocity and patterning performance, but I'm still tyring!

The other new load is the one-ounce International load offered by Federal, Winchester and Fiocchi. Lacking any experience with the latter two, I can say that the Federal load features copper-plated shot, hits almost 1300 fps and patterns like no other one-ounce load I have ever seen.

On paper, it is the ballistic equivalent of the ubiquitous "promotional loads" that pop up each fall. But in the field and at the pattering board, it is like comparing a Corvette to a Hyundai. Shooters who like a fast-stepping one-ounce load should like this one.

Heavy Loads: The load most experienced shooters point to when making a case for toting target loads afield is the live pigeon load. This 1¼-ounce, 3¼-dram load delivers velocities in the 1160 to 1190 fps range and seems to possess the innate ability to pattern beautifully from any 12-gauge barrel. In size 7½, it is quite probably the finest long-range dove load available, as well as offering more than enough knockdown power for flushing pheasant and similar-size birds at ranges under thirty-five yards. Federal denotes it as their H-125 "Flyer Load," although the Winchester product is just as good.

My attempts to duplicate this load didn't quite hit the mark as far as velocity was concerned. My own load exceeds the factory figures, but with no increase in recoil or loss of patterning performance. That load is a Federal Gold Medal hull, 12S4 (1¼ ounce) wad, 24 grains of 800X, and Lawrence Brand Magnum shot, with a Federal 209 primer, for a velocity of 1230 fps.

Although originally developed to duplicate a "target load," I quickly discovered this was the finest 1¼-ounce load I have ever used.

Back in the days when you still could toss lead pellets at ducks and I was operating a duck guiding service on Florida's Lake George, topping the basic recipe with hard #5 shot produced the best decoy load I have ever used. I had a lot of opportunity to compare it, shot for shot, with most of the 3¾-dram, high-brass factory loads, and it emerged a winner every time.

Shifting to #4 shot, it was an excellent pass shooting load. Whatever it gave up in velocity it gained back in its ability to deliver consistent patterns, combined with the penetrating ability of the heavier lead pellet.

Nowadays, I generally stuff it with #7½s when I feel I need a fifty-yard dove load, although I have plugged in some #6s on those occasions when an out-of-state trip offered cornfield pheasants, sharptails or Huns.

Regardless of the shot size chosen, it did — and still does — do just what any good target load should: deliver dense, uniform patterns, be easy on the shooter and drop game birds just as well as any shell coming in a box featuring a picture of a critter on the label.

That's probably the biggest reason I keep taking "target loads" afield. — *Chris Christian*

WATERHOLE DOVES

This Fast-Paced Action Comes In Small Packages

Cardboard decoys are not nearly as effective as full-bodied plastic models, but they do have their uses. Author often lays out a spread of the decoys where he does not want birds to land. This funnels the birds to his shooting position.

Author believes a fast-handling skeet gun with 1-1/8-ounce #8 target loads is likely the best tool for waterhole doves.

THE LATE afternoon sun was a welcome addition to what had been a gray and chilly fall day. Welcome enough that I was spending more time reveling in its warmth than paying attention to the skies surrounding the small central Florida pond. When the first bird came barrelling in, I wasn't even close to ready!

A sharp turn of the head by my dog, Lucy, brought me to attention, as the dove rocketed across my front, and I suppose, subconsciously, I knew there was no point in taking the shot. When you're caught napping that badly by a speeding dove, admit defeat gracefully and wait for the next bird.

Unfortunately, the Ruger Red Label already was up and swinging in a futile attempt to catch up with the streaking target. But as the dove disappeared over the trees the load of #8s produced nothing more than a shower of leaves.

Missing a bird is no big deal. I do it frequently. The bad part is when I do it in front of my springer spaniel, Lucy.

Like most of her breed, she takes hunting seriously, and when it comes to missing a bird, she has absolutely no sense of humor. This time, I got the full treatment.

Rising slowly from her sitting position beside me, she ambled casually over to the spot where the dove should have fallen had I done my part, dropped her nose to the ground, took a quick sniff, then sat down and stared at me.

Point made, she ambled back to her position beside me, sat down and gave me one more baleful look before turning her attention back to the skies in front of us.

I've seen some Olympic-caliber shotgun coaches that didn't do it any better!

Muttering a few unkind words about dogs with opinions, I slipped a fresh shell into the empty chamber, and had no sooner closed the action when a dove streaked over from behind!

This time, I got it right, and watched the dove crumple in mid-air as its momentum carried it a good twenty yards into the pond. That immediately put me back into Lucy's good graces, and as she hit the water at full speed, two more doves streaked in from the left!

That set the scene for the next hour, and while I certainly missed my share of shots — and maybe a few more — by the time the sun dipped below the tree line there was a twelve-bird pile at my feet. I don't know whether it improved Lucy's opinion of my scattergunning skills, but it made me feel a lot better. That's one of the reasons I find gunning the waterholes for doves so rewarding.

Mention dove hunting to most shotgunners, especially those hailing from one southern side of the Mason-Dixon line, and you'll likely conjure up an immediate vision of a traditional field shoot, and a grand tradition it is.

Here, a number of shooters station themselves in and around a field used by feeding doves, and as the birds arrive for dinner, they are greeted by a literal barrage of shot. This keeps the birds up and moving and can result in some mighty fast-paced shooting. In many areas of the Deep South, this has evolved into an early fall ritual, complete with pre-hunt barbeque.

Lucy obediently presents author with T/C-downed dove.

some of the faster wingshooting available north of the Mexican border.

Doves, much like the hunters who pursue them, enjoy finishing the day with a little tipple. They invariably seek water before flying to roost for the night. The hunter who can locate those watering holes in current use may find a large percentage of the local dove population beating a path to his door!

Locating the best waterholes, however, does take some scouting. Doves can drink anywhere they can find a teacup of the stuff, but just as hunters have their favorite watering holes, so do doves. Even in areas with an abundant supply of standing water, doves often show a decided preference for waterholes with certain physical characteristics, and will use them instead of other sources. Here is what to look for.

Doves don't care whether the water is clean or muddy. They're just as happy tippling from a churned-up stock pond as they are from pristine sources. But, they definitely require "clean" banks.

Doves, like many other gamebirds, can't simply dip their head to drink. They must dip their whole body, which

This diminutive Mossberg .410 pump is one of author's favorite waterhole guns. Briley choke tubes are quickly interchanged in the field to match shooting conditions.

Unfortunately, as enjoyable and productive as a good field shoot is, it does have a lot of drawbacks for those who enjoy pursuing doves throughout the rather lengthy season. The biggest problem is simply being able to collect enough shooters regularly to man a field. Without a sufficient number of hunters to keep the birds moving, even the most popular field will likely see far more birds on the ground than in the air.

It's not too difficult to round up suitable numbers during the early season, but as one moves farther into fall, and other outdoor opportunities become more prevalent, their numbers fall off considerably.

Even if a group can be assembled, one must operate on their schedule, which definitely restricts an individual's choice of hunting times and places.

This certainly is not a knock on field shoots. They offer excellent sport, but, realistically, any hunter who can participate in a half-dozen per season should count himself as fortunate. For many wingshooting enthusiasts, this simply isn't enough. Luckily, there is an alternative, and one that can provide gunners with the opportunity to experience

Author's springer spaniel eagerly took to retrieving, despite sarcastic displays regarding author's shooting ability.

leaves them head down and vulnerable. They instinctively know this, and as a result they insist upon a lot of open space around them.

You won't find doves landing in tall grass or vegetation, nor will they drink next to it. The first and most important requirement for a good watering hole is that it has clean-cut banks of either sand, mud or cropped grass.

This makes stock ponds a top choice, since livestock invariably beats down vegetation around the banks. Even a pond with extensive vegetation should not be ruled out, however. All that is required is a suitable section of shoreline.

One of my favorite ponds is a good example. This one is a manmade, almost perfectly square, one-acre affair. Three and a half sides are heavily overgrown with tall grass that grows right down to the water's edge. But there is a thirty-yard strip on one side that is sand beach. Every dove using this pond invariably lands there. Knowing where every bird is ultimately going to wind up makes choosing a stand site quite easy!

Another important characteristic is a dove's inherent caution. Few doves rocket directly into a feeding or watering spot. Most often, they will find a convenient perch first, so they can look things over before dropping to the ground. A pond that has one or more tall trees located around it will see far more use than one on flat, barren ground.

Doves aren't particularly lazy, and they don't mind flying a considerable distance to seek food and water. But they aren't adverse to convenience, and any waterhole lying adjacent to a feeding field — or between a field and a roosting area — may well see considerable use. If a hunter knows the area well enough to predict feeding and roosting sites, locating productive watering holes can be made easier.

Once potential sites are found, you need to determine the amount of use they are receiving from the doves. The easiest way to do this is simply to grab a pair of binoculars and watch them for a few evenings before the season opens. The peak time for watering doves is the last hour of the day, and a hunter who spends a few evenings observing a waterhole can learn quite a bit.

Once potential sites are found you need to determine the amount of use they are receiving from the doves. The easiest way to do this is simply to grab a pair of binoculars and watch them for a few evenings before the season opens. The peak time for watering doves is the last hour of the day, and a hunter who spends a few evenings observing a waterhole can learn quite a bit.

For example, is there a particular pathway the doves use coming in? Doves often will "funnel" through treeline breaks, or along the edge of the treeline. If this occurs, it

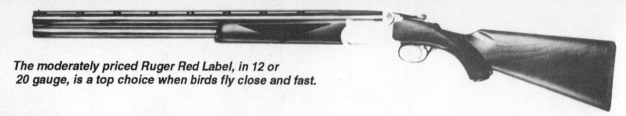

The moderately priced Ruger Red Label, in 12 or 20 gauge, is a top choice when birds fly close and fast.

Interchangeable choke tubes add versatility to shotguns; author contends most shooters overchoke their guns.

aids the shooter in selecting a stand.

Is there a particular tree the doves land in first? In what section of the pond do they prefer to land? Knowing this also helps in placing your shooting site in order to set up "easier" shots.

One pond I hunt often is located in a section of planted pines. On one side of the pond is a section of young growth, while the other side is composed of taller, more mature trees. The doves fly right down this natural contour and I can choose my position to give me incoming shots at about twenty yards! This pond is so "easy" to shoot that I often leave the long guns at home and tote my Thompson/Center .410 Contender!

Scouting waterholes is important for another reason. If you intend to do much shooting, you will need more than one to hunt.

Even the most popular waterhole can be burned in a hurry. My experience has been that shooting one more than once a week will cause the birds to move elsewhere. Since I often hunt two or three evenings a week, I find I need a half-dozen different sites if I am going to enjoy consistently good shooting. I view a good waterhole as something to be cherished, not abused. From a practical point of view, it also makes sense to go easy. As difficult as it can sometimes be to find a productive watering site, there's no point in burning it out and seeing all your scouting time go to waste.

This is one reason why most of my waterhole shooting is done solo or with just one other trusted companion. That may sound a bit greedy, but there is another practical reason for it: Most waterholes in my neck of the woods simply aren't big enough to host more than one or two shooters. This is one case where good things do indeed come in small packages.

Once a hunter locates productive waterholes, the stage

is set for some fast-paced wingshooting, but only if hunters exercise some care in mining the gold.

Some doves may water at midday, but the vast majority do so during the last hour and a half of the day. It makes little sense to arrive much earlier.

Since the action is going to be compressed into a relatively short period of time, it's a good idea to use some care in setting up for the shoot. Unlike a number of people I know, tippling doves do not get stupid, and while they may be intent upon watering at that site, it won't take much to make them change their minds. Needless to say, camo is an advantage in the clothing department, and savvy hunters will take the time to construct at least a hasty blind around their shooting site. If you treat waterhole doves in the same manner you would ducks coming into decoys, you'll fare far better. In fact, it can often pay to use decoys!

The sight of doves already on the banks seems to reassure arriving doves that the world is at peace. On the occasions when I have seen doves barrel right into the bank

A few inexpensive, full-bodied plastic decoys placed at the water's edge reassure incoming birds that all is well.

Waterhole shooting is a close-range affair. Many of author's waterholes are suited for his T/C .410 hand/shotgun which does a great job out to 25 yards.

for a landing — foregoing the usual "perch in the tree/look things over first" routine — it has been when I have put out a spread of dove decoys.

I've read that simple cardboard cutout decoys can work wonders, but after experimenting with them at length, I've come to the conclusion that the one who penned those lines wasn't shooting at the same species of dove I was. My success rate with them has been less than spectacular, although on some occasions, they produced results.

I remember one large stock pond I used to shoot each year until the property changed hands. It was big enough that doves could land well out of range, without ever even getting close to my stand. The cardboard decoys? I placed them everywhere I didn't want doves to land and they funnelled the birds to me! That's the only time I've had any use for them, and nowadays I tote a half-dozen full-bodied plastic decoys in a shoulder bag. They work the way decoys are supposed to and they are readily available in many sporting goods stores and mail-order outlets.

When it comes to selecting a shotgun for waterhole doves, the field is wide open. Most waterhole shooting is quick and close. You'll take the majority of birds at less than thirty yards. Unfortunately, many shooters handicap themselves by choosing smoothbores choked too tightly. With a few exceptions, a full choke is more of a hindrance than a help. Even modified is often too much!

The deadliest dove gun for waterhole shooters is a fast-handling 12-gauge skeet gun. Match this with a light recoiling 1⅛-ounce load using hard #8 shot, and you won't be able to blame misses on the gun and load!

The 20-gauge also is an excellent choice with any one-ounce load, and a shooter armed with a light 28-gauge double-choked skeet/skeet or IC and modified also will find himself well heeled for the sport.

One of my favorite waterhole guns is a worn Mossberg .410 pump. Although I'm not a big fan of pumps, there is something about the petite little cornshucker that appeals

to me. I've had this gun fitted with Briley interchangeable choke tubes and find that the IC tube and Federal's three-inch Classic high brass #8 shell do the job quite well out to thirty yards. That's a lengthy shot on some of my waterholes.

The point made here is simple: If you've scouted your waterhole properly, your shots will be close and quick, requiring nothing more than a fast-handling smoothbore that will throw cylinder-bore patterns at twenty-five yards.

The only exceptions I've found to this are waterholes that are really too big for one man to shoot effectively on his own and waterholes that have been overgunned. If you've overstayed your welcome, you'll find the birds flying farther and higher, as they check the area out from the air. This is one case where you will need to shift to a gun more suitable for long-range pass shooting and a full or modified 12-gauge stuffed with Federal's H125 Flyer Load in size 7½ can be an asset.

There is one additional factor that waterhole shooters must consider, and that is recovering their birds. Anytime one shoots over water, some birds will do their Mark Spitz imitation. Sporting ethics dictate that every effort be made to recover downed birds, and so does common sense. Landowners gracious enough to give permission to hunt their waterholes may have a change of heart, if the hunter is thoughtless enough to leave dead birds bobbing on the water. Dead doves float a long time.

Some hunters solve this problem with hip waders, and often tote a fishing rod equipped with a heavy topwater plug bristling with treble hooks to aid in reaching those birds in deeper water.

The best solution, of course, is a good retriever. My springer took to the job enthusiastically and much prefers it when a bird hits the drink. Any dog suitable for ducks will do well for waterhole doves, although if you shoot like I do it's advisable to obtain one with a sense of humor.
—*Chris Christian*

CHAPTER 20

IS THERE A PERFECT DOVE GUN?

It's About As Likely As The Mythical Free Lunch!

Ruger's Red Label 12-gauge is a good, all-around choice, if you remember to bring your choke tubes and wrench.

The author favors his Franchi Prestige autoloader for some dove-taking situations, but it does have its limitations:

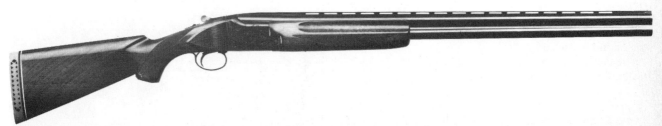

The author suggested that Bob Stead bring his Winchester Model 101 for heavy-cover dove hunting in Florida.

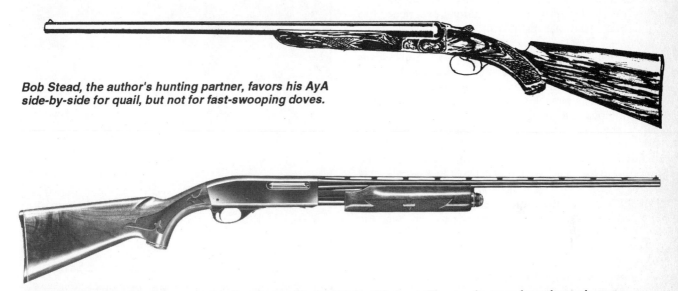

Bob Stead, the author's hunting partner, favors his AyA side-by-side for quail, but not for fast-swooping doves.

Stead finally settled for his venerable Remington Model 870 for this hunt. The results were less than adequate.

THE FIRST dove appeared so quickly it was as though it had popped out of a magician's hat. But that was expected.

The little half-acre waterhole was tucked into the middle of the planted pine plantation, which meant I wasn't going to get much warning. Under the best circumstances — and that assumes one is looking right at the spot where the bird would appear — that first glimpse would be of a brown-gray streak barreling between the fifty-foot pines at twenty-five to thirty yards, coming fast!

You don't analyze those kind of shots, you just react. By the time I'd swung the barrel of my lightweight .410 pump through the target and unleashed a load of #8s, the bird was less than fifteen yards away when it folded in a puff of feathers.

It was the kind of fast-paced action that will keep any wingshooter on his toes, and I was enjoying myself immensely. Unfortunately, my cohort didn't share my enthusiasm.

When I invited Bob Stead to spend an afternoon at one of my favorite waterholes, I clearly remember telling him it was close, quick shooting. Knowing Stead to be an enthusiastic and competent skeet shooter, I even suggested that his Winchester Model 101 28-gauge skeet gun stuffed with three-quarter-ounce loads of #8s would be the perfect choice. I figured that was adequate warning, since I knew Stead was an ardent dove hunter. I did not know, however, whether he ever had shot such a tight waterhole.

As it turned out, I should have explained the situation a bit further, because after the word "dove" everything else seemed to get lost. If Bob Stead was going dove hunting, he was going to bring his "dove gun."

To understand that, I guess you have to understand Bob

Stead. That won't require a lengthy explanation, though, because every one of us knows more than a few hunters like him.

In his mid-fifties, Stead has been prowling Florida's woods and waters for well over forty years, and he is firmly convinced each of his chosen tools is as perfect as any hunting tool can be. For example, when deer season rolls around, he doesn't agonize over his choice of equipment. He simply plucks his well-worn Ruger Model 77 out of his gun rack, grabs a box of .270 ammo and checks to make sure his 2x-7x scope is sighted to put his rounds three inches high at one hundred yards. For the last decade, that combo never has failed to put his annual allotment of venison in the freezer.

When duck season arrives, it's a Mossberg Model 835. For quail season, a quick-handling, little AYA 20-gauge side-by-side gets the nod.

Bob Stead has what he considers the proper firearm for any hunting endeavor. When I invited him to hunt doves, he didn't hesitate. He automatically grabbed his "dove gun" — a well-worn Remington Model 870 with a twenty-eight-inch ribbed barrel and a modified fixed choke.

Since virtually all of his dove-hunting experience has been under what one might call "classic field shooting situations," Stead's choice isn't surprising. A modified-choke 12-gauge stuffed with 1⅛-ounce #7½ trap loads is tough to beat under those conditions. And although the gun is an older model without interchangeable choke capability, Stead is a savvy enough wingshooter to know that just a change of load will change his choke.

If he needs to open his patterns, shifting to one of the popular promotional loads (pushing an ounce of soft shot at 1300 fps) will deliver improved cylinder patterns. If the doves are flying high, Federal's Flyer Load, with its 1¼ ounces of hard #7½ shot at moderate velocity, does the job. It may not equal the paper target patterns of a true full choke, but in the real world it will whack and stack the doves just as well.

As far as Bob Stead is concerned, he has the perfect dove gun. Unfortunately, he never had been required to test that gun under conditions where a twenty-yard shot was a long one.

It took him a while to get the long gun onto the short birds, and when he finally did connect, he probably wished he hadn't.

His first score was about twelve yards off the end of the muzzle, and when my springer spaniel, Lucy, bounced obediently out to retrieve the bird, she was confronted with the inevitable results of 1⅛ ounces of #7½ shot on a four-ounce target at powder burning range. Being a highly intelligent little dog, she just nosed around until she found the biggest piece, brought it back to me, then trotted back out to gather up the rest. From then on, Stead's day sort of went downhill.

The gun that had worked so well under conditions of leisurely twenty-five to forty-five-yard shots seemed to swing like a two-by-four when the doves were up-close-in-your-face-and-fast. "Smoking a dove" took on an entirely new meaning. In fact, after Stead's third or fourth hit, Lucy wouldn't even go out to retrieve his birds. She doesn't do piece work.

On the other hand, my little .410 was doing quite well.

Open-field shots are handled well by modified-choked 12-gauges and 1-1/8-ounce trap loads. If you change the scenario, however, and have the wrong gun, a favorite dog isn't going to have much retrieving work to do.

Fitted with Briley choke tubes, I had the skeet tube installed and further encouraged quick-opening patterns through the use of factory three-inch eleven-sixteenth-ounce loads of #8s. The partially protected charge resulted in lots of flyer pellets, and if you were to pattern that combo at thirty yards, you'd find it as full of holes as a rusty bucket.

But, at fifteen yards — where the doves were — it was as deadly as a Patriot missile. The patterns were open enough, too, that Lucy could retrieve the entire bird on one trip.

Does that mean a skeet-choked .410 is a better dove gun than a modified-choke 12 gauge? Not under most conditions, but at that time and place, it may well have been the "perfect dove gun."

Which just goes to show there ain't no such critter. Nor could one logically expect there to be such a thing as a per-

This skeet-choked load from the author's .410 delivers dove-downing patterns at the 20-yard range used here. Beyond that range, holes open quickly in the pattern. At 15 yards, Hunter insists it is the perfect dove gun.

fect dove gun. Not when you consider the dove is not only the most numerous, and widely distributed, North American gamebird, but can be hunted under some of the most varied conditions in which feathered game is found.

If that is surprising, consider this: While the vast majority of dove hunters ply their trade in open fields where shots can be rather leisurely affairs, they can seek and find doves under conditions so far removed as to render a proper "dove field gun" a distinct handicap. Here's a look at some of the more interesting ways to put doves on the table, and why your special dove gun may not be the best choice.

Gunning the waterholes: If there is one predictable trait inherent with doves, it is that they will fly to water immediately after feeding and again before going on the roost for the night. In an area with a good dove population, this makes gunning a productive waterhole in the late afternoon some of the most exciting wingshooting around.

Locating productive waterholes does require some scouting, because while doves need water, not all waterholes will be used. Doves have some truly specific requirements, and if they are not met, the doves will just keep flying until they are.

The most important consideration is that at least some portion of the bank be clear-cut right down to the water's edge. Doves will not land in nor walk through any vegetation tall enough to prevent them from seeing approaching predators. Since a dove doesn't stand more than six inches tall, it doesn't take much grass to render a waterhole unusable for them.

Another consideration is that there be a tall tree or other convenient perch close to the pond. The first wave of doves to water generally prefer to alight and look the area over before going in. In arid areas, where water sources are limited, this is not always a factor. But where water is abundant, the doves will choose the ponds that best suit their needs and a convenient perch is a big plus.

Locating good ponds is best done in mid- to late afternoon with a pair of binoculars. This is a pre-season ritual with me, and it tells me a lot more than simply which ponds are being used. After you've watched the birds come in, it will tell you their flight path, where your best position will be — and what shotgun you'll want to use.

In choosing the best shotgun, my primary concern is that the gun and load combo produce the widest usable pattern, with sufficient density, within the distance range the majority of doves using that particular pond will be encountered. Since ponds vary, so too does the most effective scattergun.

One of my favorite ponds — the one mentioned at the beginning of this piece — rarely gives me a shot beyond twenty-five yards. Twelve to eighteen yards is the range encountered most often. That requires a quick opening pattern, and (with the exception of custom-loaded "spreader" shotshells) nothing does that as well as the lowly .410, especially with factory three-inch shells.

From a skeet-choked .410, factory three-inch loads of eleven-sixteenth-ounce of #8 shot will produce patterns a third again as large as a skeet-choked 12 gauge with 1⅛ ounces of the same size shot at ranges under twenty yards.

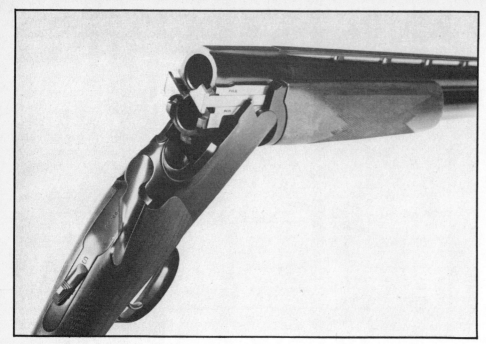

The author favors Ruger over/unders in 12 and 20 gauges, one with a pistol-grip stock, the other with an English-style straight stock for the various types of dove hunting he encounters in his central Florida environs.

The patterns are dense enough to drop any bird within them, yet not so dense as to create "instant doveburger." Yes, the pattern blows apart quickly past twenty yards, but if that's going to be your longest shot, who cares?

Change the pond, however, and the little .410 becomes as useless as a politician's election year promises.

Another favorite pond of mine is a man-made, one-acre-square affair. My shooting station is a small patch of reeds that juts out into the pond on a little point in the center of one bank. Most shots here are in the twenty- to thirty-five-yard range, with a high percentage being crossers.

This pond generally sees me toting my Franchi Prestige 12-gauge gas autoloader, with the improved cylinder tube installed, and the magazine stuffed with 1⅛-ounce #7½ traploads, or an equivalent reload. If I feel like toting an over/under, my 12-gauge Ruger Red Label, with custom Skeet I and Skeet II tubes and the same shotload, gets the nod.

Two different waterholes, two different gun/gauge/load combos. Think of waterhole doves as a shooting version of golf: pick the proper club for the lie.

Selecting a three wood when you are seventy yards off the green is a good way to ruin a round. So, too, is selecting the wrong gun on a waterhole, regardless of what preconceived notions one may have concerning the "perfect dove gun."

Gunning the waterholes requires a varied approach in shotgun selection; how well you make that selection can determine how successful you will be. The next offbeat dove hunting scenario, however, doesn't require a lot of thought at all.

Rolling them out of the trees: Few dove hunters consider it a midday sport. But it can be, and it also can be some of the most challenging wingshooting available.

Doves tend to loaf around during the middle of the day, generally perched comfortably in whatever tall trees lay in the vicinity of the fields in which they are feeding. When approached by a hunter on the ground, it doesn't take them long to come barreling out!

Prowling tree-lined field edges can provide fast-paced midday wingshooting that's challenging enough to give even a veteran grouse hunter fits.

It generally goes like this: Moving slowly along the inside edge of the treeline, the gunner might catch a glimpse of one or more doves flitting around and changing position in the trees ahead, but not always. Usually the first indication that powder and shot are about to be expended occurs when the sudden whistling of wings is accompanied by the simultaneous evacuation of a tree full of doves. A dove vacating a tree bears a strong resemblance to a drunk falling off a bar stool: they just sort of half-roll out, tumble a foot or so toward the ground, manage to right themselves, then they're off!

They also are incredibly good at accomplishing the above maneuver while keeping some of the present vegetation strategically placed between you and them.

Since doves generally are accommodating enough to allow you to get within twenty yards or so before leaving, one might conclude that the smaller gauges could be effective. Not so.

Doves invariably flush away from the threat, and when the intervening greenery is considered, this becomes a game for guns capable of tossing 1⅛ to 1¼ ounces of shot, delivering patterns appropriate for twenty-five to thirty-five-yard encounters.

My first choice for this is a three-shot, 12-gauge autoloader. I don't always require that third shot, but on enough occasions to make it worthwhile, there will be one or two laggard doves that flush late and can make relatively easy targets — if you have a round left.

It's a good idea to increase your shot size, as well. While I normally favor #8s for anything inside twenty-five yards, and #7½ shot for all other dove chores, I opt for #6s here. And if I happen to be out of those, I don't feel bad about loading #5s.

The heavier shot punches through the inevitable greenery much better, and in thicker cover I like doves to drop as close to where they are hit as possible. My favorite load here is a 3¼ dram shell carrying 1¼ ounces of hard #6s. Most of the time, an improved cylinder choke is the best choice, but I make certain I have a modified and a full tube — plus the proper wrench — with me. If the birds have been hunted and flush wildly, you'll need them.

Flushing feeding birds from the fields: One of the prerequisites for a classic field shoot is that you have enough shooters to keep the birds in the air. If the field isn't ringed properly with gunners, the birds land, feed and leave.

Assembling that many hunters can be tough late in the season when many outdoorsmen drift off to pursue other game. That doesn't mean, however, that you need to abandon the field. Just shift gears, let the birds land, then walk them up. This is a radically different way to pursue doves, and requires an equally extreme shift in your choice of shootin' irons.

A dove flushed from the ground comes almost straight up — and quickly. Those who have competed in live pigeon matches or have shot Olympic-style trap will find themselves right at home. The vast majority of the shots presented will fall right into the thirty- to forty-five-yard range common to both of those games.

Obviously, the best gun and load combo here would be the same one that would excel there: a tightly choked 12 gauge capable of at least two shots, and fitted as a high gun; one that will place it's pattern twelve to eighteen inches high at forty yards. Feed it 1⅛-ounce #7½ trap loads or, better yet, a 1¼-ounce pigeon load like Federal's Flyer, and you're ready to enjoy some offbeat, yet highly productive, late-season gunning.

Those lacking a multi-shot trap gun can achieve the same high-shooting effect with any flat-shooting field gun through the use of one of Meadow Industries' (P.O. Box 754, Locust Grove, VA 22508) various detachable cheek pads. Either the variable recoil slip pads or their variable Convert-A-Stock pad can be used to raise combo height in controllable increments, and thus raise pattern impact point.

When not needed, the pads can be removed easily to return the gun to a flat-shooting field stock. I have them on several of my guns and would not want to be without them, since they also help cushion the cheek and reduce felt recoil.

Such a diversified collection of scatterguns may seem a lot of trouble to go through just to bag a limit of doves. And if one is content to confine his wingshooting to traditionally classic field shoots, that selection would hardly be needed.

But if you're one who desires to take full advantage of abundant birds, lengthy seasons and challenging situations, you will discover quickly that, like the mythical "free lunch," there is no such thing as the "perfect dove gun." — *Rod Hunter*

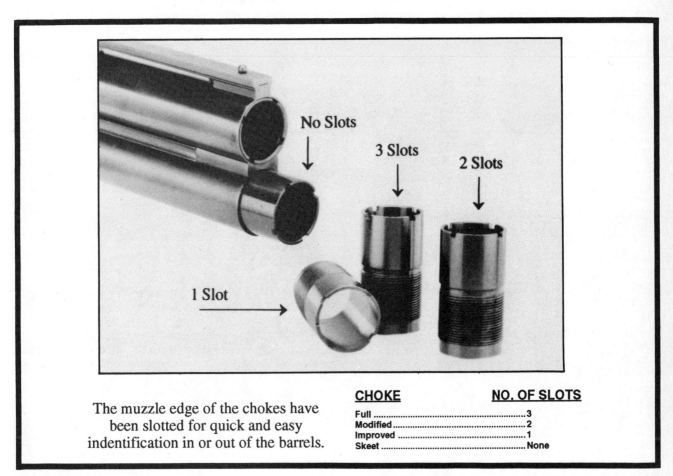

The muzzle edge of the chokes have been slotted for quick and easy indentification in or out of the barrels.

CHOKE	NO. OF SLOTS
Full	3
Modified	2
Improved	1
Skeet	None

Ruger shotguns have screw-in chokes that have slightly different barrel configurations from the fixed-choke models. Due to dimensional variations screw-in chokes cannot be retrofitted to the existing barrels of Red Label over/unders.

CHAPTER
21

LONG-RANGE UPLAND HUNTING

Not All Of These Shots Are Close; Here's What To Do About It

When upland birds flush at maximum range, heavy loads and tight patterns are preferred if your goal is clean kills.

The speed of outgoing birds actually offsets some of the pellets' retained velocity. This must be considered when selecting the right load. The No. 6 lead pellet is about the minimum that should be used for long-range uplanding.

WHEN UPLAND game hunting is mentioned in many parts of our country, thoughts quickly turn to smallbore shotguns with light loads, open chokes and short barrels. The prevailing theory, of course, is to have a bird gun that will snap onto a flushing ruffed grouse or woodcock before it gets behind screening cover, or will double on a covey of quail before the birds fan out.

But not all upland birds flush at close range, nor do they inhabit thickets where poke-and-hope is the only legitimate technique. Put heavy hunting pressure on pheasants, for instance, and street-savvy ringnecks will sprint or sneak a long way before they flush well out in the corn or swale. Let wind whip across Nebraska or Manitoba, and spooky sharptails will rocket away at the far fringe of shotgun range. And there are days when doves hang high or when canyon-dwelling chukars run forever before pitching downhill. Thus, there are times and terrains when and where uplanding becomes a truly long-range proposition from the flush, calling for shot-making skills and tight patterns that are well beyond those of the poke-and-hope scattergunner, as well as open chokes with light loads of 7½s and 8s!

Even the second shot in rather normal upland gunning can take on long-range proportions. If a pheasant, sharptail or chukar that jumps at moderate range is missed on the first shot, it'll be yards farther for the follow-up pattern.

What we always must realize is that an added ten yards can change an effective pattern into a crippler. For unlike a modern high-powered rifle which, with its flat trajectory, allows the big-game hunter to misjudge range by fifty yards and still hit, the shotgun goes from close to moderate to long range within just forty to fifty yards. A twenty- to twenty-five yard shot can be called close range in bird hunting circles, twenty-five to thirty-five being moderate range, while long-range shotgunning starts at around thirty-five to forty yards.

Even the ruffed grouse, which many equate with classic close-range uplanding, will offer testy long shots when hunted hard or when made skittish by high winds and/or leafless, late-season cover. Moreover, grouse can be prone to jumping in the distance when a dog creeps in too close. A poorly disciplined dog, in fact, is a sound reason for selecting long-range equipment, as a rampaging mutt will unseat more than a few game birds beyond skeet-gun range!

An intelligent hunter, then, will accept the reality of long-range shots and will equip himself for their eventuality.

The idea that an open-patterning piece can handle such demanding conditions consistently is a pipe dream. For although there are isolated occasions when that proverbial "Golden BB" will make a clean kill at long range via a lucky one-pellet neck or brain hit, such weak patterns and

When doves hang high, it is better to use the No. 7-1/2 lead pellet rather than the seemingly favored No. 8.

light-hitting shot will mainly feather or cripple and waste game when stretched beyond their intended and sensible ranges.

The essence of long-range upland gunning is making multiple hits in the bird's vital areas with pellets that are heavy enough to penetrate effectively. Unfortunately, there is an opposing theory that has been going around since the early 1900s to confuse the issue.

This theory argues that multiple hits with light shot such as No. 7½s, 8s and 9s will generate an intense shock effect on the bird's nervous system to kill it quickly in midair without the need for deep penetration. The "fine-shot" school has an appeal among hunters who dote on marginal equipment such as the lesser gauges and lightest loads, for the fine-shot theory is, in effect, a justification of their equipment selection. And over the closer ranges, especially when a good retrieving dog is handy, the light-shot loads do take birds.

But although there can be some nerve-shock effect from light pellets at close range, along with some mild shock at long distances, honest field observations indicate that game birds can shrug off the hits and be running before a hunter can get to the spot for his positive retrieve. How many outgoing pheasants have you seen killed cleanly in midair by a load of No. 7½s at forty-five yards?!

Anyone who is observant, honest and truly experienced afield knows the fine-shot theory *doesn't* work reliably for long-range wing-gunning. Small pellets shed too much energy in flight. Air drag slows them to reduce their already low-energy values, and whatever shock effect they may have had at fifteen to twenty yards has worn off by thirty yards. This slowing can be disastrous on outgoing birds, as their speed absorbs some of the pellet's velocity.

An accompanying table illustrates some of the differences in downrange energy for lead No. 4s, 6s and 7½s. These data are from the latest calculations and are based on a published starting velocity of 1255 feet per second, which is a nominal figure for 12-gauge, 1⅛-ounce loads with a 3¼ drams equivalent powder charge.

A careful look at the data shows a significant difference between the No. 7½ and No. 6 at forty yards. The No. 6 still carries nearly two foot-pounds of energy, whereas the No. 7½ has dropped back to slightly more than one foot-pound.

This is important, because most experts have accepted the thinking that at least one foot-pound of energy is needed on the smaller upland birds for meaningful impact and penetration, meaning the No. 7½ has become marginal by forty yards and is certainly underpowered at forty-five to fifty yards. Moreover, the larger upland birds could take more energy. The No. 6, however, still retains a 1.5-foot-pound energy level at fifty yards for a more positive impact. And the lead No. 4 is cruising along briskly at fifty yards with nearly a three-foot-pound punch. Thus, the minor differences in shot size diameters do mean a lot when it comes to exterior ballistics.

Which specific sizes fit the many different field demands? With the exception of dove shooting, the No. 6 lead pellet is about minimum for long-range uplanding. Regardless of gauge, a hunter must not deem it improper to chamber heavy loads with energy-laden pellets of the larger birdshot sizes.

An unheralded pellet these days is the lead No. 5. With a diameter of 0.12-inch and counting about 170 to 175 per ounce — depending upon the antimony content — lead No. 5s split the difference between the pattern density of

This isn't a long-range shot yet, but it will be if this hunter misses. That's when the second barrel becomes critical.

No. 6s and the energy of No. 4s. It is a great size for the larger upland birds such as pheasants, sharptails, sage grouse and prairie chickens, when they must be taken from thirty out to fifty yards. A 1¼-ounce shot charge is minimum for this long-range work, and some hunters have had superb success with 1⅜-ounce reloads of lead or copper-plated No. 5s.

Some hunters like No. 4s for pheasants, claiming a need to break bones. However, No. 5s also have enough energy for that, while normally supplying another hit or two because of their greater starting number. Indeed, if any lead pellet should make a comeback, it is the overlooked No. 5. It will drop and hold game where the next smaller size often will leave game running after the fall.

The No. 6 lead pellet can be a good upland size for the smaller and medium-size game birds. In the late fall, for example, No. 6 lead shot works wonders on wild-flushing ruffed grouse in the thicket and timber. Likewise, lead 6s can be a blessing on the running, far-flushing species of desert quail. Countless hunters have been frustrated on the desert by quail that take a hit, go down, but then can't be found. Some pretty savvy retrievers also have been unable to locate downed desert quail taken at thirty to thirty-five yards or more over the cactus by No. 7½s or 8s. A switch to No. 6s can change that in a hurry. The quail won't be torn up, either, as they are so small they can't receive many pellets; however, those that do hit are more potent than any No. 7½ or 8 can hope to be. At ranges of thirty yards or more, two No. 6s exhibit more holding power than three to four hits from the lighter pellets.

When doves hang high, the No. 7½ lead pellet has greater lethality than the No. 8s which seem to be more popular. For really long-range shooting at doves, the No. 7

is excellent. Unfortunately, not much No. 7 lead shot is available these days, but Fiocchi of America has reintroduced it in a heavy field load.

Hungarian partridge — also known as the gray partridge — also can present long-range shooting. There does seem to be a difference between those Hungarian partridge of the Montana flatlands and the upper Midwest, though, with those of the latter area being far more skittish. In any case, when Hungarian partridge feel pressed, they can jump at the fringe of sensible scattergun range, and a tight pattern of No. 6s is about minimum.

Another partridge, the red-legged chukar of the Western canyons, is a runner that can carry lead, and a husky load of lead No. 6s isn't out of order. Indeed, one mistake that hunters can make is trying to equate pellet selection with a bird's size; just because a game bird is rather small doesn't invariably mean it is killed easily. Knocking one out of the air is only part of the sequence. Killing it cleanly and making a positive retrieve are included. As shotgun ranges stretch beyond thirty yards, the heavier pellets do a better job of these latter two steps.

Chokes for long-range upland shooting are obviously the tighter ones, namely, modified, improved modified and full. When the range definitely will be past thirty-five yards, full choke is the best selection. Theoretically, a good modified choke performance will place fifty-five to sixty-five percent of the original shot charge into a thirty-inch circle at forty yards, improved modified will place sixty-five to seventy percent in said thirty-inch ring and full choke will print seventy percent or better. To concentrate enough shot on the target for a killing impact by placing multiple hits in vital areas, optimum density is required.

An important thing to realize is that a full-choke pattern

will open at about the rate of one inch per yard of flight, which gives it about a thirty-inch spread somewhere between thirty and thirty-five yards. That's already an effective distribution, and a hunter needn't worry about his pattern being too tight. The handicap is between a hunter's ears when he tries to be too deliberate and to aim a shot rather than simply pointing and making the same smooth swing he'd make with a wide-open skeet pattern at close range. A smooth swing will center a full-choke pattern the same as it does an improved cylinder spread! Full choke is *not* out of place in the uplands if you're regularly taking shots beyond thirty yards.

Modified choke is considered by many to be an all-around choice. A study of comparative patterning, however, indicates that much depends on the exact load. Some loads will deliver little more than tight improved cylinder patterns from a modified choke, others will do a solid modified-choke pattern, while a few others actually can run full-choke percentages through a modified-choke constriction.

Buffered loads, along with some reloads stoked with slow-burning powders, can wring rather tight patterns from just a modified barrel. Thus, one always should pattern to make certain of any load's performance through modified choke: patterns of fifty-five to sixty-five percent aren't automatic!

Moreover, a study of modified choke patterns that do deliver fifty-five-plus percent densities indicates that modified is at its most efficient level from twenty-five to forty yards. Somewhere between thirty-five and forty yards a basic modified choke pattern can become weak. A final point is that, at that yardage, there is little difference between the hitting areas of a modified choke and a full choke, except that the modified choke pattern now contains fewer pellets.

People who never pattern assume that modified choke opens more liberally to provide added hitting area over that of a full choke, but pattern reading doesn't show that to be true. Both chokes exhibit basic thirty-inch-diameter patterns, the full choke results showing a heavier pellet concentration. Modified choke, then, is not a panacea. Stretching it to forty-five to fifty yards is like stretching improved cylinder to thirty-five to forty yards: both will provide weak patterns.

A combination of modified and full isn't wrong for a double pointed at long-range upland gunning. Some hunters may try to split hairs and pair improved modified with modified or with full choke. Whether the choke tandem is M&IM or IM&F, the concept is dubious. Improved modified choke doesn't automatically give a pattern that is a little tighter than modified choke and a little looser than full. What improved modified does is to put somewhat fewer pellets into the thirty-inch circle at forty yards than a full choke does while essentially having the same effective spread. Moreover, to get a perfect improved modified pattern, one must do substantial load testing and pattern reading. It isn't unusual to find that improved modified chokes will shoot to virtually full-choke pattern diameters with modern shotshells having hard, high-antimony or copper-or nickel-plated shot.

An interesting choke duo for double barrels is improved cylinder in the first barrel and full choke in the second. An

Ruffed grouse aren't noted as long-range targets but they can far flush. This trio was taken with one-ounce lead No. 6s in a 20-gauge SxS during late season hunt.

improved cylinder choke will give about twenty-five to thirty yards of certain range before its pattern weakens, and full choke throws the density needed for lengthy follow-up shots. Indeed, improved cylinder/full choke combo is more positive than improved cylinder/modified if the birds are jumping at moderate distances, as the full choke pattern stands a better chance of making multiple hits to the bird's vital areas.

Although ultra-short barrels are being boomed for upland birds these days, such stumpy guns aren't ideal for the smoothness needed in long-range wingshooting. A more disciplined piece is needed. The short-barreled bird guns, meaning doubles with barrels of less than twenty-eight inches and repeaters sporting tubes shorter than twenty-six inches, can be overcontrolled too easily. They are whipped by aggressive hand/arm action, and they do not contribute any of their own momentum to extend the swing smoothly into a definite follow through. Indeed, short-barreled shotguns tend to die in one's hands; if the shooter doesn't have a perfect pivot, the gun may slow when it reaches the mark instead of accelerating through it into a

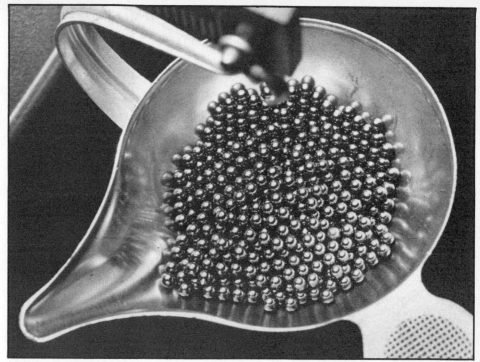

For long-range potency, pellets should be heavy and hard. This will enable them to retain as much of their original energy/velocity values as possible. Author recommends using copper- and nickel-plated lead shot.

forward allowance. Thus, while the new breed of short-barreled upland guns — meaning those repeaters with barrels of twenty-one to twenty-three inches and doubles with barrels below twenty-six inches — may promise explosive starts on close-in flushes, they also leave some things to be desired for longer range shooting.

When long-range upland gunning is the order of the day, a twenty-six-inch barrel is about minimum on a repeater, and twenty-eight inches is better. On doubles, twenty-eight inches is minimal with thirty inches being quite effective. The hunters of yesteryear weren't all wrong when they insisted upon thirty-inch barrels! Such pieces swung smoothly and helped with the dynamics of a swing by supplying momentum.

TABLE OF RETAINED VELOCITY AND ENERGY VALUES

RANGE	No. 7½	No. 6	No. 4
Published Starting	1255 fps 5.2 fp	1255 fps 8.0 fp	1255 fps 12.9 fp
10 Yards	1069 fps 3.2 fp	1085 fps 5.12 fp	1101 fps 8.71 fp
20 Yards	878 fps 2.16 fp	904 fps 3.56 fp	933 fps 6.26 fp
30 Yards	741 fps 1.54 fp	772 fps 2.60 fp	808 fps 4.69 fp
40 Yards	635 fps 1.13 fp	669 fps 1.95 fp	709 fps 3.61 fp
50 Yards	550 fps 0.85 fp	627 fps 1.50 fp	587 fps 2.83 fp

Legend

Load: unbuffered shot
Velocity expressed in terms of feet per second (fps)
Energy expressed in terms of foot-pounds (fp)
Starting velocity (1255 fps) is published velocity, not muzzle velocity

Shotgun hunters who get interested in sporting clays will observe the revived attention being given longer shotgun barrels these days. Some popular sporting clays guns are available with thirty-two-inch barrels, and this length has had attention overseas from high-scoring competitors. It isn't a joke!

Whereas many American hunters and sporting clays shooters think they need a gun that literally jumps into action, the savvy British and Europeans, who are quite advanced in shotgunology, don't put an emphasis on lightning-like gun mounts. They stress smoothness and a follow through, both of which are assisted by a longer barrel. Thus, the stumpy shotguns with novel barrel lengths below twenty-six inches may jibe with fast-action, poke-and-hope uplanding on close targets, but they leave much to be desired for the longer forward allowances that must be set off on wild flushes and long crossers. If a twenty-one to twenty-four-inch barrel were the answer to all upland gunning, British and European sporting clays experts would be using them instead of their thirty-two-inchers!

This brings us to gun handling and wingshooting technique. A hunter whose nerves are set on hair trigger may indeed hit a satisfying number of close-range flushes with an open-choked, short-barreled scattergun with the above-mentioned poke-and-hope method. The range is close, so it takes virtually no time for the shot charge to go from muzzle to target. And a widely scattered pattern compensates for shooter error. Woodcock, bobwhite and close-lying pheasants lend themselves to moderate successes with snap-shooting techniques.

But long-range uplanding is a different matter. While a woodcock at twelve to fifteen yards requires little lead, a crossing sharptail at forty yards takes a lot. Air drag slows pellets quickly, be they lead, steel or whatever. As the accompanying chart shows, a No. 6 lead pellet with a published starting velocity of 1255 feet per second is down to 669 fps at forty yards. It takes that lead No. 6 about 0.1331-second to go from the muzzle to forty yards, during which time a bird crossing at a ninety-degree angle with a speed of forty miles per hour will fly about eight feet. Snap

A manageable 12-gauge is the top pick for long-range uplanding. It handles smoothly, but hits like a duck gun.

Trapshooting presents upland hunters with targets, including doubles, that are a lot like those of flushed game birds.

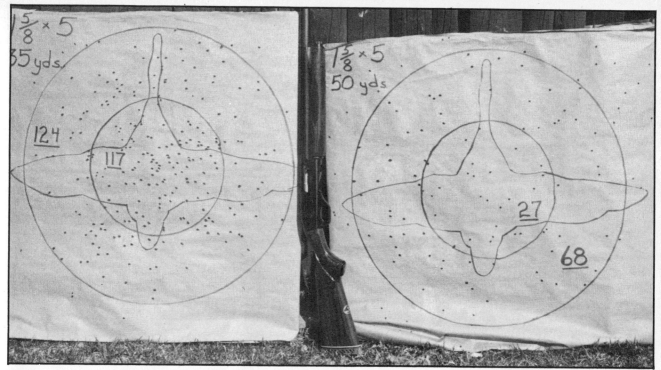

Tight patterns are needed for long-range coverage. These patterns illustrate how the shot charge weakens as the range increases. The pattern shot at 35 yards (left) shows considerably more density that the one fired at 50 yards.

and spot shooting don't work on those long loads; they've got to be swung and timed.

The name of the game here is smoothness. Delays, herky-jerky mounting, slow movement, aiming with the matted receiver and front bead all cause misses. A shotgunner simply cannot take a squinty-eyed aim like a rifleman and hope to hit a moving target. Wing-gunning is predicated upon eye/hand coordination; trying to be precise is anathema in shotgunning.

A full-choked shotgun with 1¼ ounces of lead No. 5s can be lethal on the larger species of upland birds for nearly half a football field — provided you can make the coordinated mount-point-swing move which puts the shot string at a point that intercepts the target! Slow, deliberate gun handling that doesn't build the speed of the target into the swinging gun is a primary reason for failures afield. This doesn't mean a hunter must jump into the gun mount, of course. The mount must be smooth, too, and the hunter cannot hitch his swing as he second-guesses himself.

One reason why hunters react too slowly, too deliberately on distant game is because things appear slower when they are farther away. But that's an optical illusion. An airliner landing well out on the runway seems to be floating in like a mallard on cupped wings. If one were alongside the runway, however, that airliner would whistle past at more than one hundred miles per hour!

Thus, a hunter must deliver his shots at long-range birds with confidence and dispatch without being jumpy and/or panicky. The smooth, coordinated gun mount that scores for champions at sporting clays and low-gun skeet also jibes with long-range upland gunning.

This technique is predicated on eye/hand coordination. When the bird flushes well out, the hunter focuses sharply on it and remains so focused through the action. He doesn't bring his eyes back to the gun to line up beads or the rib. His hands make a minor outward move toward the target, centered by his eyes, as they elevate the gun. This helps establish pointing accuracy and direction as well as ensuring that the butt will clear his armpit. As this elevating move is made, the shooter already should be pivoting to the target so that, when the gun is shouldered, the shot can be triggered instantly.

The first point of contact should be under the shooter's on-side eye, not against the shoulder. By bringing the gun to the face, not to the shoulder, one establishes immediate eye-muzzle-target alignment. If the gun is placed first against one's shoulder, a hunter must hunch and scrunch about to get his eye properly placed, which wastes time. Moreover, a shotgunner's eye is the rear sight and when it isn't centered behind the receiver it is like a rifle's rear sight being knocked out of zero.

Once the comb comes in contact below the eye, the hunter can roll his shoulder into the butt and shoot. A little dry-firing practice with this mounting sequence, emphasizing the minor outward thrust and gun-to-eye elements, will prove how efficiently one can get on distant birds without wasting time or smoothness while still retaining alignment.

For long-range upland shooting, then, the ideal piece is one that swings with grace and patterns like a duck and goose gun. The hunter who takes his sport seriously will want to spend some off-season time with it on the trap line, as trapshooting gives excellent practice on distant, outgoing targets.

Some practice on trap doubles will get one in shape for follow-up shots afield. And if you don't like the established way of shooting American trap with a fully mounted gun, lower your bird gun and mount as the target emerges. Trapshooting becomes an entirely new sport when you hold a low gun! — *Don Zutz*

CHAPTER
22

THE EVOLVING SLUG GUN & LOADS

Is This Still A Shotgun Or A New Breed Of Big-Game Taker?

This two-shot trail group was made by a benchrested Mossberg M500 with rifle sights using the Winchester Foster Slug at 50 yards.

The modern slug gun and load have the accuracy and energy to collect trophy bucks at 100-125 yards.

THERE WAS a time when, for both military use and hunting, lead balls were fired from smoothbore barrels. The resulting accuracy was horrible. If the lead ball took on a spin as it rambled through the bore, the "English" caused it to curve. And if the ball wasn't spinning as it left the muzzle, air resistance (drag) worked on it variously to produce boundry vortices which gave it an unpredictable flight akin to that of a major-league pitcher's knuckleball. From these primitive beginnings sprang our modern slug guns and loads.

The unfortunate thing about our current state of slug gun and load development is that casual hunters still harken back to those early times when it was anyone's guess where a lead ball might fly. We continue to hear disparaging sport shop remarks about the performances of shotgun slugs. No hunter is willing to take the blame for his own misses, so it isn't unusual to find hunters damning the slug's supposed inaccuracies whenever the ol' gray buck gets away.

The fact is, however, that through the decades, important strides have been made to refine the slug gun and slug load, and many of them can now rival the one hundred-yard accuracy of some centerfire rifles. It isn't unusual to find a slick slug gun that can outduel a .30-30 carbine! The important thing nowadays isn't finding good equipment, but rather understanding the newest technologies.

The first important step made in improved shotgun slug accuracy came in the late 1800s, when it was realized that a conical projectile was needed for better aerodynamics and to eliminate erratic spin. The basic form was a hollow-based lead unit with a hemispheric nose and cylindrical tail segment. By theory, this kind of slug would enhance smoothbore accuracy because the cylindrical part would bear along the bore walls to keep it aligned, and the rounded nose would keep it on line because the preponderance of weight up front made it fly like a sock with a rock in its toe.

People at the time also knew a rifled barrel would give better accuracy, but rifling shotgun barrels wasn't then a part of tradition. The British did make a certain concession in that direction, however, occasionally putting a short length of rifling at the muzzle of one barrel of a double to stabilize a solid projectile. These were known as Paradox guns, and they became important to career officers and government administrators who could carry only one sporting arm to the far-flung reaches of the British Empire. In one double, they could use fine shot for birds and solid Paradox projectiles for big game. It was nearly a hundred years before stateside gunmakers and hunters began to equate improved shotgun slug performance with rifling.

First, the so-called rifled slug was tried. It was much like the original round-nose slugs, except that a minor rifling spiral was moulded into the cylindrical segment. Known more precisely as the Foster-type slug, its raised rifling lands were not intended to produce a stabilizing spin in the bore. Instead, it was thought that air pressure in flight would cause the slug to spin. This idea apparently came

Slugs are an important part of American hunting and Remington's M11-87 with cantilever mount is a popular rig.

from a belief that a rifled slug would react much the same as an arrow in flight; the arrow's fletching did generate a rotation of the shaft for enhanced accuracy. Initially, though, shotgun slug accuracy with the rifled Foster-type projectile didn't deliver what the public expected, and the tandem of a smoothbore plus slug was still open to criticism.

That doesn't mean the Foster-type slug was all bad, of course. It did have its strengths. The rifling lands reduced friction and bore leading, since only about half the unit's circumference bore on the walls. Moreover, they were an aid to keeping the slug centered. But there still was much that the public and ammo makers had to learn about slug gun accuracy.

Not the least of this was the need to keep slugs matched to bore diameter so that, like a rifle bullet, they remained co-axial with the bore and exited the muzzle uniformly, shot after shot.

If a slug is undersized, it will glance about in the bore as it moves from chamber to muzzle, deforming as it goes and, potentially, taking on a tilt. In turn, the glancing, tilted slugs will strike the muzzle region (choke taper) at a different point and, thus, fly at different angles from the bore axis. All of this frustrates the physics of accuracy shooting, which includes the need for the projectile to exit with its base squarely at a ninety-degree angle to the bore axis.

A number of American ammo manufacturers added to this problem by turning out undersized slugs. It was believed a bore-size slug would ring-bulge tightly choked barrels and cause some liability claims. For a time, many American-made slugs shot best from a full-choked barrel, not the improved cylinder chokes recommended by industry sources which feared barrel damage. In recent years, however, manufacturers have begun bringing their slugs to somewhat larger diameters for better co-axial fit without the glancing and tilting. For example, Remington's line of "Slugger" Foster-type slugs have been given a wider diameter for 1993.

It must be noted that some European barrels with narrow bores of 0.722-inch or thereabouts have tended to give exceptional accuracy with American slug loads, as the Foster-type rifled slugs which are a loose fit in Yankee bores are snug fits in overseas barrels. A Beretta BL-4 over/under repeatedly gave this writer four-inch, five-shot groups at fifty yards, using nothing more than the gun's basic bead and receiver for sighting equipment. When a casual hunter failed to match his slug to his smoothbore's bore diameter, then he merely added to the potential for poor grouping.

Another problem typical hunters had in the early going was finding the point of impact. A smoothbore normally

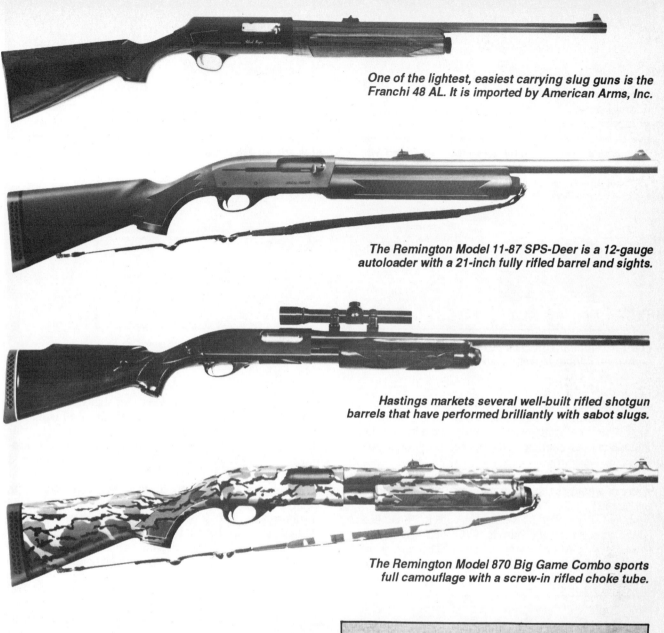

One of the lightest, easiest carrying slug guns is the Franchi 48 AL. It is imported by American Arms, Inc.

The Remington Model 11-87 SPS-Deer is a 12-gauge autoloader with a 21-inch fully rifled barrel and sights.

Hastings markets several well-built rifled shotgun barrels that have performed brilliantly with sabot slugs.

The Remington Model 870 Big Game Combo sports full camouflage with a screw-in rifled choke tube.

doesn't put its slug point of impact where it centers its birdshot patterns. A slug load sets up different vibrations in a shotgun barrel than does a shot charge, and since the velocities of the two loads also can be different, they will exit the muzzle when it is at different points in its vibrational pattern.

A slug load, often being faster than a shot charge, may well exit while the muzzle is in a downward mode, thus hitting lower than a pattern of birdshot from the same gun. Thus, it is wrong to believe a hunter can expect his duck gun to shoot slugs directly to the point of aim taken with the receiver's matted top and the front bead or by aligning two beads on a ventilated rib. Indeed, much of the "bad mouthing" that slug rigs have taken is due to hunters who didn't understand this variation between slug and shotshell impact points. The best bet for solving the problem, of course, is an adjustable sight.

Not much really was done to improve shotgun slugs, guns or the sighting equipment thereof until well into the

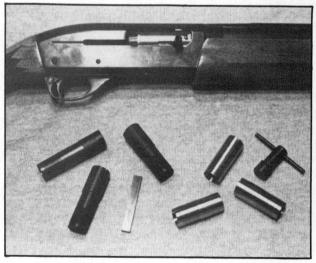

These screw-in chokes from Hastings will transform any smoothbore into a slug gun worthy of taking afield.

Browning's BPS 12 is a top performer, equipped with rifle sights and an extended rifled invector screw-in tube.

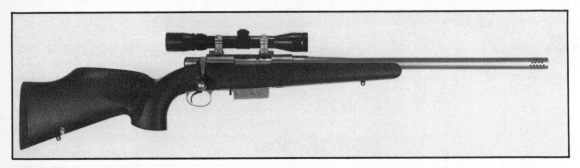

The Tar-Hunt slug gun is a custom job with a barreled-action made solely for shotgun slugs. The best benchrest concepts were used in the gun's development to eliminate accuracy-destroying vibrations.

1960s. In that decade, the whitetail deer herd began expanding back into many of its former ranges of the Midwest. This was farming country, rather heavily populated, and when deer hunting was reopened the law mandated shotgun slugs only.

The following seasons produced an army of new hunters, many of whom clamored for improved slug-gun accuracy and greater range. The industry's initial response was the so-called slug gun or, as Remington calls it, "Deer Gun." There were shortened barrels with open rifle sights on them, but they still were smoothbored. The industry hadn't done much to enhance the grouping performance of a smoothbore with slugs, but at least the sights got hunters to place their ragged groups closer to the point of hold.

Gradually, innovators began to experiment with different concepts. Rifled barrels were tried and found to produce excellent results. However, that direction was blocked at first by state laws which had decreed that only smoothbore guns could be used in certain areas in connection with shotgun slugs. Gradually, this opposition has been erased by most states, and rifled shotgun barrels can be employed. It took a while, but state governments were convinced eventually that a 12-gauge slug still is a 12-gauge slug, whether it comes from a smooth or rifled bore. But bureau-

Remington's Copper Solid has a plastic sabot like that of Remington's Accelerator centerfire rifle ammunition.

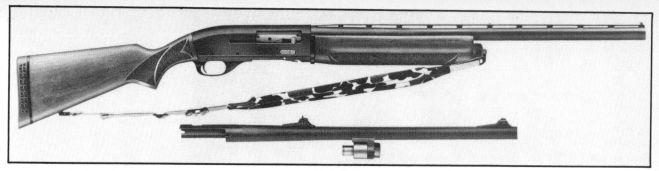

Remington's SP-10 magnum combo 10-gauge comes with REM chokes and an extra 22-inch barrel with rifle sights.

crats are bureaucrats, and they all like to study changes within their slough of the swamp.

With the advent of rifled shotgun barrels came the growing interest in sabot (pronounced "sab-o") loads. In its original French meaning, *sabots* are wooden shoes. But in the early French labor disputes, workers used them to damage machinery and railroads — hence, the origins of the word "sabotage." Like the wooden shoes, the plastic sabots of modern slug shooting are encasements. They hold the slug centered in the bore, minimize deformation and separate after muzzle exit. In general, most of the early sabot slugs were wasp-waisted, giving them the shape of an aerial bomb.

Some of the first sabot slugs were disasters. They were fired through smoothbore barrels, and they were erratic. They were known to keyhole, spin and even snap apart at their waist. It wasn't until rifled barrels made their appearance that sabot loads finally became consistent. Once they were paired with rifled barrels, though, sabot loads became exceedingly accurate, and for that reason they gained considerble notoriety.

Unfortunately, sabot slugs did not enjoy the same reputation afield. Numerous reports of hit and lost deer followed them: Sabot slugs did not have the diameter of Foster-type slugs, nor were they made to expand reliably on thin-skin game such as whitetails. Sabot slugs were cast relatively hard compared to Foster-type slugs, and hunters complained of "penciling," meaning the projectiles shot through without observable shock effect, leaving the animal on its feet, running.

Some manufacturers have altered the sabot slugs for improved on-target dynamics by using slightly softer alloys and/or a hollow point. Winchester announced a softer alloy for better mushrooming with their sabots, which were formerly the BRI loads, at the 1993 SHOT Show.

But as of this writing, there still is a problem with the 20-gauge sabot slug loads, as these projectiles have smaller diameters and offer considerably less frontal area for impact

Winchester's new version of the former BRI sabot load has been given a softer lead alloy for improved expansion.

The Convert-A-Mount rig changes a conventional bird gun into a scope-equipped slug outfit in a few minutes.

and mushrooming. Because of this potential pencil effect, it is wise for any hunter to wait out a sabot-struck deer if it runs. Wait for it to lie down and bleed out, which may take a half hour. Just don't take the trail immediately, as such a deer can travel a long distance when fueled by adrenalin. This will require some self-discipline, but it's the best way to handle such a hit.

At this writing, two ammunition makers have taken a hard look at the sabot slug's weaknesses and have come up with different concepts to provide equally good accuracy with impressive mass and cross-section. The first of these is the Brenneke Golden Slug, which isn't a sabot load, but is, instead, a wide-diameter cylindrical lead slug with a hard golden coating to reduce lead fouling while delivering excellent accuracy through a rifled barrel.

It is Brenneke's contention that a sabot assembly isn't necessary for great accuracy with shotgun slugs and that, without the plastic encasement, a slug can be given greater frontal area for a more potent impact.

The Ithaca people make a rifled-barrel version of their grand old Model 87 pumpgun with a one-in-twenty-five-inch rifling twist that's especially suited for this Golden Slug. Loaded to 1475 feet per second, the Brenneke GS isn't recommended for smoothbore barrels. A micrometer tells us the Golden Slug has a 0.730-inch diameter on its driving band and runs about 0.725-inch on its frontal edge, which is indeed wider than the normal wasp-waisted, 12-gauge sabot slug's .50-caliber (half-inch) diameter. Moreover, the Brenneke GS scales at 1⅜ ounces as opposed to the nominal ounce of sabot lead slugs.

Remington is the second company to mull over the sabot concept, then take a different tack. The new-for-'93 Remington Copper Solid shotgun slugs are sabot-types in concept, but they have an entirely different sabot design and a totally new slug styling. The sabot emulated the design employed for years in Remington Accelerator centerfire rifle ammunition.

It looks like an eight-finger shot cup, albeit with sturdier fingers. This multi-fingered sabot cups an all-copper, round-nose slug that is machined, not moulded. Scaling twenty-eight grams (432 grains), the Copper Solid is a .52-caliber projectile with its nose hollow-pointed and quartered by four longitudinal slits running about five-sixteenths-inch.

On contact with game, the Remington Copper Solid's nose elements begin to flare out from the forces built up in the hollow point. These flare to about double caliber for added radial damage and increased shocking power, then break off and continue as secondary missiles for added tissue damage while the main cylindrical section continues to penetrate. Such a performance is hardly conventional, as most shotgun slugs heretofore were of lead, and their expected terminal action was thought of in terms of mushrooming. But whatever works...

The Remington Copper Solid has shown extremely good accuracy. They are made only for use in rifled barrels and may show dicey accuracy in smoothbore guns. However, with a Remington M11-87 Deer Gun using a rifled Remington barrel and cantilever mount plus nine-power scope setting, this writer has punched two-inch, three-shot groups at fifty yards, and with early batches of the loads

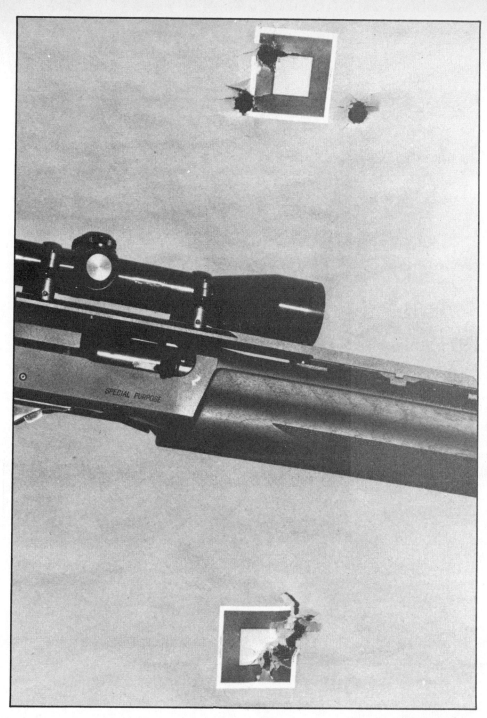

Note the accuracy of the Remington Special Purpose gun with cantilever mount and Weaver scope at 100 yards using Winchester's one-ounce Foster-type slugs.

hammered a pair of four-inch clusters at one hundred yards from benchrest. Thus, both the Brenneke Golden Slug and the Remington Copper Solid offer promise for hunters who want the accuracy of sabot slugs with added slug girth and frontal area for knockdown impact.

As mentioned, shotguns also have undergone change for slug-shooting specialization. Hastings of Clay Center, Kansas, was one of the first to offer a broad line of rifled barrels, obtaining them from France for use on most popular American repeaters. But stateside gunmakers and importers soon caught on, and most leading brands now have a rifled barrel available.

Of extreme importance is the sighting equipment for slug guns. Open field sights, while far ahead of the coarse receiver/bead method of aiming, leave some things to be desired. Many shooters have a tendency to shoot high with them, because of either holding their head high or not pulling the front bead or blade down far enough into the rear sight's notch. Also, open sights can be difficult to use in the poor light of early morning or late afternoon. Receiver sights, alias "peep" sights, also are less than perfect, as it is virtually impossible to see through them during the first half hour of hunting time before sunrise in the depth of a dark swamp.

The new Remington Copper Solid sabot uses technology developed by Remington for its Accelerator rifle sabots.

The best sight for a serious slug gun is a low-power scope. Anything from 1½ to 3x will do nicely, provided it has a broad field of view. If one hunts open farmland where shots can be one hundred to 125 yards, a 4x isn't all bad, for modern slug loads carry adequate energy to make such shots legitimate, and with a well-tuned gun/load combo there will be adequate accuracy to place the slug into a deer's vital heart/lung area. I know of several whitetails having been dropped out to 113 yards by conventional Foster-type, 12-gauge slugs. The important part of the equation is the hunter's ability to tune his equipment, sight-in properly and learn his trajectory.

There are several approaches to scoping a slug gun. Some are mounted on the gun's receiver, while more recent attention has been given to using the cantilever (extended) mount on the barrel.

In theory, the sight that is mounted on the barrel will retain its accuracy better because the barrels on modern repeaters do shift about under firing forces, and if the scope is attached directly to the barrel, it will remain aligned with

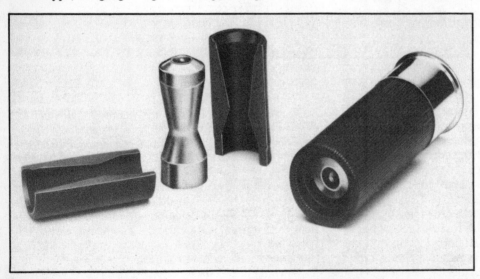

The Federal Hydra-Shok has a typical sabot assembly. The plastic encasements fit about the slug, keeping it aligned and protected from scrubbing against the bore.

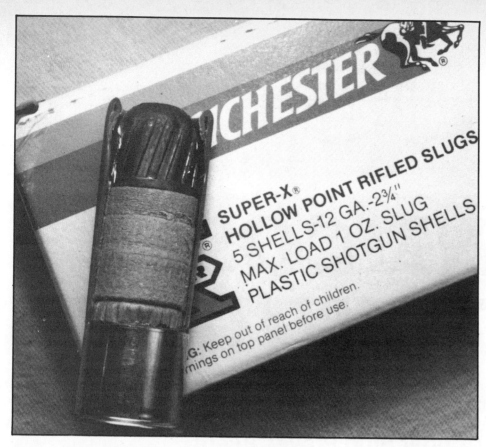

Winchester's one-ounce Foster-type slug is a good fit in many smoothbores.

the bore. On the other hand, a scope that is mounted on the receiver may not always be in perfect alignment with the bore if the barrel shifts during firing. The cantilever theory carries this matter of slug gun accuracy to its maximum and rates attention.

However, I have shot with a number of receiver-mounted shotgun scopes without seeing inaccuracies that would cause a miss on the deer's heart/lung area. One such rig is Weaver's Convert-A-Mount, which fits easily to such guns as the Remington M870 and M1100/11-87, Ithaca M37/87, Mossberg M500, Winchester M1200, Browning A-5 and Beretta MA303, plus Browning's BPS pump. These attach via screws or drift pins, according to the gun in question, and they can be removed in minutes for a return to bird hunting. The Weaver V3 scope is an exceptional partner for the Convert-A Mount, providing a range from 1 to 3x with a comfortably long eye relief.

Using the Weaver mount/scope assembly on a Remington Model 1100 with a Hastings rifled barrel, I was able to pound four-inch, three-shot groups repeatedly over one hundred yards from benchrest using Winchester one-ounce Foster-type slugs. This 2¾-inch Winchester loading has given stellar accuracy for years from both rifled and smoothbore barrels. It will be interesting to see what Remington's revamped Foster-type slugs will do with their new increased diameters; however, none were yet available for testing as this goes to press.

Hunters who like to level a howitzer-like blow can do so with the 10-gauge magnum. Federal's 1¾-ounce Foster-type rifled slug has tremendous energy and is, obviously, wider than any 12-gauge rifled or sabot projectile. Remington's SP-10 autoloader now is available with a rifle-sighted barrel, and one can only wonder how long it'll be before

Browning follows suit with their freshly announced 10-gauge semi-automatic.

Accuracy buffs will drool over the highly specialized slug gun being custom built by Tar-Hunt (RR 3, Box 572, Bloomsburg, PA 17815). A bolt-action built to 12-gauge dimensions, it has a McMillan fiberglass stock wrapped around a solid, specially machined barreled-action hosting a Shaw rifled barrel. The method behind this seeming madness is to build an ultra-accurate slug gun using the best refinements of benchrest riflery. The makers claim two-inch groups at one hundred yards using a scope! The gun alone will set you back more than a cool thou, but if you're a dedicated deer hunter in slug country, why not! It makes no difference if the money goes into a custom slug gun or big-game rifle, if hunting satisfaction is the end result.

In reality, the current trend in shotgun slug equipment causes us to wonder if it has to do with shotguns at all. We have developed, and are beginning to refine, an entirely new big-game sporting arm. It is associated with the shotgun because it continues to employ shotshell cases, and many of the currently popular pieces are based on scattergun designs. But full-length rifled barrels are hardly commensurate with shotgunning traditions and purity.

Whatever the terminology or nomenclature, the modern shotshell-based slug guns are vast improvements over the days when lead balls were rammed into smoothbore barrels. But hunters must get into this evolving specialty to understand its subtleties before they can appreciate and apply the slugs and sabots with positive field effectiveness!

Missing or crippling and losing a deer is no longer a fault of the equipment — it's a failure of the one behind the butt. Modern slug guns can shoot accurately, when teamed with the right ammo! — *Don Zutz*

CHAPTER
23

ANTICOSTI ADVENTURE

Wherein Remington's New Solid Copper Slug Proves Itself!

The sabot houses the all-copper slug. When the sabot meets air resistance after leaving the bore, the eight petals open like a flower, releasing the slug.

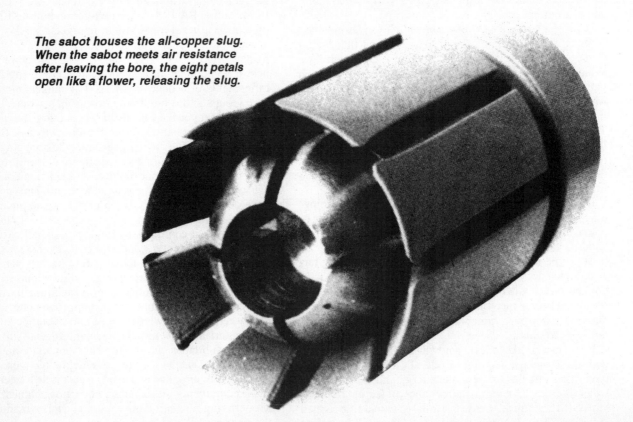

The new Remington Copper Solid slugs and a Remington 11-87 semi-auto 12-gauge proved a worthy hunting combination for the author. This is one of two bucks he took on Anticosti during the testing of the new slug.

HUNTING WITH shotgun slugs and specialized guns for them is a different proposition in the 1990s than ever in the entire history of smoothbore big-game getting. Because of the added interest in slug-gun hunting, triggered by the proliferation of laws forbidding the use of rifles in many of the more populated areas, the industry has responded with an evolving array of products which put this activity in the arena of high tech and high performance.

The reality of this came through in total clarity when I ventured to Anticosti Island in the extreme northeastern part of Canada's Quebec province. There, on that game-rich island, whitetail deer abound — so much that the legal limit is two bucks per hunt. Each year, hunters take only about 8,000 of the 125,000 deer on the massive island.

For the hunt, I used a Remington Model 11-87 Premier Cantilever Scope Mount Deer Gun. This specialized piece of hunting gear is a far cry from the rig I had used with slugs back in the 1950s when I first considered going after deer with a shotgun. Although the 11-87 Deer Gun from Remington is a 12-gauge, it behaves like a rifle within the

distance parameters of a shotgun. Hence, it represents the best of both worlds: rifle-like accuracy and the safety of a smoothbore.

But calling the Remington Deer Gun a smoothbore would be a total misnomer, because it sported a fully-rifled twenty-one-inch barrel with a cantilever scope mount on top. The scope mount for the hunt sported a Leupold 2-7x scope. The rifling twist of one turn in thirty-five inches was just right to stabilize Remington's one-ounce solid copper slug. As much as the gun was a marked departure from the traditional norm, so was the ammo.

When it introduced the new Copper Solid slug, Remington performed another quantum leap in the hunting market. The slug is nestled in a plastic sabot jacket which engages the rifling as the payload shoots down the barrel. Yet, once the slug is out of the barrel, the sabot drops away, and the sleek slug spins toward the target, totally stabilized.

Although the company claims accuracy of a couple of inches at one hundred yards with a combination of the fully rifled barrel and the saboted slug, the rig I was using cut that grouping size in half. It truly was more accurate than are many of the centerfire deer rifles being used.

That was the first opportunity I had to check out the rifled barrel with the cantilever scope mount system. The way it works is simple and effective. The cantilever scope base is attached securely to the barrel itself, not to the action. This means the scope need not be resighted whenever the barrel is removed and reinstalled. But it is more than that.

Such an arrangement is inherently more accurate in the first place. When a scope is mounted to the receiver on a centerfire rifle, there is little problem, because the barrel is attached snugly to the action. However, when one is talking about shotgun actions and removable barrels, there is no way that the connection is as snug nor as rigid. This contributes to inconsistency, and inconsistency means a drop-off in accuracy.

To make the rig quick-pointing and effective when a scope is mounted, the stock has a raised Monte Carlo comb, which puts the eye right in line with the reticle. A standard shotgun stock with more drop-off would make it a bit tougher to use the scope, and it would force the shooter to raise his or her head slightly off the comb to see through the scope. Not only is this a slower proposition at the moment of truth, but it also can be downright uncomfortable when the stock bucks up during recoil, hitting the face rather than simply pushing against it.

With the twenty-one-inch barrel, the overall length of the rig was a handy forty-one inches, and the weight, with scope, sling and fully loaded with slugs was in the ten-pound category (the basic gun so configured weighs 8½ pounds). Although the gun came equipped with a synthetic sling and quick-detachable swivels, I had little use for it — until it was time to drag the two downed deer from where they fell to a four-wheel-drive vehicle so they could be transported back to camp and to the skinning shed.

Normally, I do not sling a long gun while hunting. Such a carry precludes any chance at a quick shot of opportunity, and in the thick, northern woods, such shot options are routine. Hence, whenever moving, I carried the rig at a modified form of port arms, ready for action. And for the second buck of the hunt, such a procedure paid off big time.

Granted, a ten-pound rig can start pulling convincingly on the forearms and shoulders as the day wears on, but years ago I decided such strain was simply a part of hunting. A hunter spends too many precious hours in search of game to afford a built-in handicap like a slung rifle or shotgun. However, once an animal is down, and it is time to drag it any noticeable distance, a sling is worth many times its retail price. So it was nice having it on the rig.

Although the rig weighed about the same as the loaded M14 rifle, once used in the Army, the 11-87 Deer Gun carried better and was much more responsive and alive than the rifle ever had been. After all, the 11-87 is a full-on shotgun, and that means it points and swings like a shotgun — superbly.

Before heading into the woods after whitetails, I checked the rig on a fifty-yard range near the base camp. I wanted it to put a hole in the target exactly two inches high at fifty yards. That would mean that it would be right on target at one hundred yards, and less than a half foot low at 150 yards. Translated into real-world hunting terms, that meant

that I could place the crosshairs at the vertical midpoint behind a buck's shoulder from the end of the barrel to 150 yards, squeeze the trigger and score.

A single shot at the fifty-yard range confirmed that the rig had remained perfectly zeroed during the multi-leg airline trip to the remote island. There was a .50 caliber hole two inches above dead center. Although the hosts for the trip were SEPAQ, the official government agency in Quebec which operates the hunting on the island (SEPAQ-Anticosti, 3000, rue Alexandra, Bureau 102, Beauport, Quebec G1E 7C8), there was another purpose of the expedition. I was among several hunters who were using Remington's new Copper Solid slugs for the first time on actual game animals. These projectiles had worked supremely in the lab, but the real proof is in the woods when the target is made of living tissue, not ballistic gelatin.

Shooting game animals with solids is the basis for many a long conversation around the world. Normally, one encounters such conversations when the subject turns to large, dangerous game like elephant, rhino or Cape buffalo. For those creatures, hunters through the years have opted for solid bullets, as compared to soft-pointed, expanding ones, because they value the added penetration that the non-expanding solid offers. However, because solids can slip through an animal and not cause quick death if the animal is not hit in a vital area, or if the bullet does not break through bone, such bullets are not allowed for the hunting of thin-skinned game in many parts of the world, including most of the states in the United States.

To that end, however, it is necessary to note that Remington's Copper Solid slug is a far cry from the "solid" bullets used by African hunters. Frankly, the Copper Solid slug is a complex mechanism which includes the fragmentation of the entire nose section following impact.

The slug has a hole drilled in the center, as well as two cross-cuts made vertically to the slug's axis. When the slug augers into the animal, the four remaining "petals" of the nose section are forced outward and back, breaking off and continuing in four tangential directions as the main body of the slug continues to drill straight on through.

In addition to resulting in four small wound channels and one large one, this fragmentation process is intended to impart more energy into the animal when it is far enough inside to disrupt vitals. It is rather an ingenious design.

Traditional slugs are less accurate and shed their velocity much more quickly than do any of the saboted slugs, including the ones from Remington I was using. Also, when the more traditional design, termed the Foster slug, hits the animal, it tends to flatten, especially when it encounters heavy bone. Although this is not a problem at close ranges, it can cause marginal performance whenever the shot is beyond the seventy-five-yard line.

Designers of saboted slug rounds, including the Remington Copper Solid configuration, have attempted to create a projectile that will have more retained energy and more performance at greater distance. This also means more penetration at the one-hundred-yard line and beyond. Remington's designers were convinced that they had a slug that would have no penetration problems at 150 yards.

Experiences of hunters on the trip showed there was plenty of penetration at the one-hundred-plus-yard distances. For close-in shots. the slugs zipped through the whitetails so fast and cleanly that the deer barely acted as

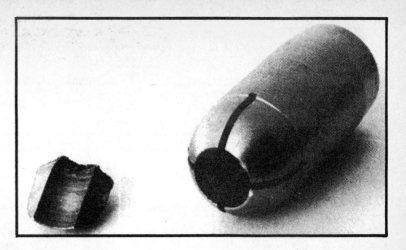

The petal (left) was removed from one deer the author took using Remington's new Copper Solid. The slug has a rounded nose with four petals that fragment upon impact.

though they had been hit, even though the shot was fatal. And, when I hit one buck at extremely close range with a slug that found the animal's front shoulder bone, it flipped the deer like a load of No. 5 shot bounces a rabbit.

But it was the gun itself that offered some of the most telling data. For most shotgunning, I prefer the Model 870 pump to any of the other offerings in the Remington lineup. And there is a full-on deer rig available in the 870 mode. However, for slug hunting, I must admit to a preference for a gas-operated semi-auto. Such a gun shoots noticeably softer.

Although I never have backed away from a credible rig just because it kicked a little, there is more to the equation than some modified form of machismo. There is such a thing as recovery time for a follow-up shot. Slugs kick enough to make the recovery time differential noticeable between a pump and an auto. The auto wins.

When most of the terrain being hunted is covered with conifers and brush, the hunter is afforded precious few open spots or fields of fire. It is common to have nothing more than slender visual alleys through the foliage. This means it is totally important to keep the animal in view and to be able to crank off a quick follow-up shot if the initial blast doesn't drop the animal in its tracks. Lacking this ability, the deer can disappear in a heartbeat, only to trigger a lengthy tracking session, or worse, to escape wounded.

Certainly, the concept of a single, well-placed shot being sufficient is alive and well. However, I would far prefer to expend one more shell and end everything in an instant when the classic scenario fails to play out as scripted. And, in the real world, it does happen that way sometimes.

The first day of the hunt afforded ample time for me to become intimately acquainted with the shotgun. I did a whole lot of carrying and no shooting. It was a 2x1 guided hunt, which meant one guide for two hunters. All hunts on Anticosti are guided by regulation, and that is fine. I was hunting with Dick Dietz of Pennsylvania (retired public relations manager for Remington) and guide Alain Marchand.

For the first day, the game plan was simple. I was to still hunt along an ascending ice-covered dirt trail for about a mile, then set up an ambush position overlooking a beaver pond along the ridge top. Deer had been crossing the trail at the beaver pond for the past several days, and no one had bothered them. It sounded like a good plan, so I trekked off

into the woods. That was shortly after daybreak, and I was to meet Marchand and Dietz back at the drop-off point at midday. Then, if necessary, they could help me drag out a buck, or if I was unsuccessful, we could head to another spot.

Meanwhile, Marchand and Dietz drove off about a half mile and began hunting along a large creek bed (or small river bed, depending upon how one classifies such things).

As I walked slowly and quietly along the trail, I spotted a few deer tracks, but nothing fresher than a few days old. As I reached the ridge, however, things changed. I began spotting fresher tracks, including one set that was made the night before or earlier that morning.

As I continued along the trail, I noticed that the tracks would come and go, disappearing into the thick woods, then reappear farther along the trail. They were not terribly large tracks, so my interest was less than intense.

The gun felt good as I carried it in the modified port arms fashion, or when I cradled it in my left arm, keeping my right hand wrapped around the pistol grip and ready for action. I knew that if I did get a shot of opportunity in that area, it would be a quickie. There would be no time for fumbling around.

I would stop occasionally, listen and look around. Nothing showed. It didn't take too long to get to the beaver pond, even though I was going slowly. As I approached, I looked for likely spots to sit — places that would help conceal me, yet afford a good field of fire. Although there were several likely spots, one looked particularly inviting because it precluded the need for me to sit in the snow on the ground. A tree had been blown over, and the trunk at one point was not only free of bothersome branches, but was chair-high. Yet, it was right in the middle of some bushes that would break up my profile, but still open enough to allow a clear shot in any of several directions.

From that spot, I could see the trail in both directions, I could see the pond and I could see anything coming or going. It was perfect, and the air was dead calm. After sitting there for about a half hour, I began to daydream a bit. All that time, I would steal glances at the gun. I would envision my actions should any of several shot opportunities present themselves. It is always handy to have a plan figured out before the moment of truth.

I recalled how nicely the trigger had felt on the range, and how responsive such a shotgun rig was, compared to many kinds of bolt-action rifles I normally used when hunt-

Author tested the Remington Copper Solid slugs in a Remington Model 11-87 SP Deer Gun. The autoloader, with three-inch chamber, has a cantilever scope mount and interchangeable rifled and improved cylinder REM chokes.

ing in the West. Although a hunter tends to think of such things while sitting on stand, the senses are no less keen. I could hear the wingbeats of birds as they flew by, and I could hear a bit of a wind picking up in the higher branches of surrounding spruce trees.

It was that increasing wind that began causing concern. It was not coming from some dominant direction. Rather, it seemed to be swirling above. By the time I had been sitting there for a couple of hours, the breeze was noticeable at ground level, and it was still swirling.

Yet, I could hear noises — noises that my anxious mind insisted had to be deer in the woods, just beyond where I could see into the thick foliage. Several times I thought I detected the muffled sound of a hoof breaking through the crusty snow, or the sound of an animal breaking a small twig on the ground. It was nearing midday, so I stretched and decided to still hunt back to the rendezvous point.

I hadn't walked twenty paces when I heard the all-too-familiar snorting of a doe and the crashing sound of a deer, breaking through the brush that filled the voids between the conifers. My suspicions had been correct. The deer had remained just out of sight, and I could have remained sitting there all day without success.

The return to the rendezvous point was uneventful, except for a couple more noisy interludes when deer crashed through the woods. I never saw one of them. However, by the time I returned to the pick-up spot, I was pleased with how well the 11-87 Deer Gun rig had carried. It had not seemed heavy, and my arms telegraphed no feeling of fatigue from having carried the rig a couple of miles. That was comforting, but I had little time to revel in it, because Dietz and Marchand drove up in the truck just as I arrived at the spot.

Their morning had been more successful. While walking along the creek bed, Marchand had spotted some deer, and one of them was a nice buck which Dietz bagged with a single shot at about one hundred yards. He was using a rig identical to the one I had, and his shot was well placed. The slug went entirely through the deer, which dropped within a few yards of the spot where it was hit. We drove the deer back to camp, hung it in the skinning shed and returned to the woods following a welcome lunch.

Day one ended as unsuccessfully for me as it had begun. Since Dietz had scored the first day, though, he still-hunted alone the second day while Marchand and I went off together. Marchand is an expert rattler and showed during the second day just how effective the noise of banging together old deer antlers can be.

Following a rather frustrating morning's outing, we headed to a spot more than a mile off the truck road for the afternoon expedition. Following a bit of a hike, Marchand began rattling, and it was almost as though the buck had been trained. He strutted right out into the open, about one hundred feet away. It was a nice buck, and the 11-87 went to my shoulder like it had a mind of its own.

As the buck stopped to take a look around, I squeezed the trigger. The buck did a 180, bounding off exactly in the direction from which he had come. Having a quick follow-up shot is really handy.

We found no evidence on the ground that the buck had been hit — no blood spots or cut-off hair. But about fifty yards away, there were a few blood spots on the snow, and as we followed the buck's tracks, the frequency and size of spots increased steadily until we came to the base of a birch tree where there was a frothy crimson pool in the snow.

Within fifty yards of there, the buck lay. A postmortem examination revealed he had been hit twice: once near the base of the neck (the first shot which sent him running back, but which had not severed the vertebrae) and once through the rear of the chest area, taking out lobes on both lungs.

Since the shot was only slightly more than thirty yards, the slugs had zipped through the entire animal cleanly, having failed to encounter any major bones on the way.

I was particularly pleased with the way the 11-87 rig had pointed for the first shot and the way it stayed with the buck for the second shot. It had been a series of fluid movements in a scant moment of time that had put the buck on the ground. It felt good.

That night, I had ample opportunity to replay the event many times in my mind, building confidence at every turn. After all, it had been the first time I ever bagged a deer with a scope-mounted shotgun. Frankly, before that deer, I wasn't totally convinced scoped shotguns were for me.

In fact, I had wondered whether I might have preferred either barrel sights or an aperture sight setup. Scopes are nice for long-range shots in the Rockies in those cross-canyon situations, but in the woods, I was still a bit of a traditionalist. No longer. The scope setup works and it works well. But some explanation is in order.

I could have made those shots with a gun sans sights and with just a plain barrel. Or I could have made them with open barrel sights. With either of those alternative arrangements, though, I would not have been in a position to make a more precise long shot had it presented itself. And since the scope arrangement proved to be totally effective on a standing shot — and on a follow-up shot at a bounding deer — it offered all the pluses and none of the minuses. It was credible.

The next day, it was Dietz' turn to accompany the guide, so in the morning, I walked off into the woods, still-hunting my way along a small valley as the other two headed off in the opposite direction. Not long into that morning's hunt, I spotted some very healthy-looking deer tracks that were fresh enough to be steaming if the buck had a hot foot.

Lacking any better plan, I decided to stay on his track and see if I could get close enough for a shot. The spacing of the tracks in the crusty snow indicated the buck was walking, only occasionally taking a slight bound to clear a bush or downed tree. He was staying ahead of me, and I was convinced he also was remaining just out of sight deliberately.

I made periodic side-trips a few yards off his trail, hoping to keep him going generally in a forward direction and, at the same time, not pressuring him enough to cause him to flee. It worked.

After about half a mile, I sensed things were about to get very interesting very quickly. Although I had been walking slowly all along, my pace slowed to a crawl. I would take a couple of steps, stop, listen and look. Then I would take a couple more steps and repeat the process. I was still hot on his trail, and that was no time to make a tactical blunder.

I held the 11-87 at the ready as I inched along. The safety remained on, but my hand was positioned to click it off and mount the gun simultaneously, if necessary. My mind continued to replay the action from the day before. I was totally confident that if a buck showed himself, I would be ready and that the shotgun rig would do its part. As I burned the game plan into my brain, I came alongside a thick spruce tree that blocked my vision to the left. As I took a deliberate step forward, I looked around to the right and slightly to the rear, hoping to spot a deer.

Then I heard a slight click. There was a slight breeze in my face, and it was moving the branches of the trees ever so delicately — but moving them, nonetheless. The click reminded me of the noise an antler makes when it hits a small branch. The hair on the back of my neck crawled when it dawned on me that the buck was likely just on the other side of the spruce tree, hoping to double back and leave me proceeding on through the woods. What a sneaky animal!

I froze in my tracks, instantly formulating a game plan if my suspicions were correct and the buck was just on the other side of the tree. I looked ahead in the direction I had been walking, then glanced back to the way from which I had come. I wanted to determine where would be the best place to have the buck flush, if indeed he was there.

There was more open area behind than in front, so I decided I would try to make the buck go out that way if I could. Although there were several options, I decided that first I would see if I could get him to sneak around behind, yet still give me a shot.

I took two — almost a full three — baby steps forward, as I kept my head turned over my left shoulder. The 11-87 was at the ready. I had decided that, if he appeared, I would shoulder the gun and be ready to fire in one fluid movement — much the same way a shotgunner takes a flushing bobwhite. I recall being fully aware of how well the rig had han-

dled on the first buck, at the same time sensing a comforting level of confidence.

As I stopped after the third small step, which actually put me no farther from the back side of the tree than I had been when I first sensed the presence of the deer, the buck appeared, hunched down and trying to sneak away behind me. I did several things all at once, all in one continual move.

First, I determined he was a credible buck. At the same time, I mounted the gun, taking it off safe in the process. As the rubber recoil pad made contact with my wool coat and the crosshairs found their mark low in the buck's chest, I depressed the trigger and the shot rang out.

I had been curious about a couple of things from the day before, wondering just how cleanly one of those slugs would slip through a close-up whitetail if no major bones were encountered. Hence, I wanted to make the first shot a lethal one, but figured there was enough space for one or two quick follow-up shots to put the animal down, if he didn't drop from the first.

At the shot — which was all of about ten feet away — the buck bounded in the direction his nose had been pointed, exactly the way I had hoped to structure the episode. As he hit the ground from the initial scurry and the second bound, I had recovered from the recoil of the first shot and the crosshairs had found the spot right on his left shoulder, as he tried to angle away to my left. That meant that, for an instant, he was presenting me with a side-on shot at not more than thirty yards away. The follow-up shot rang out and the slug hit the buck's shoulder bone with such force that it literally flipped the animal to the ground. A postmortem examination revealed that the first shot had taken out part of the heart and lungs, and that the second slug had shattered the near shoulder bone, continued through the deer and broken the bone on the far side.

The gun had performed flawlessly, effortlessly and quickly. Because it pointed and swung so well, I had options in the game plan that I would not have had with a less lively and responsive rig. Although neither of the bucks had presented me with a long-range slug shot, I felt the hunt had been a total success because I had learned some other important things which a longer shot opportunity would not have allowed. Given the rifle-like accuracy of the rig, I had no doubt that a precision longer shot would be relatively easy. Fortunately, the other hunters on the trip, including Dietz, proved that their rigs, which were the same, were capable of one-hundred-plus-yard, one-shot kills.

Although the rig I was using was the Premier model with blued steel parts and nicely finished walnut stock and forend, there are even more tactically rugged variants available, like Remington's own camo synthetic 11-87 Deer Gun. That is probably the ultimate for such hunts, but I have no complaints about the rig I used. After all, it bagged two nice bucks in two consecutive days of hunting. That's not bad in my book.

Meanwhile, the lesson continues to ring through clearly. As much as I might be a traditionalist in most things, this new genre of shotgun slug deer hunting rigs with scopes, rifled barrels and saboted slugs is a far better bet than that which went before. Indeed, substantial progress has been made. — *Steve Comus*

CHAPTER 24

BASICS OF RELOADING

One Decision Involves The Choice Of Rolled Or Folded Crimp!

The folded crimp is found on most modern factory-loaded shotshells. To know what is behind the crimp you must examine the label.

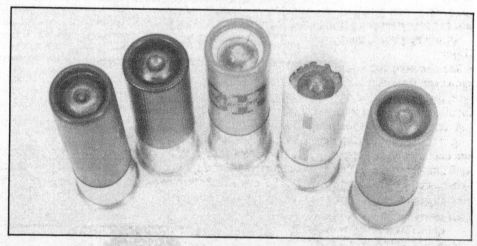

About the only shells with roll crimps are slugs. You can easily identify the slug from the top, not the label.

BASIC SHOTSHELL reloading is simple, if you follow directions for the load you are working up. This is not like rifle or pistol reloading, for you must follow the formula for the specific shotshell load being worked on, whether it is upland bird hunting or buckshot. A slight variation in the load column can increase pressure beyond the safe level.

A good source for shotshell reloading information is the third edition of the *Lyman Shotshell Handbook* that is found on most gun store shelves. This lists loads ranging from bird to slug shooting and has various powders and shot for anything you may want to take with the scattergun, including using it as a single-shot slug gun if you like.

Lyman is working on their fourth edition handbook, which will be available late in 1993 with updated material.

A second source for information on the more modern shells would be Ballistic Products, Inc., 2105 Daniels Street, P.O. Box 408, Long Lake, MN 55356. Dave Fackler, the in-charge man at BPI, has a list of many loads and several specific books he has put together incorporating his knowledge of shotgunning, and has listed loads for buckshot, slugs, steel and buffered loads.

Ballistic Products sells many of the items you may find hard to obtain for wad column-type reloading. The company also stocks such shells as Fiocchi and Activ in both three-inch and 2¾-inch lengths.

Ballistic Products also lists many loads for the wad component system that allow you to tailor your load for the game being hunted. You can get fast-spreading systems or tight, full-choke applications that will pattern well and down geese if that is what you hunt.

We all are acquainted with the many types and sizes of hulls that can be purchased, picked up at the trap range and often are given to us by non-reloaders. What many data sheets and books don't tell you is the danger of changing the wad column in various hulls.

Lyman lists a good example in their third edition handbook regarding a reload that utilized the same hull, same powder and shot charge; all they did was change the wad. Using a 2¾-inch Winchester compression formed case, they loaded 1⅜ ounces of shot in front of a Winchester 209 primer. The powder was 26.0 grains of Hi-Skor 800-X. The pressure varied from 10,220 pounds per square inch using the Winchester WAA12R was, to a maximum of 12,300 pounds per square inch pressure merely changing the wad to a Federal #12S4. This high pressure only changed the velocity from 1263 feet per second with the WAA12R wad to 1281 fps, when using the Federal wad. This is how radical wad column effect can be if you don't follow the formula.

What is considered maximum safe pressure? You won't find many loads above 10,000 or 11,000 pounds per square inch in most reloading books, but they state that 15,000 is max. Maybe you want to pull the trigger on that much pressure, but pressure resolves into recoil against your body and that could be painful to say the least. Follow the formulas in the reloading books and don't deviate.

When loading a rifle cartridge, we usually start with a relatively low powder charge and slowly increase that charge until we spot pressure problems, then back off. Don't do that when reloading shotshells. Follow the formula as stated.

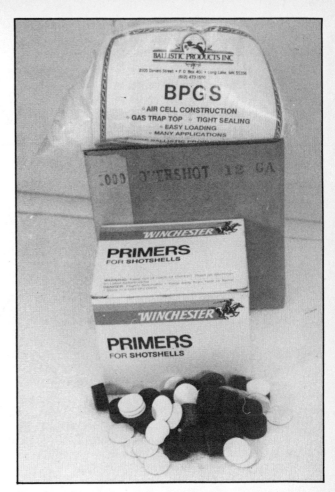

To load 00 buck, you'll need Winchester 209 primers, overshot cup BPGS, felt wads and .030 overshot wads.

During a coffee session after some night varmint calling, a discussion became an argument as to what back-up gun or load one would want in the blind in case a bobcat or some other nasty little critter jumped into the blind with you.

One person advocated a sidearm such as a .44 magnum. Another said he could handle it with a rifle, if it wasn't too close. I flatly stated that, if you can't see it, you can't hit it with a single-bullet firearm. My choice was a 12-gauge loaded with a double 00 buckshot. Up to twelve round lead pellets can be going at that critter in a single trigger pull. The 00 buckshot is .33-inch in diameter, which is larger than most rifles used for varminting— and smaller than the .44 magnum, of course.

Later I noted there were no 00 buckshot loads in my kit, so I decided to make some up. Lyman lists many loads for various buckshot sizes, but one that looked interesting called for the Winchester AA hull with a Winchester 209 primer and twelve pellets of 00 buckshot. This would travel at a velocity of 1295 feet per second, generating LUP (lead units of pressure) of 9800 units. Powder listed is SR 4756 — using 37.5 grains of it for that load. The Lyman manual specifies a folded crimp. A similar loading by BPI lists an Activ 2¾-inch hull primed with a Winchester 209 primer, the same SR 4756 powder, using 33.0 grains for a velocity of 1230 and LUP pressure of 10,500. Similar loads, either folding or rolled crimp are listed as optional. The BPI load also used the old-style wad column rather than the single-unit plastic system.

A fast search of my hull stock disclosed there were no AA hulls on hand, but there were plenty of newer Activ

Above, the shortened hulls are set for depriming and priming which will be done on a Lee Load-All, right.

hulls waiting to be reloaded. The option of folding with the star crimp or using the older-style rolled crimp offered a new question: What is the difference?

The Lyman folks contend there is little difference. They state the fold-type crimp does give a touch more LUP, but this is minimal and not a problem.

If you are into serious shotshell reloading, you have either a single-station reloader or a progressive style. For the roll crimp and the appropriate component sytem, the single-stage works better for most of us, since one removes the shell at each loading station and takes it to the next.

We can't put 00 bucks hot down any of the shot tubes; the shot just jams up, causing problems, so this becomes handloading at its most basic.

If you don't want to use a roll crimp, merely make a few simple changes and use the fold crimp on your machine. Be certain to use the right crimp starter station for either the six-point or eight-point crimp. If you use the wrong starter, the crimp won't form properly; a simple problem, but often overlooked.

When working up special loads such as this 00 buck, it helps to be able to identify the shot quickly when you take them out to stuff into the tube of your shotgun. Once the crimp has been formed on the folded style, you have no idea what is in that hull until you shoot it.

However, there are ways you can mark your special loads. Some people take those mailing circles you buy in the stationary store in different colors and stick them on the shell. That works but what do you do at night when you don't have time for a light? You can load a hull such as the Activ and remember that those are 00 only loads. That works quite well, since the Activ has a distinctive hull with no brass showing at the base.

Another solution that never fails and can be used even in the pitch black of night is to make up *only* that special load with a roll crimp. This is identified easily merely by placing your finger on the end of the shell. If you can't tell the difference between the fold crimp with the six or eight points and no open center, and the roll crimp which has a distinctive ridge around the outer rim, you have problems.

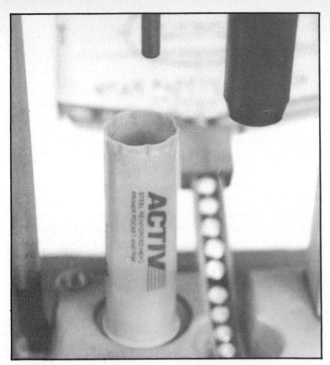

This hull is in the Load-All deprimer station. It will then be moved to the right for priming with a Win. 209.

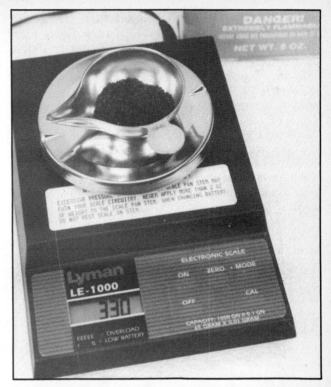

An electronic scale like Lyman's LE-1000 is used to ensure the proper amount of powder for each load.

The author's Lyman 55 Ideal powder measure is a real veteran, but dispenses powder well for this operation.

When you decide to roll crimp shotshells, you need to purchase some items that will make it easier for you and result in good looking, finished shells.

The first item would be that single-station reloading system mentioned earlier. A progressive reloading press could get complicated, as we will see.

The difference between a single-stage and a progressive reloader is primarily in the number of shells one can turn out per hour. One single-stage unit at a modest price is the Lee Load-All. This unit is made primarily of plastic, with metal parts where needed. It is inexpensive, works great with standard plastic wads, and speed depends on how fast you can work. This Lee product is available in 12-gauge and is simple to adjust from 2¾-inch hulls to three-inchers by moving one screw and raising the wad guide unit. The Lee unit has charge and shot bushings, and one can create most loads wanted using just this system. It is fast, simple and inexpensive, yet is convertible from 12- to 20-gauge.

The Lee Load-All manual lists the tool intended for use with plastic wad columns only.

Our hull has been chosen, the load checked and decided upon, but we still need the proper device to obtain that roll crimp. We need the wad column, overpowder plastic, overshot wad and a drill press or even a hand drill with which to form the roll crimp. These items aren't expensive and most of us already have them in the shop.

We might find some wide-eyed stares when we go to a gunshop and ask for an overpowder felt wad component and overshot card. Many shops today don't carry these items, since there is little demand for them. This is where BPI comes to our aid. They make and stock all the above-listed items and offer fast delivery. Choice of wad sizes ranges from an unlikely 8 gauge down to and including the .410-bore. These are available as the hard nitro card type for overpowder loading and the softer felt or fiber cushion wads. If you don't know what you need, the staff is quite helpful, since they reload and shoot, too.

Ballistic Products also sells the required roll crimp unit in sizes 10-, 12-, 16- and 20-gauge. We will use this in a drill press to form the roll. Also needed is a hull cutter to cut the length of the hull for rolling back from the fold crimp memory the plastic hull has retained. It helps to buy a hull vise or make your own, if you have the time and inclination.

All the decisions have been made, the needed supplies and tools are at hand, and it is time to set up and make a batch of roll-crimped 00 buckshot shells.

Set up your reloading press and select your primer and powder. Check your bushings for the proper load, remembering to keep the charge in the range of the formula you are using. If anything, go under but not over when it comes to powder measurement. The Lee chart shows that of the bushings for SR 4756, powder drop from one too high and another was too low by a few grains. Normally with smokeless powder, we work in half grains — or less — for consistent loads in any system.

That presented no problem. Lyman's 55 Ideal powder measure was chosen since it will throw a big load and is infinitely adjustable. We won't use the powder slide on the reloader, so leave it empty. Getting the wads and other components for the load into and through the wad fingers presents no problem, but we do have some preliminary work to do.

The first item is to clean the hulls if they are dirty; this is normal procedure. Next, we take a D-Loader if we have one and cut a quarter-inch off the end of the Activ or other chosen hull. The folded crimp gives the plastic a memory and this type of shell does not roll well at all. If you don't think so, try it!

If you didn't get a cutter unit, use some good, sharp shop scissors to cut that plastic hull.

For myself, twenty-five hulls were prepared since more than that would be negative thinking. Also, 00 buckshot works for deer, ducks, geese — and home protection. If you had an intruder coming down the hall and you let this load go, it would do permanent damage to more than the intruder, including your hall and room behind it.

A loading block is quite handy, since we will be going through separte stages, and such a block offers a good holding system. Again, you can buy one or make it.

Put all the hulls in the block and move them one at a time to the depriming station of the press, and punch out spent primers. Move each hull to the primer seating station and punch in a new Winchester 209 primer. This is where the standard reloading system varies. Move the primed hull to a powder measure preset for the 33.0-grain SR 4756 load and drop that load into the primed hull. It's back to the press, placing the hull into the wad guide station, then taking the BPGS (Ballistic Products Gas Seal) unit in the fingers, ram it down on the powder. This serves as your overpowder shot cup and is more eficient than a nitro card.

Above, shells on the right, with .030 overshot cards, are ready for roll crimping. Right, the shell is held in hull clamp while the BPI roll crimper does its job.

Place one one-eighth-inch wool felt wad in the guide and try to get it down the hull. If it won't go or it twists to the side and jams the press, carefully remove that hull and forget using the Load-All for the wad column.

Now what do you do? Simply go back to the real basics and use a round wood dowel to seat the felt wads — two for the proper load — and you will be ready to load the 00 buckshot.

The Load-All works great with that for which it was designed: plastic wad units. When the wad section is rammed down on the powder tightly, you can count out twelve of those round lead balls to fit into the remaining space in the hull of the shell. You can't cram in more than that, but you could load fewer, if that is the load you want. This shot will lie nicely in four layers of three. It takes only a few minutes to load all twenty-five shells if you complete each stage as you go.

You should have at least a quarter-inch above the shot for the roll crimp.

Move the loading block to the drill press and start finishing off your loads. First, they require two overhsot cards to give the correct height for forming the roll crimp. These cards lock the buckshot into the hull and give us something to write the load on when finished. These light .030-inch cards are inserted with the finger and pushed into place around the rim of the hull mouth.

We now are ready for the final step. The two roll crimping units — one from Lyman, the other from BPI — vary slightly in design. The Lyman has a long stem for attaching it to the drill chuck, while the BPI has a shorter stem but is longer in body. The Lyman has a slanting inner rim that ends with six half-rod like units evenly spaced around the center open core. The BPI has the same converging rim, but has only one bar at an angle.

How do they work? You place the crimper in the drill chuck. Drill press speed at about 1500 rpm was found to work best in the press. Clamp or otherwise hold the loaded shotshell under the roll crimper and lower the spinning unit onto the top of the hull. The hulls are of plastic, and plastic melts or softens with heat. Hold gentle pressure on the hull

top until you feel lessening pressure on the drill arm. That indicates the plastic is softening and you can apply slow, gentle pressure to form the roll crimp over the top of the white overshot card. You can raise and lower the crimper to check progress, but be certain to keep it straight. It will deform the edges if not in alignment. The speed of 1500 rpm provided a clean, rounded edge on the roll and the depth was easily determined by the pressure and noise you get if you should get too low and hit the 00 pellets on top. The latter sign isn't good, since it means the shot may be deformed and become fliers when you shoot.

Your first roll crimps may appear a bit tacky, trying to do them too fast and the plastic turning white in appearance from too much pressure at high speed. By the time you finish the first twenty-five rounds you set out to make, you should be making a nice, clean crimp. — *C.R. Learn*

Above, the hull clamp is released, revealing crimp. Left, here are a few of the 25 shells loaded by author.

LOAD 'EM UP!

Lee's Load-Fast Makes A Boring Job Easy — And Fast!

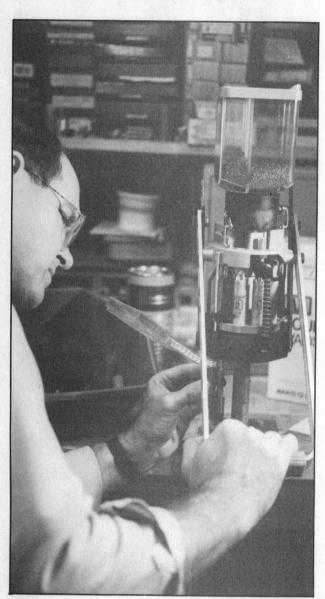

Author cycles Lee's Load-Fast progressive shotshell press. Unit comes complete from the factory ready to begin loading skeet, sporting clays and trap target loads.

THE FRIENDLY folks in Hartford, Wisconsin, have done it again. On the drawing boards for the better part of fifteen years, Lee's Load-Fast finally has reached dealer shelves. Unless we miss our guess, it will find wide acceptance among sporting clays, skeet and trap shooters, and with hunters as well.

Offered now only in 12-gauge, 16- and 20-gauge versions may follow in a year or so. The Load-Fast is an eight-station progressive shotshell loading tool expressly designed for 2¾-inch shells.

The Load-Fast comes from the factory already adjusted to turn out target and hunting loads using 1⅛ ounces of shot. Along with the shot bushing, the press is supplied with a 151 powder bushing that drops 2¾- to 3¼-dram equivalent charges, depending on which powder you choose.

If you invest $15 or so in a set of the same powder and shot bushings that fit Lee's Load-All II, the Load-Fast can handle virtually any combination of components used in standard-length 2¾-inch 12-gauge shells.

John Lee, designer of the press, says a kit to adapt the press to three-inch shells is under consideration. Required would be a longer center column and a lengthened wad guide post, as well as other slight modifications.

The question in Lee's mind is whether the shotshell loading public will find it worthwhile to load three-inch shells on a progressive tool. Another question is whether components will become available for loading the 3½-inch 12-gauge, which is becoming a favorite among water-fowlers.

As it stands now, the Load-Fast is a fairly straight-forward machine. A spud, projecting from the center post, engages a spiral cam-way in a nylon bushing which rotates the steel shell plate 22.5 degrees, when the operating lever is pulled down. Lowering the handle also raises the shell plate. Raising the handle lowers and turns the shell plate another one-sixteenth of a circle.

A large spring-loaded steel ball bearing, housed in the

With the optional automatic primer feeder in place, the author slips a fired shotgun hull into the resizing station.

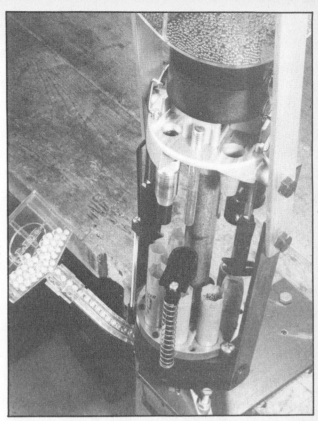

Author's Load-Fast overhangs bench so spent primers, falling through center of the press, drop into a container.

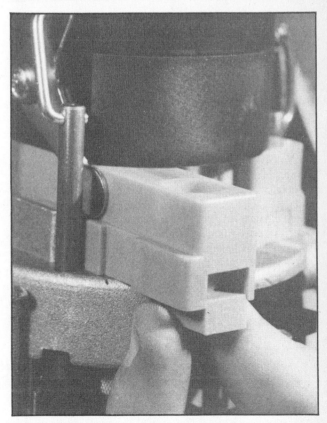

The Load-Fast uses the same powder and shot bushings as the Lee Load-All. Changing the bushings is a snap.

glass reinforced nylon shell plate carrier, engages detents, locking the plate firmly in position at the bottom of the shell plate's travel.

Eight holes, each the minimum diameter of a resized 12-gauge brass case head, with an additional step to resize the rim, have been bored in the shell plate. The plate rotates counter-clockwise through traditional sizing, decapping, powder charging, wad seating, shot charging, crimp starting and final crimp/full-length sizing stations. At the eighth station, the shell is ejected from the press.

Twin charge bars — one for powder and the other for shot — ride on an aluminum casting from which dies are suspended. The Load-Fast incorporates a pair of disconnects that make it virtually impossible to throw a charge of powder or shot without a case in position under the drop tubes. The key is a claw-like nylon block which is forced into position by the presence of a case.

With a case in position, the block engages a bar which activates a lever to pivot an arm, sliding the charge bar forward as the shell plate rises and back when the shell plate is lowered. To change bushings, push the bar forward with

The powder and shot reservoir is removed by rotating it a quarter turn. The tubes are drained by detaching them from the charge bars and sliding them back and forth.

The acid test for the Load-Fast was the loading of steel BB-size shot. While the pellets tended to bridge in the drop tube, the author loaded 25 shells in 20 minutes.

your fingers. The bar will slide past the edge of the casting and you then can swap bushings.

A few of the early production models of the press were equipped with powder measure disconnects that would jam. This resulted in no charge, even though a case was in position. The problem was cured by adding a bevel to the bottom of the inboard arm of the disconnect. Check the powder charge disconnect. If it is not beveled, call Lee at (414) 673-3075. They'll supply a new one at no charge.

Priming is accomplished at the second station. A spring-loaded cup sits on a post which screws into the base of the press. The post is held securely with a lock nut. The upward movement of the shell plate carries the case over the de-capper. The spent primer falls free and is deflected through a port in the hollow center column. Place a primer in the cup and lower the shell plate. You can feel the primer seat home.

As an accessory, for about $15, Lee offers an automatic priming system for the Load-Fast. This consists of two trays, each holding fifty primers, a trough that feeds primers to a shuttle that then moves one primer at a time onto a slid-ing priming post. The automatic primer feed is attached to the underside of the shell plate carrier by two screws.

When installing the automatic primer feed, remove the single primer post from the base of the press. In its place, screw in the ¼-20 hex-head bolt, being sure that elastomer ring — it looks like a thick plastic washer — is in place. Adjust the bolt so it clears the bottom of the primer feeder

by the thickness of a dime. Otherwise, serious damage to the primer feeder can result.

At the bottom of the shell plate carrier's travel, the primer post contacts the hex-head bolt. You can adjust primer seating depth by raising or lowering the hex-head bolt.

A tapered pillar projects down from the bottom of the primer seater. Pushing the pillar to the right allows a primer to slide from the feed trough into the primer shuttle, which is under spring tension. When you release pressure on the pillar, the shuttle slips back into its original position, plac-ing a primer atop the priming post.

Automatic priming systems are the bugaboo of most progressive presses, but Lee's solution seems to be almost foolproof — it has to be for my fumble fingers — and it works smoothly.

After a case receives a primer, the next pull of the operating lever raises the case, triggering the powder mea-sure. Unless a case is in position under the powder drop tube, the measure will not dispense a charge of powder.

Once charged with powder, the case is rotated through the wad-seating station. Wad-seating pressure is adjusted by loosening a nut and screwing the wad punch up or down as appropriate. As it came from the factory, the punch needed no adjustment for seating wads for my clay target loads.

The shot measure works the same way as the powder measure, employing a similar disconnect that engages

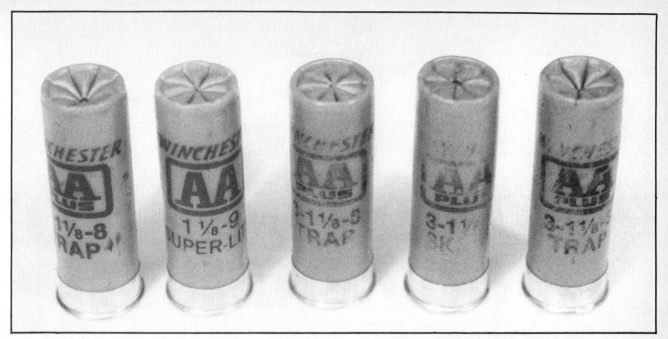

The center shell is a new, unfired Winchester AA trap. The two rounds at right were loaded with steel shot and the two on the left were loaded with 7-1/2s, all on the Load-Fast. The crimps are uniform and the rounds fired flawlessly.

when a case is in position. It's virtually impossible to goof and dump a load of shot into the workings of the press. For this I am grateful.

Bins for powder and shot are contained in a large reservoir that sits atop the press. Rotating the reservoir a quarter-turn closes off powder and shot ports to the charge bars. You then can lift the reservoir off the press to dump powder or shot.

Clearing charge bars requires either manually moving them back and forth in their tracks until the system is empty, or you can slip an empty case over the end of the powder and shot tubes, engage the disconnects, then pump the press up and down until the charge bars and feeding ports are empty.

While the press tosses 1⅛-ounce target loads of lead shot with absolute ease, I wanted to give it a torture test. From the steel shot loading manual from MEC (Mayville Engineering Company, 715 South Street, Mayville, WI 53050), I chose a load for 1⅛ ounce of steel shot in Winchester AA hulls.

To make matters even tougher, I opted to load BB-size shot. BB shot has a diameter of .18-inch. Steel lacks the lubricity of lead and is prone to bridge across drop tubes. It is a pain to load.

Yet the Load-Fast performed more than adequately. I used the 1⅝-ounce bushing to throw 1⅛ ounces of the big steel pellets. Of course, speed was not possible. Shot bridged on every fourth shell, but use of the short end of a one-eighth-inch Allen wrench easily freed shot stuck in the tube.

To load steel shot in the 2¾-inch cases, I lowered the wad-seating post about one-half-inch to ram the wad firmly over the powder. That was it. Going slowly, I loaded a box of steel BBs in about twenty minutes.

From the factory, the press delivers nearly perfect eight-point crimps in Winchester AA and Remington RXP cases. The crimp starter automatically indexes to the folds in the case. After loading five hundred rounds or so, it never missed a beat. A six-point crimp starter is included for cases requiring same.

Leaving the crimp starter, the case moves to the final crimp station where the shell is sealed and resized in a full-length nylon die. At the final station, the completed round is punched out of the shell carrier, down a ramp and into your waiting hand.

Lee recommends mounting the press on a raised platform so that completed shells will tumble down the ramp into a box or tray. But the main reason for mounting your press on a platform has to do with ejection and collection of spent primers.

During the decapping process, as I mentioned, spent primers are ejected into the hollow center column of the press. Lee recommends drilling a three-quarter-inch hole under the column through your loading bench so the fired primers will fall through into a receptacle.

I chose a different route. I decided to mount the press on 4x8x¼-inch scrap steel plate. After marking the location of the center column, I drilled out a three-quarter-inch hole. The press is attached to the plate with three ¼-20 hex-head bolts. The plate I bolted to my loading bench overhangs the edge of the bench just enough for spent primers to fall free into a waste basket. This system works fine.

I've used a number of progressive presses over the years. The Load-Fast from Lee is one of the few you can take out of the box, bolt to the bench and begin loading within the hour.

And its price is attractive, to say the least — less than $130 straight retail and available for less than a *C* note from some discount houses. In all, the Load-Fast is quite a bargain. What else would you expect from those fertile minds up in Lee-land? — *Chris Christian*

CHAPTER 26

POWDERS DO MAKE A DIFFERENCE

This Experimenter Finds That Shotguns Can Be Fussy About The Flakes They Digest!

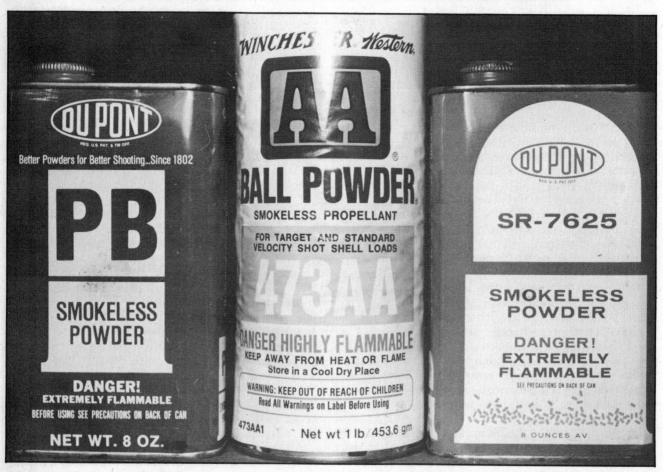

There are a lot of shotshell powders. The one you select can make a difference in a gun's patterning performance.

Deformed pellets also can influence pattern development. They will slow down and often flip out of the main string.

WHENEVER YOU see it written that "each gun/load combination is a physical law unto itself," believe it! Also believe that the law doesn't apply only to rifles and handguns. Shotguns can be just as fussy about which load they'll pattern best.

In fact, shotguns may even be more fussy, for they don't throw just one solid projectile at a bullseye. Scatterguns launch oodles of pellets that become patterns, but the pellets' flights can be influenced by such things as the barrel's vibrational characteristics and the load's component structure.

Experts long ago not only accepted the fact that overall pattern percentages (efficiencies) change from load to load, but also that pellet distributions and densities vary within the main thirty-inch-diameter circle. For that reason, pattern reading involves more than merely eyeballing a bunch of holes in cardboard and proclaiming them a nice pattern. What may look pretty good at first glance to those who have no inkling of pattern analysis or standards often pales under the scrutiny of scientific analysis.

For the purpose of this chapter, then, patterns will be judged on three bases: (1) the number of pellets in a twenty-inch-diameter "core" drawn about the center of mass; (2) the number of pellets in the outer ring, which is a five-inch area between the twenty-inch core and the main thirty-inch-diameter circle; and (3) the total density for both core and ring. What the reader must be alert to is the potential for differing densities within the core and ring as we go from load to load using the same gun and degree of choke. When measured by more scientific methods, patterns do show obvious variations on a load to load basis.

All the components of a shotshell can impact patterning. However, it is the hardness of the shot and the burning rate of the powder that can have the major influences on patterning. The role of pellet hardness has been discussed in many magazine articles and books. Suffice it to say here that pellet deformation suffered under the pressures of firing setback and bore travel can upset patterning substantially.

Steel shot invariably patterns tighter than most lead loads, because steel doesn't deform. Among the varieties of lead shot, nickel-plated shot is the least likely to deform, while unplated lead shot finds the so-called "hard" or "magnum" shot withstanding setback and bore travel forces better than chilled shot. The hard or magnum grades of lead shot have greater antimony contents, and because antimony is a hardener, these grades generally will increase the pattern efficiencies by ten to twenty percentage points over ordinary chilled shot. Thus, anyone who tries to study

During author's tests, Winchester's Super-Lite Ball Powder produced excellent ring density.

patterns must understand the role of shot hardness factors and not try to compare the results of different hardnesses. Do all comparative patterning with one hardness of shot! The reloads listed in this chapter all used Lawrence brand high-antimony magnum shot.

While it may be difficult for many casual shooters and reloaders to accept this, gun powder can impact the characteristics of a pattern. Some powders will tighten patterns; others will loosen them. Some powders will give liberal pellet distributions throughout a pattern; others will tend to concentrate pellets in the center while leaving the outer ring weak, while others will weaken the center and hammer the outer ring. And this can be true for all degrees of choke!

For example, one would think a wide-open skeet choke with flared flats would spread its pellets broadly, regardless of the load, and it would invariably give about the same pellet count with any and all reloads and powders. But serious pattern reading tells us that some powders do it differently than the others. Recent experiments with a Remington Model 1100 skeet gun with unaltered factory skeet barrel have proved how powder charges can change the shot distribution pattern.

The experiment was based on two powders — Green Dot and Solo 1250 — which in the past had shown that they did indeed affect opposed patterning characteristics: Green Dot tended to hold'em tight, as Solo 1250 was inclined to a wider distribution. But in a skeet gun?!

Well, yup. Let's look at typical results for a twenty-yard patterning test with said pair of powders. On average, Green Dot laid 300-310 No. 9s in the twenty-inch-diameter core with about 200-210 No. 9s in the outer ring.

On the other hand, Solo 1250 put only 170-180 No. 9s into the core, with a healthy 220-232 going into the outer ring. Both are reasonably good skeet clusters, but how many skeetmen don't want another twenty or so pellets in their pattern's outer reaches for a larger sure-hit area?

To further illustrate the influence of powder on the patterning of an open-bored shotgun, a series of five different

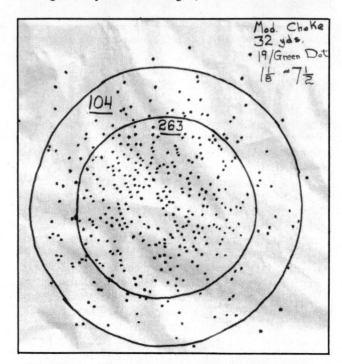

Above, despite being fired from a modifed-choke barrel, this Green Dot load yielded high center density. Left, this pattern was made with Winchester Super-Lite powder. While it shows a lighter core density, there's more shot in the outer ring.

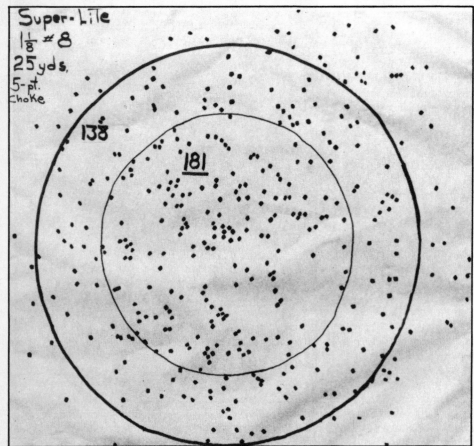

reloads was patterned through a Beretta Model A303 sporting clays gun, using a Hastings five-point (0.005-inch) choke tube.

Shooting was done over twenty-five yards, because that is a practical working range for skeet and improved cylinder. The reloads all used Lawrence brand No. 8 hard shot in 1⅛-ounce charges. Each reload was patterned five times, after which the pellet holes were tallied and averaged for each core, ring and total thirty-inch circle. The results may surprise shotgunners who thought all gun/load combos shot alike:

Load	Ring Hits	Core Hits	Total
A1 (Unique)	127	238	365
A2 (Solo 1250)	174	250	424
A3 (Solo 1000)	128	230	358
A4 (Super-Lite)	140	183	323
A5 (Green Dot)	104	263	367

As one can see, the reloads with Solo 1250 gave the heaviest outer ring coverage, while the reloads with Green Dot tightened the core more than any of the other rounds.

In other cursory patterning done with open-choked shotguns, a similar result occured, namely powders like Solo 1250 and Winchester Super-Lite tend to deliver broader spreads with more shot in the outer ring.

A newcomer, Hodgdon's Clays, has also indicated an ability in this direction in open-choked guns. On the other hand, Green Dot invariably has thrown tight core densities, as further discussions will prove.

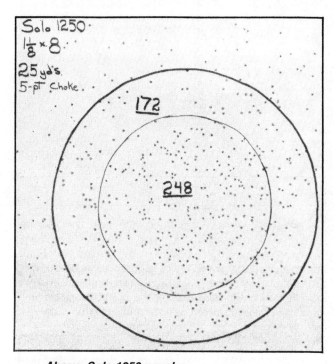

Above, Solo 1250 powder showed a greater overall density and a heavier outer ring saturation. Right, this pattern is typical for Solo 1000 when fired through a five-point choke tube.

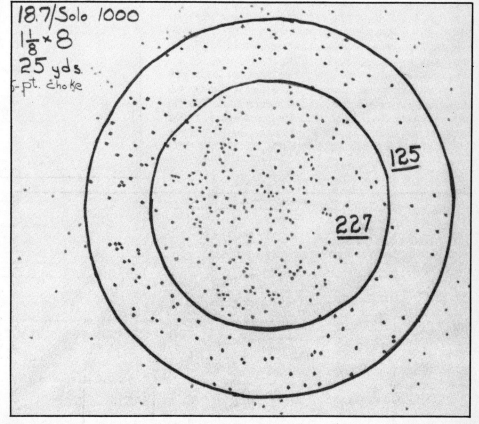

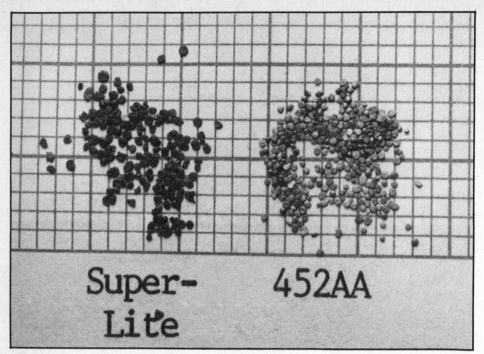

Winchester's Super-Lite Ball Powder has a different burning characteristic than Winchester 454AA. This means better ring density for the Super-Lite loads.

An interesting thing is the disparity between two powders from the same line of Scot Powder, Solo 1000 and 1250. Solo 1000 came nowhere near matching the density of Solo 1250 in any of the three measurements. For the record, the two extreme patterns — A2 and A5 — were assembled thus:

Load A2

Winchester AA hull
Winchester 209 primer
24.5 grains of Solo 1250
Windjammer wad
1⅛ ounces of hard No. 8s
Published pressure: 7400 1.u.p.
Published velocity: 1200 fps

Load A5

Remington Premier hull
Remington 209P primer
19.0 grains of Green Dot
1⅛ ounces of hard No. 8s
Published pressure: 7300 psi
Published velocity: 1145 fps

Some readers may point out that Load A2 used a higher velocity than load A5, and they may try to invoke the popular concept that slowing a load and/or lowering its chamber pressure will tighten patterns. However, some reloads with Red Dot and Hi-Skor 700-X also were tried at 1145 feet per second without duplicating the density of Green Dot or the spread/density figures of Solo 1250. Rules of thumb regarding shotshell velocity don't always work!

An interesting tale about modified choke performance fits this discussion: One spring I did some reloading for a high school trap shooter, using the light-recoiling load of Green Dot listed above (A5). The young man's gun was a Remington Model 870 with a twenty-eight-inch, modified-choke barrel, and when I watched him shoot, he literally smokeballed targets; that Model 870 was hammering clays as if it were a full choke, not just a modified choke. So I borrowed the Remington one day and did some patterning with it, using several different reloads.

But the first thing I did was take an inside dial micrometer to its bore to find out exactly what kind of choke constriction it had. The mic gave it a bore diameter of 0.727-inch with a constriction of 0.020-inch, which is

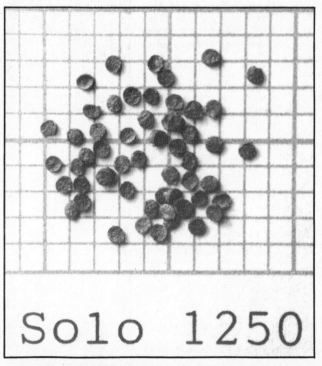

During the test, Solo 1250 gave high overall density with a broad distribution.

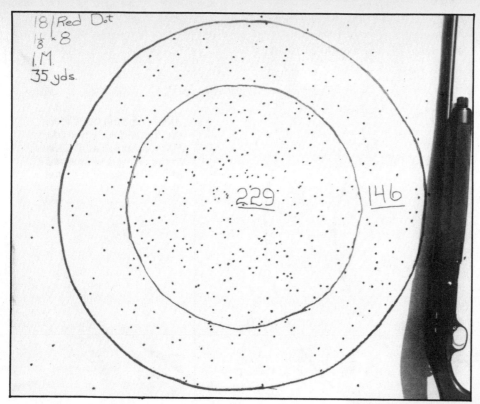

18/Red Dot
1⅛ × 8
I.M
35 yds.

229   146

Left, the best improved modified patterns were thrown by Red Dot, one of the oldest propellents. Below, reloads with Green Dot and No. 9s produced this pattern from a skeet choked Remington M1100.

within the parameters of modified choke and certainly isn't anywhere near the 0.035- to 0.040-inch constrictions of full choke.

I did my patterning at thirty-two yards, which represents a midrange point where modified choke fits in afield as well as being the range where a trapshooter would be breaking his singles shot from the sixteen-yard line. The results with Green Dot are shown in an accompanying photo, and they

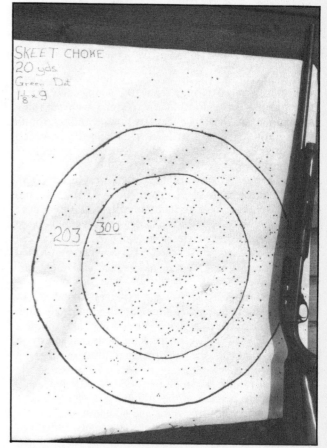

SKEET CHOKE
20 yds
Green Dot
1⅛ × 9

203 300

Green Dot

During author's extensive testing, Green Dot powder tended to tighten patterns and hold high center density.

explain why the high-schooler was making trap targets evaporate in midair: the gun/load combo was performing like a full choke, slamming a preponderance of shot into the twenty-inch-diameter core of the thirty-inch-diameter pattern.

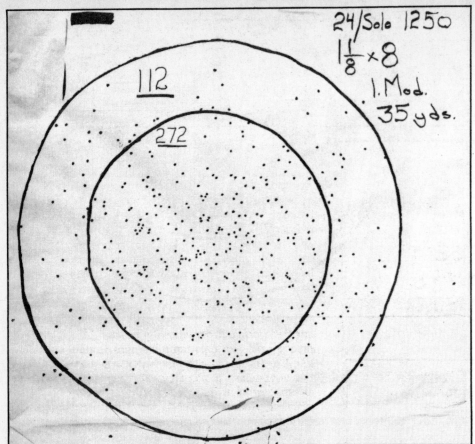

24/Solo 1250
1⅛ × 8
I. Mod.
35 yds.

112

272

Although Solo 1250 threw the tightest core densities, it placed the fewest pellets in the outer ring and, thus, shot like a basic full choke.

The outer ring picked up just a few pellets, leaving some weak spots along the fringe. Thus, the young shooter had little more than a two-foot effective pattern — but anything picked up inside those two feet was ground and re-ground by the ultra-dense shot string! It was indeed a modified choke that shot like a true full choke, because of the load being used.

What happened when other reloads were used? With powders like Red Dot, Hi-Skor 700-X, SR-7625 and Clays, it went right back to shooting patterns with less core density, and when I tried some ball-type propellants there were a few instances when the gun fell to a tight improved cylinder. Modified choke, then, also is sensitive to load changes. And Load A5 continued its tight-shooting characteristics.

Improved modified is little known among hunters, but many trap shooters employ it for sixteen-yard singles and the first barrel on trap doubles. Some sporting clays shooters also have been trying it for the long shots, especially in FITSAC, which is the International form of sporting clays.

Essentially, improved modified is supposed to put sixty-five to seventy percent of the original shot charge into a thirty-inch circle at forty yards and spread it about more evenly than does full choke. But it's extremely difficult to find a load that will give patterns within that range of just five percentage points while also distributing its pellets evenly. The shooter who thinks he'll get a bona fide improved modified performance from any and all loads through a barrel so choked is dreaming.

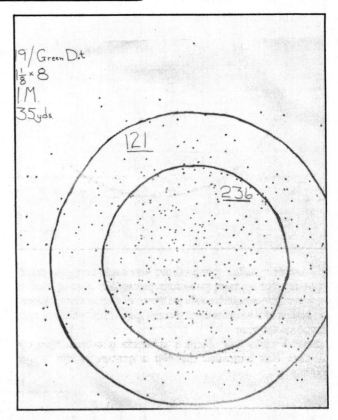

19/Green Dot
1⅛ × 8
I.M.
35 yds.

121

236

Green Dot also hammered the 20-inch core from the IM tube, but it placed more shot into the outer ring.

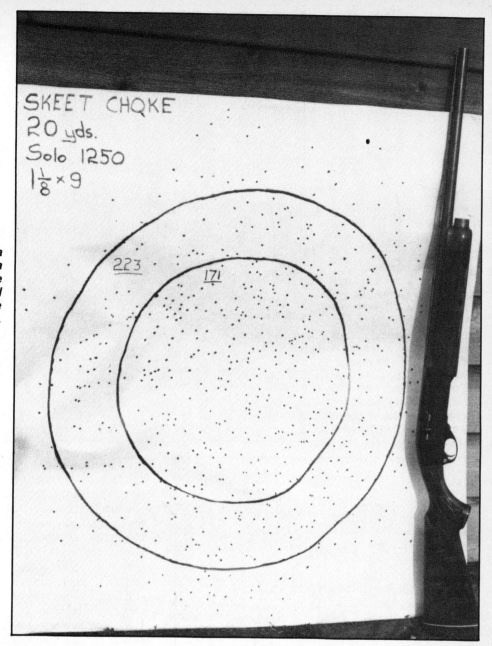

SKEET CHOKE
20 yds.
Solo 1250
$1\frac{1}{8} \times 9$

223

171

An open skeet choke on a Remington M1100 threw a heavier ring, lighter core density with Solo 1250 and No. 9s compared to the same load using Green Dot.

In a recent patterning run, reloads with Red Dot, Green Dot, Solo 1250, Hodgdon's Clays and Hi-Skor 700-X were tested in a Beretta Model A303 12-gauge autoloader using a Hastings improved modified choke tube (0.25-inch constriction).

The tendencies of all reloads, except one, were to pound high center densities like a full choke and leave the outer ring variously weak. Reloads with Solo 1250, which had scattered pellets broadly in the skeet and improved cylinder chokes, held a rifle-like core density while placing just 112 pellets, on average, into the outer ring. The Green Dot reload remained true to its tight-patterning ways, and Hi-Skor 700-X placed only 125 pellets, on average, into the outer ring. But there was one powder that gave both a solid core density with increased outer ring density.

That was Red Dot. Although Red Dot has had a lot of competition from other powders lately, it still can get the job done. In this particular improved modified choke, it put

an average of 147 pellets in the outer ring with a normal count of about 230 in the twenty-inch core. No other reload tested through that IM choke has put more shot, on average, into the outer ring of a thirty-inch-diameter patterning outline. The exact reload which brought out the best result from this improved modified tube was:

Federal Gold Medal hull
CCI 209 primer
18.0 grains of Red Dot
Federal 12S3 wad
1⅛ ounces of No. 8 lead shot
Published pressure: 8200 psi
Published velocity: 1145 fps

It's another instance of one powder outshooting most others to bring out the best pattern from a given degree of choke. And in this instance, it also flies into the face of the

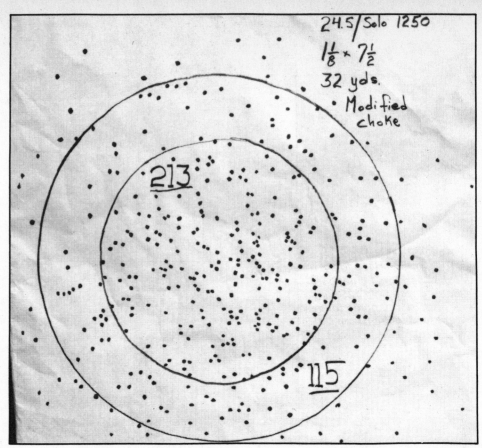

24.5/Solo 1250
1⅛ × 7½
32 yds.
Modified choke

213

115

Right and below, this pair of patterns, fired through a bona fide modified-choke M870 at 32 yards, shows a significance in density and distribution. The reload with 19.0 grains of Green Dot (below) put over 260 No. 7 1/2s into the 20-inch core. The same choke put less than 220 in the core when Solo (right) was used.

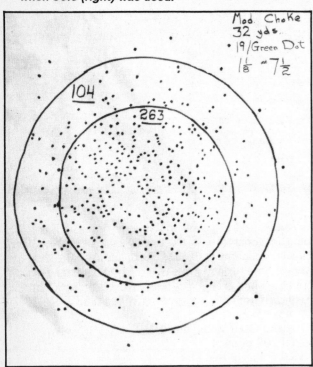

Mod. Choke
32 yds.
19/Green Dot
1⅛ × 7½

104

263

theory that high velocity is needed to expand a pattern, as 1145 feet per second is considered just a light target load, not a high-velocity one!

After considerable experimentation, one not only can find a perfect powder for an individual shotgun, but also can begin to notice tendencies on the parts of various shotshell powders.

As mentioned repeatedly, Green Dot is inclined to throw snug core densities as is fine for handicap trap shooting and doves. Because Green Dot also holds a center density in open-choked barrels, it also could be employed for sporting clays reloads and shot through skeet or improved cylinder choke tubes when the range gets a bit lengthy for normal skeet and IC patterns.

Hodgdon's new Clays, a super-clean-burning powder, has a fine tendency to follow the dictates of most chokes. It'll punch wide skeet patterns, do well through modified, then can be relied upon for a good full-choke performance. Hodgdon's newer International shotshell powder is slightly slower burning than Clays, being in the burning range of Green Dot, and initial tests indicate International's lower pressures can produce some tight core densities, too, for trap handicap and dove loads.

Winchester's Super-Lite is a ball powder that was a result of experiments with steel shot propellants. Steel shot needs a slow-starting powder to effect the proper ejecta flow (because steel doesn't compress), and Super-Lite's burning characteristic is to start slowly, then intensify as the ejecta moves forward; hence, Super-Lite has a push-type recoil sensation unlike that of Winchester Super Target and Super Field.

But patterning with Super-Lite has uncovered a tendency for it to place more shot into the outer ring of a pattern than do many ball-type propellants. Some full-choked trap guns also will deliver variously wider, but still highly effective, patterns with Super-Lite than they will with Winchester's former ball powder, 452AA. It's worth a try!

IMR Powder Company's slow-burning Hi-Skor 800-X

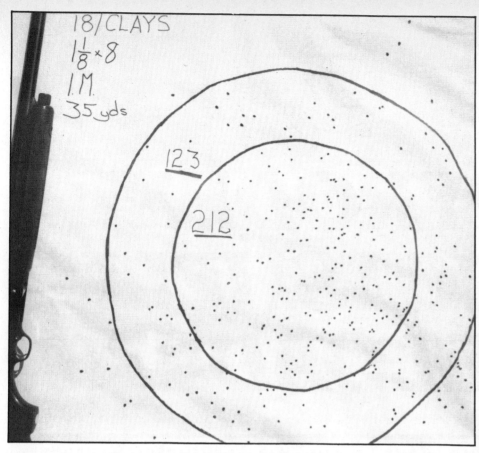

18/CLAYS
1⅛ × 8
I.M.
35 yds

123

212

Left, Hodgdon's Clays fans the pattern a bit wider than Green Dot or Solo 1250. Below, Solo 1250 produced a full-choke pattern that filled entire 30-inch circle.

(note 800-X, not 700-X!) also has tended to be tight-patterning from a lot of modified, improved modified and full-choked shotguns. It can be a bit boomy with the lighter 1⅛-ounce 12-gauge loads, but it has been known to deliver really lethal trap handicap patterns with No. 7½ lead shot. In 1⅜- and 1½-ounce 12-gauge short magnums, it is a stellar powder for long-range shooting with No. 4 and 5 lead shot plus some steel-shot reloads. Hi-Skor 800-X also seems viable for the new bismuth shot that's coming on line.

Nitro 100 from Accurate Arms Company is a good, all-around shotshell powder for target and light field reloads. It has been tested under cold conditions and has been found to be extremely efficient with little loss of pressure/velocity values. It is an exceptional cold-weather trap load, but it doesn't experience chamber pressure increases when taken to the desert for doves or quail, either. Clean burning, Nitro 100 is made of nitrocotton for uniform ballistics, and it gives representative patterns from all degrees of chokes.

It would have been great to have been able to have shot patterns with all available shotshell powders, but that would have been exhaustive. The above examples, however, should prove the point of this chapter's title: powders *do* make a difference! To find that difference in your guns, you'll have to do some trial-and-error testing. Gather lots of published data sheets and manuals, select the shot charge weights and velocity levels you wish, and then follow the printed component lists.

Substituting components may not blow up a gun, but it can vary the pressure/velocity values, which in turn, can influence patterning qualities by altering a gun's vib-

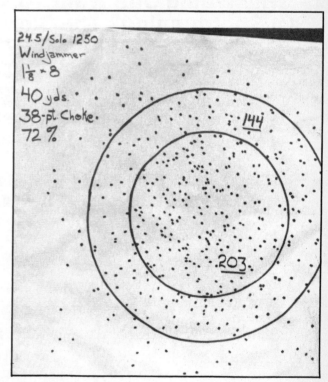

24.5/Solo 1250
Windjammer
1⅛ × 8
40 yds.
38-pt. Choke.
72 %

144

203

rational characteristics, the impact of the wad upon the shot charge at emission and the deformation of pellets on firing setback.

Indeed, developing a great-patterning reload for a shotgun has much in common with finding the best accuracy load for a rifle or handgun. — *Don Zutz*

PYRODEX SHOTSHELL RELOADS?

Why Would One Want To Try This Antiquated System Of Shotgunning? The Simple Answer Is: "Because…"

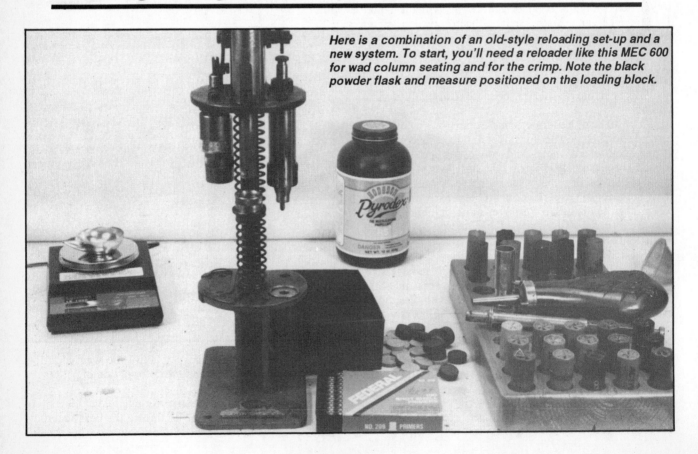

Here is a combination of an old-style reloading set-up and a new system. To start, you'll need a reloader like this MEC 600 for wad column seating and for the crimp. Note the black powder flask and measure positioned on the loading block.

The hulls used included Activ, Fiocchi, Federal, Winchester AA, Blue Peters and Winchesters of unknown origin.

TAKE A measured amount of saltpeter, add some sulphur and charcoal in the correct proportions, then stir well. When you finish, you will have created one of the original bangers for any type of rifle, pistol, shotgun — or cannon. It is called black powder!

This explosive still is used today by the traditionalists using the front-stuffer shotgun. That might be fun, but you also can load black powder shells for modern shotguns. Along with the heavy, smelly dense smoke it creates, you get the job of cleaning your favorite scatter gun afterwards.

You can get one step closer to smokeless powder by loading a shell using a powder that is like black powder in that it has some of the smoke, less of the smell and little of the fouling inherent to the older propellant. This is Pyrodex, a product made by Hodgdon Powder Company, Inc. It might be considered one step up from black powder, but has similar propelling factors.

Those who are into front-stuffer rifles and shotguns need no introduction to Pyrodex, but shooters who haven't heard of it are missing a traditional type of load that will offer almost equal power as a similar smokeless powder loading — but with only about half the pressures.

Pyrodex-loaded shells never have been offered to hunters or trap shooters by any company to my knowledge, but most shotgunners reload, since it is the best means of being able to shoot a lot without spending a small fortune for factory-loaded shells. The average reloader has just about all that is needed for this project.

The need, of course, is a shotgun. You can use any type you want, but keep in mind that even though Pyrodex burns more cleanly than black powder, it still is more fouling than the smokeless types. One can shoot this load from a semi-automatic gun, but the gas ports probably would foul with just a few shots and the gun would be a temporary single-shot in a short time. In short, this load isn't recommended for autoloaders.

A good pump-gun can work well enough with Pyrodex loads, since it doesn't rely on gas actuation for chambering the next round. Pumps take down easily for cleaning and the degree of choke doesn't matter, since shooters will be using that favorite load of bird shot.

Perhaps, though, the best choice for Pyrodex loads would be a double-barrel, but a single-shot would do just as well. These guns take down easier than the more complicated shotguns and clean more easily. Believe it when you're told you will really have to clean them, since this powder *does* leave more residue than smokeless.

Shotgunners can use this load — with the right components — in the 10-, 12-, 16-, 20- and 28-gauges as well as in the .410-bore. Loads and components have to fit the different shells, of course, but that is common sense.

Most scatterguns use a 12-gauge, so let's concentrate on that.

Required loading information for breech-loading shotguns is printed on page 746 in the New Hodgdon Data Manual (Twenty-sixth Edition). There is about a half-page of data for Pyrodex use in these guns that caught my eye while checking loads for old-style, front-stuffing shotguns.

The unusual part of this load is that you can use the hull from any brand of shotshell. With any other load data, you first must select your hull to be loaded and find the data for

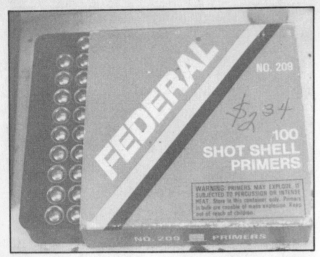

Federal 209 primers were chosen, because they tend to burn hotter than most other brands except magnums.

A carefully measured 72 grains of Pyrodex RS powder sits in the grain scale scoop, awaiting transfer to a hull.

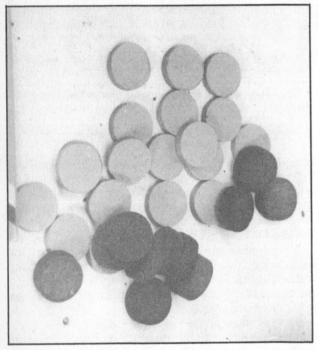

A .125-inch hard card was used for the overpowder wad. This was topped with a 3/8-inch felt wad. Later, this was changed to a 1/4-inch wad for better crimping.

The Hodgdon manual lists 12-gauge loads for 1⅛, 1¼ and 1½ ounces of shot for Pyrodex.

Select hulls that measure 2¾ inches, as load data the manual lists is for this length; no loads for the three-inch shell.

The 1⅛-ounce load calls for a card plus filler; 72 grains of Pyrodex (weighed charges only, please) for a velocity of 1043 feet per second with pressure of a mere 5700 pounds per square inch. The pressure generated by Pyrodex is about half that of any comparable smokeless load — and that equates to less recoil.

Pyrodex RP powder is similar in most respects to FFg black powder and will offer virtually the same results in the bang and velocity department without all the mess and smoke, but Pyrodex is *not* a smokeless powder! It is designed to provide properties similar to those of black powder, but it is safer to handle, less volatile — and just a bit harder to ignite, Hodgdon states.

One can use any modern reloader that will allow removal of the hull from any of the different stations with little trouble. A single-stage tool such as the MEC 600 works quite well for this project. Progressive reloaders may work okay, but check whether that hull can be removed from the mechanism at the various stages.

Sort the hulls, and when selected, place them in a loading block with base down. This will facilitate reloading, since each shell will be moved several times. The selection I made for this project included hulls for Winchester AA,

that hull and the use for which you need it. This is not the case regarding the Pyrodex load — and that is good.

Over the years, most of us have picked up hulls at the trap or skeet range; while quail hunting we may stoop to retrieve spent hulls in the field, if they appear to be in good shape. Friends may give us a sack of hulls they can't use. They mean well, but some of these hulls are not worth reloading — some are totally out of date and some no longer have reloading data available.

There is no sense in reloading an unsafe hull, so use good ones only. These can be loaded with #7½ shot for quail, dove and trap, using the 1⅛-ounce load.

Loading can be done faster, yet accurately, using a powder measure. This ensures exact volume is used.

This brass shot cup, graduated to measure one-ounce, 1 1/8-ounces and 1 1/4-ounces, makes loading shot fast.

Fiocchi, Activ, Peters, Federal and some black plastic jobs with a Winchester stamp on the base. This black plastic seemed a bit on the thin side, but work well enough for this project.

Use the right rear station on the 600 press to deprime the hulls. This is standard procedure and should be no problem. I selected the Federal 209 primer, since the manual states Pyrodex is a bit hard to ignite compared to black powder. The Federal is one of the hotter primers available.

The hull is moved from the deprimer, a new primer placed in the cup at the repriming station and the primer seated with a downstroke.

Then the first problem was encountered. Five high-brass Remington hulls had been included for reloading, since the manual stated we could load any hull. The problem was that these were old-style Remingtons that require the smaller 57 primer. I had none on hand and these primers no longer are made or sold, so the hulls were placed back into the discard sack and five others brought out. Do not try to load a 209 primer in the 57 hull, it just won't fit and if you try force, it could ignite. Believe me, you never want that!

After priming, I was ready for the Pyrodex load. The Hodgdon manual specifies weighed charges. Those who haven't worked with the older-style, black powder front-stuffers may not understand the need. In shooting black powder, we use a brass measure that is graduated in ten-gain increments, usually from about 50 to 120 grains. We set the rod on the proper weight mark, lock it in place, then pour that amount of black powder into the measure from a powder horn. We then transfer this weighed load to the shotgun and pour it down the barrel. The same is done with Pyrodex, since it is a volume-for-volume system with Pyrodex providing the same combustion power at that setting as would FFg black powder. Pyrodex takes up less space than black powder. It also has more boom to the grain than black powder, so pay attention to the load data or a real monster load could be created without you being aware.

The data calls for 72 grains of Pyrodex CTG, RS or Select. I use the RS-type powder. The others are different in granulation, but all work well, and that is the important part.

The manual also has a volume-to-volume comparison

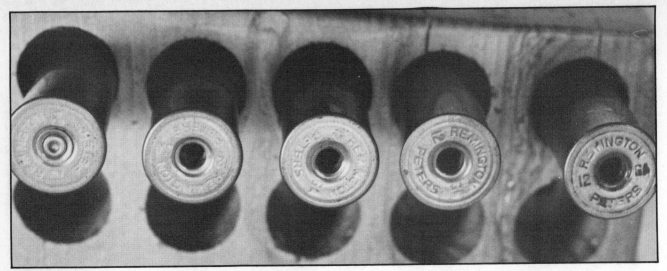

These Remington hulls need 57 primers. Since this size isn't made any more, they went back into storage.

The logo and plain, easily read markings on Hodgdon Pyrodex RS makes it easy to keep powder in order.

chart. According to this chart, one can pour about 75 grains of Pyrodex by setting a powder measure used for black powder at the 100-grain mark. If you don't have any of this black powder gear, you can substitute easily.

A Lyman LE 1000 electronic grain scale was used for getting the right load by weight. This Pyrodex load then was checked against the powder measure system of volume-for-volume by extending the marking rod to full load, pouring in the weighed charge and raising the rod until the Pyrodex was level with the top of the measure. This powder then was returned to the scale. The marked measure was checked and did indeed show 100 grains, as the manual had assured us it would. Even a five-grain difference is allowable in most black powder loading, since it isn't as powerful as smokeless powders. This might seem a sloppy procedure, but if you check with a black powder shop to ask how much grain variation is allowed for most charges, you might be surprised.

Since the mark on the measure gave us an equal volume of Pyrodex, we saved time by using the measure for loading this particular powder into the hull. This can be duplicated by a measure system such as that provided by the Lee dippers. These give you the needed volume and the correct weight. Pour the weighed load into the hull, and place it into the wad column station.

The data requires a card-plus-filler system, the style used for all shotgun reloading many years ago. When still used, it works quite well. The card chosen was a Circle Fly .125-inch nitro card. This is a hard card of .125-inch thickness that is compressed to make it tough, since it will receive all the power and burn on ignition from the primer. Similar cards can be purchased from BPI or Dixie Gun Works.

The next part of the formula is a filler, which is usually of a softer material. In this case, I used a compressed felt wad of three-eighths-inch thickness. These cards and filler materials are made to fit the gauge you are loading, so I used only 12-gauge components in this project.

After using the wad column seating station to insert the nitro and wad cushion over the powder with at least fifty pounds

A Federal 209 primer sits in the pocket of a MEC 600 reloader. It now is ready to be seated in shell.

This Activ hull has been reprimed and is ready for reloading with Pyrodex powder and #7-1/2 shot.

of pressure — the 600 has a pressure station on that section — you are ready for your shot.

If the 600 wasn't such a popular unit, I wouldn't have had the problem that came about. I didn't have the shot bushing for my machine. It had been loaned to a friend, since he didn't have a bushing of that size. Now, I learned, he was on vacation. Not a real problem, it really was just a nuisance.

Manufacturers of black powder gadgets also make a brass volume measure for shot that is graduated in 1⅛- and 1½-ounce measurements. One of these measures was set for the desired load of 1⅛ ounces of #7½ shot and used in shot loading.

I dipped the brass measure into a tub of shot, leveled it off, then poured it into the hull on top of the wad column. You can make a shot dipper from almost anything, since you have the grain scale with which to back up your load system until you determine the correct amount of shot.

A black powder measure makes it easy to maintain appropriate volume control. First, overfill the measure, tap the bottom five or more times to settle the powder, rotate the funnel around to level the powder off, then pour it into the primed hull.

The final 1/4-inch felt wad is placed on the nitro card and given at least 50 pounds of pressure on load bar.

A brass measure is dipped into a tub of shot, leveled off and is now ready for transfer to the primed hull.

To prove this, I took a plastic cigar tube and cut off a section about two inches long at the base. I dipped it full of shot and weighed it. It held far too much, so I cut, dipped and weighed until I arrived at the proper weight in ounces.

When you start to get close, another touch is to drop melted candle wax into the bottom of the tube to make the load right by volume as well as weight. The wax should adhere to the plastic, and you will have an instant dipper that measures 1⅛ ounces of any size shot.

After loading the shot, place the overshot card on top of the shot, put the hull in the crimp-start station of the press, and bring the handle down to start the fold crimp on the hull. Move the hull to the final crimp station and lower the handle. Upon raising it, you will have a completed Pyrodex-loaded shell with old-style wad components that probably will perform beyond your expectations.

Why not just use the powder measure on the MEC 600? Unless you have worked with the Pyrodex and black powder, you have a valid question. One never should place black powder or Pyrodex powder in a measuring system that can cut or abraid the granules. Black powder is highly unstable and can be ignited by friction, heat or just "cook-off" for no obvious reason, as they say. Pyrodex is much more stable and probably could be measured on the MEC 600, but it takes only a bit more time to use the brass measures, which are safe. It's better to take a bit more time and not blow up the shop.

Now that you have a Pyrodex load for your modern shotgun, how are you going to use it? Here are some ideas.

The first is to irritate your fellow gunners on a trap range.

The Pyrodex load will perform well enough, but you will have a pall of smoke issuing from your barrel. It won't smell as bad as black powder, but other shooters will wonder what is going on. It probably will play hell with their shooting rhythm, too.

The most obvious reason is "Because." That's right. Because you never have used it before. Because it will make a good working load that is cheaper even than smokeless powder per loading. Pyrodex has more expanded grains than smokeless or black powder. You might call it fluffier if you like, but it is lighter and gives more loads per pound. Because you want to enter the cowboy shooting competitions and have other competitors wonder what the hell you are doing! Never tell them; let them guess.

This cowboy shooting game is growing fast and participants often use black powder for their arms. Some will have no idea what you have stuffed into your double-gun, but others might guess, since these individuals are more into older loads and black powder than are serious shotgunners. You can shoot a black powder-loaded rifle, pistol and shotgun in modern replicas for each.

Check the rules and regulations before you enter an event. Pyrodex is safe, but some may object to the smoke.

What we have discussed here is a simple, straight-forward loading system, even though it may be different. In my opinion, the single-station unit is best for this type of loading, since one uses the pressure bar and not the powder and shot system. You could make these loads using hardwood dowels to seat the components, but let's not get carried away!

The final question: How do we identify these loads as

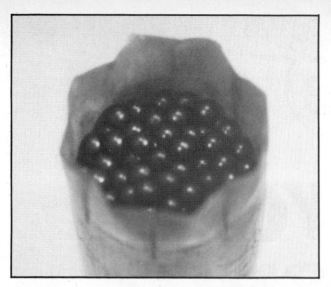

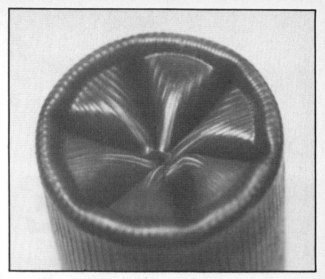

Shot is placed on top of the wad column. One-half-inch of hull is needed to achieve a good, solid crimp.

The final crimp is folded onto the loaded hull. The indent around the hull helps in chambering.

Pyrodex? You can mark them with nail polish on the brass cap. That works well, but if you use too many colors, confusion can set in regarding the many types of different shells. Colored markers are excellent for rolled-crimp shotshells, since the overshot card that holds the shot in the shell can be marked with indelible ink with any code system you choose to use.

The folded crimp worked well for these loads. However, the first three loads were a bit too full, and the crimp fold wasn't clean. I didn't change the nitro card, but a wad only one-quarter-inch-thick was substituted, and this resulted in all the remaining shells having good-looking, solid crimps. They looked just like any other shotshell.

If you work up other loads for the 1¼- and 1½-ounce shot loads, you will, of course, change the weighed amount of Pyrodex to match the data given in Hodgdon's manual.

The amazing part of this load is that all of them have such low pressures. The 1¼ gives 5800 lead units of pressures, and the 1½ gives 5900 LUP. Compare that to smokeless powder reloads!

Pyrodex reloads may not be for you, but before you settle into being totally negative, give them a try. The only difference between this and what your great-great grandfather used is in the breechloading shell. You have duplicated his propellant system with cleaner-burning Pyrodex powder.

When you finish shooting Pyrodex loads, be certain to really scrub your barrels and do a good cleaning job on all parts of your shotgun.

Have fun checking your hits through that small cloud of smoke you make with each boom. — *C.R. Learn*

The 25 various hulls have been loaded with Pyrodex.

CHAPTER 28

TAKE YOUR BEST SHOT

How To Build Custom Loads To Boost Your Sporting Clays Scores

This single Duck Pond station can offer slow-settling incomers, hard-crossers and quick-climbing outgoing targets. Savvy shooters who want to best all these offerings should choose at least two different loads for this one station.

SPORTING CLAYS has been called the most fun you legally can have with a shotgun. It also has been called one of the most challenging shotgun games to come down the pike. Both statements are quite true!

Unlike most shotgun games, sporting clays does offer an endless array of repetitive shots. In fact, it's quite possible to shoot a one hundred-bird round, and never see the same shot twice. There is good reason: that's exactly the way the game was intended to be played; and course managers are encouraged to offer diversified fare through the constant shifting of speeds, angles and flight paths. Some take a fiendish delight in doing just that.

What results is a shooting game that bears a strong resemblance to golf. And, just as there is no such thing as the "perfect" golf club, there really is no such thing as the perfect sporting clays shotgun — or load. A quick trip around a sporting clays course will show why that is true.

Sporting clays course managers display wide latitude in design of their courses. Existing terrain sometimes plays a large role in the types of shots offered or it may be dictated by local preference or tournament rules. Regardless of the exact course layout, you will likely experience some — or all — of the following stations:

Rabbit Run: This is a ground-bouncing target often using a thicker, tougher clay target to reduce breakage when it hits the ground. The target may "run" along the ground and frequently will bounce as high as six feet in the air. In some cases, the course designer may have created only a narrow opening where the gunner can break the target. Others may provide a larger window, but extend the range. The really devious ones often will include an aerial target in the scene, as well. The range may vary from fifteen to thirty-five yards, and at the longer distances, the tougher target takes a stout load to break it.

Woodock: This is usually a close — ten- to twenty-yard — extremely fast target that may be crossing, going away or coming at you. Most woodcock stations are set up to provide the shooter with only a brief glimpse of the birds as they streak through the woods. This is fast, close-range shooting.

Duck Tower: This is just the opposite! Generally it is a forty- to seventy-foot tower with up to five stations laid out around it. Shots usually are lengthy and either outgoing or crossing. A shot of twenty-five yards is considered close here, and some may stretch to sixty yards!

Dove: Another elevated tower shot, this one often resembles a high-house skeet target. Sometimes, shooting stations are laid out along the flight path of the target to produce crossing-type shots in varying degrees. You might break this target fifteen yards off the gun or at forty.

Grouse Bluff: Often referred to by less charitable names, it places the shooter on an elevated station with targets going away or crossing. Sometimes there may be several shooting stations, each presenting a different angle and distance. This can range from a twenty- to forty-five-yard shot.

Blue Bill Pass: This is similar to the duck tower in the length of the twenty-five- to sixty-yard shots. The difference is that the birds are flying fast and much lower and outgoing angled shots are quite common.

Tower shots can be at extreme ranges. Reloaders who develop an effective 50-yard load have an advantage.

Quail: The better stations do an excellent job of simulating the quick, rising flush of a quail. The really good ones make certain that "quail" has something to duck behind soon after the flush. It calls for quick shooting on outgoing targets at ten to twenty yards.

Pheasant Flush: This also is known by other names, but generally comes under the heading of springing birds:

199

Taking a bouncing, fast-moving rabbit is a challenge. A stout load is needed to break this tough clay target.

the angle of the thrower is turned skyward and the targets really climb. The ranges on this type of target may vary from twenty to sixty yards.

Rising Sharptail: This event often utilizes 60mm mini targets thrown away from the shooter at a gentle climb and high speed. Ranging at thirty-five to sixty-plus yards, the small targets often require tight chokes and dense patterns. Or you may find a devilish course manager has come up with a totally new wrinkle to test your gun, load and shooting skill. It also will test your mental powers. It should be obvious that, when dealing with such a wide array of shot possibilities, no one choke will handle them all.

Savvy shooters generally carry a selection of interchangeable choke tubes with them and frequently will change between stations. So popular has the game become that specialized choke tubes that can be changed quickly without a wrench now are available.

Unfortunately, while many shooters give a lot of thought to the choke they will use on the next station, not nearly as many consider changing their load, as well. That is a mistake that can cost targets!

The ideal load for a fifty-yard target could easily be the worst choice for a ten-yard target! The longer bird will require heavier shot to ensure a break, plus a dense pattern with a short shot string. That's a distinct handicap at close range, regardless of the choke used. That situation requires a fast opening pattern and shot size is unimportant — even the smallest commonly used size will break a ten-yard clay target.

Change that scenario to a thirty-yard target and either of those loads would be a poor choice.

"Reloaders have the option of creating perfect loads for virtually any shooting situation encountered on a sporting clays course," says Dave Fackler. "By doing so — components and load data are readily available — they are able to optimize the effectiveness of their equipment and probably see scores take a significant step upward."

Fackler certainly should know. As the force behind Ballistic Products, Inc. (20015 75th Avenue North, Corcoran, MN 55340), he has become one of the leading shotgun load designers in the country and holds patents on a number of innovative components.

Fackler's philosophy on sporting clays loads is simple:

Quick-burning and medium-speed powders are needed to achieve the type of loads critical for sporting clays.

Grouse Gulch gives the shooter the choice of a fast, 15-yard shot or waiting until the target reaches 30 yards. Having the right load can make the decision easier.

Shooters basically require three totally different loads for sporting clays — close, medium and long range. It even can be an advantage to expand that to "ultra-close" and "extra-long."

The reason for three separate loads is equally simple: Breaking targets at ten, thirty and sixty yards requires different load characteristics involving shot size, velocity and patterning. A shooter who assumes one load can do it all

Hodgdon's new powders promise the reloader superior performance for a wide variety of sporting clays loads.

will find scores suffering just as badly as the golfer who attempts to play eighteen holes with just one club.

Here is how Fackler makes certain he has a full bag of clubs everytime he steps on the course.

Short-range: Inside twenty yards, on an average sporting clays course, twenty to thirty percent of your shots will be at ranges between ten and twenty yards. Targets are scored as a simple hit or a miss. They are not graded on a scale of one to ten.

To score a "hit" you must knock only a visible piece off the target. Since a #9 pellet will do this at ranges under twenty-five yards, there is no reason to use anything else on short-range loads.

There are several reasons why #9s are your best choice. A one-ounce load of #9 pellets contains about 585 of them. In contrast, the heaviest load allowed generally is 1⅛ ounces of #7½ pellets, and there are only 394 of them. Since any of those #9 pellets can register a hit target, the increase in pellet count allows shooters to use lighter recoiling loads and produce an increased number of pellets in the pattern at close range. Since fifty to one hundred birds is a normal round of sporting clays, reducing recoil anywhere one can will pay dividends to the shooter on the later targets.

The increased number of pellets also allows the shooter to make use of a number of spreader-type wads to really open those patterns quickly!

On a fast-moving target at ten yards, the advantage of a twelve-inch pattern over one in the four-inch range should be obvious. You can make a lot of mistakes and still score a "hit."

In years past, making these special spreader loads required inserting a separate component (either a cardboard X-spreader or a PC-post) into a standard wad. One also can use a standard wad, cutting the petals back about three-

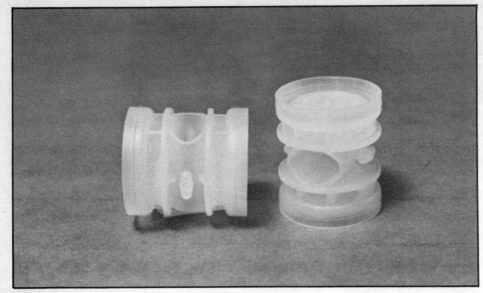

The G/BP 12-gauge Brush Wad is fast and easy to load. It achieves quick-opening patterns with plain lead shot.

quarters of their length to remove the protective shot cup. These components still are around, and still work. But, there are easier ways today.

The G/BP Dispersor X-12 wad is a one-piece, easy-to-load target wad with an intregal X-spreader moulded right into the shot cup.

As the wad leaves the muzzle, the petals fold back and release the shot in an incredibly quick-opening pattern.

Some ranges have restrictions against spreader-type wads. If yours does, then shifting to the G/BP 12-gauge Brush Wad will provide the same types of open patterns, in keeping with the rules. This is a standard one-piece wad without a shot cup — no different than taking a standard target wad and cutting away the shot cup.

Another option is the G/BP Piston Skeet wad. This produces patterns almost as open as the two previous wads, and can be a better bet at the fifteen- to twenty-five-yard range. It has no internal spreader device and thus beats the spreader ban, yet the unique petal arrangement creates quick-opening patterns. This European import is commonly used by top Olympic skeet shooters. All can be used with standard American components.

Here are a couple of Dave Fackler's favorite close-range spreader loads:

1. Federal Gold Medal Hull, G/BP Dispersor X-12 wad, Fiocchi 615 primer, 20.0 grains Scott Solo-1000 powder, 1 1/16 ounces of lead #9 shot. Pressure, 8000 LUP; velocity, 1180 fps. Comments: Extremely quick opening pattern; one of the best loads for under fifteen yards.

2. Federal Gold Medal Hull, G/BP Piston Skeet wad, Fiocchi 615 primer, 21.0 grains Scott Solo-1000 powder, 1 1/16 ounces of hard lead #8 or #9 shot. Pressure, 10,5000 LUP, velocity, 1280 fps. Comments: Extremely quick opening, high speed load for fifteen to twenty-five yards.

Using these specialized wads to create quick-opening loads gives the close-range shooter a tremendous advantage, since there are virtually no factory loads that will duplicate their performance.

Medium Range: At twenty to thirty-five yards, the largest proportion of shots on a sporting clays course will fall into this group. Longer shots require a heavier pellet to ensure a break. Once the target gets beyond twenty-five yards, a clean break with #9 shot becomes "iffy," while

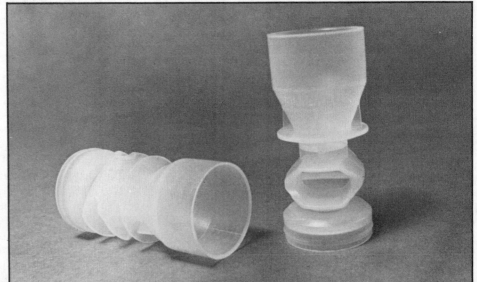

Dense, long-range patterns require special wads. This G/BP International Target Driver, originally built for Olympic shooters, will deliver good 50-yard-plus patterns with nickeled shot.

Mid-range loads can be created easily with standard target elements. From left are the G/BP Competition Special, the Federal 12SQ and the Federal 12S4 wads.

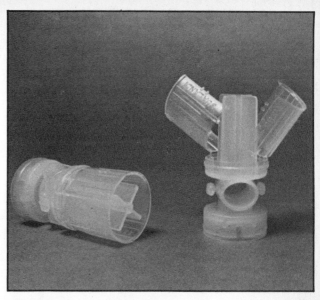

The G/BP Dispersor X-12 is a one-piece target wad that features a moulded X-spreader. This is quite effective.

#8s will perform well out to almost forty yards. For that reason, savvy shooters usually select hard #8 shot for mid-range loads.

Good mid-range reloads do not call for specialized components. All the loader really needs to do is duplicate any of the quality factory 3 dram trap loads like the Federal Gold Medal or Winchester AA. In fact, shooters opting for factory loads would find either an excellent choice.

One of Fackler's favorite loads for this range is: Fiocchi 2¾-inch 12-gauge hull, G/BP Piston Skeet wad, Fiocchi 616 primer, 20.0 grains Scott Solo-1000 powder, 1 1/16 ounces of hard #8 lead shot. Pressure, 7700 LUP; velocity, 1215 fps. Comments: An extremely good general purpose medium-range load with soft recoil. Excellent in the twenty-five- to thirty-five-yard range.

One advantage the reloader has here, however, is that he can create some extremely fast loads that are not available in factory shells. High velocity loads help reduce the lead required for tough crossing shots, providing yet another edge for savvy shooters. Here are two Fackler has developed, using two different imported European target wads.

1. Win AA 2¾-inch 12-gauge hull, G/BP mid-size Euro-target 19x16 wad, Fiocchi 616 primer, 25.0 grains Scott Solo-1250 powder, 1 1/16 ounces of hard lead #8 shot. Pressure, 8800 LUP; velocity, 1320 fps. Comments: Another good general purpose load, most effective in the thirty-five-yard range. Makes a good upland game load with #7½ shot.

2. Fiocchi 2¾-inch 12-gauge hull, G/BP Compact Euro-target 17x14 wad, Fiocchi 616 primer, 28.5 grains Scott Solo-1250 powder, 1⅛ ounces of hard lead #8 shot. Pressure, 10,200 LUP; velocity, 1400 fps. Comments: Dense, high-speed load for the toughest targets. Best range, thirty to forty yards.

The ability to tailor a load for a specific station will help any shooter to improve his scores at sporting clays.

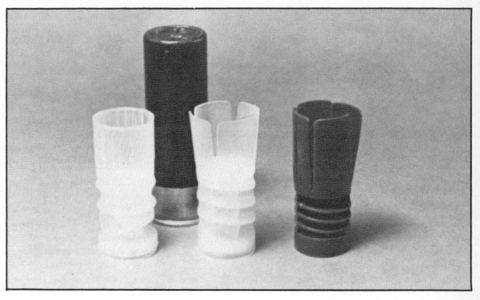

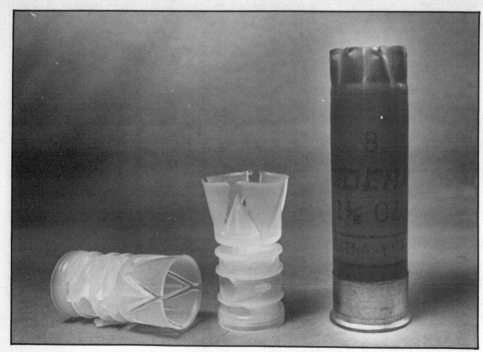

The G/BP Piston Skeet wad can open patterns almost as quickly as a spreader wad, yet is legal to use where spreaders have been banned.

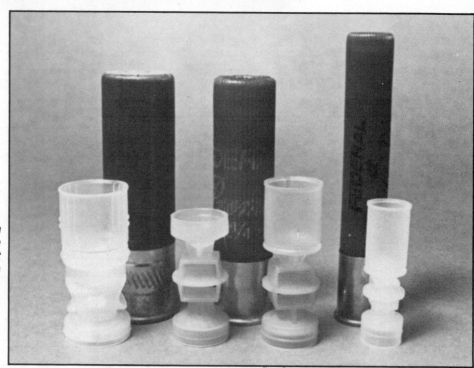

Ballistic Products offers a variety of smaller gauge reloading components that will boost the effectiveness of the shotgun sub gauges.

Long Range: At forty to sixty yards, fortunately, only about twenty percent of the shots on an average course will fall into this range. That's good news, because they are not easy!

Breaking targets beyond forty yards calls for the heaviest shot size allowable. In most cases that is #7½, although some ranges allow #7. That shot charge must hold a dense pattern, with a minimal shot string, and deliver every bit of energy the pellet possesses onto the target.

Nothing does that as well as nickel-plated shot! Some shooters balk at the expense, but consider that usually less than one box of these special long-range loads will be needed per round. When that is factored against the normal cost one will incur for travel and range fees, regardless of what shot you use, you still will expend powder, wads, primers and shot anyway. Not using the best shot for those few rounds becomes false economy in the truest sense of the word.

The harder grades of copper-plated shot can substitute, should nickel be unavailable. Black shot, even the best grades, is a distant third choice.

Holding patterns together at distant ranges calls for special wads, and Fackler suggests two. The first is the BP12, a sturdy shot cup that must be slit by the user. Developed

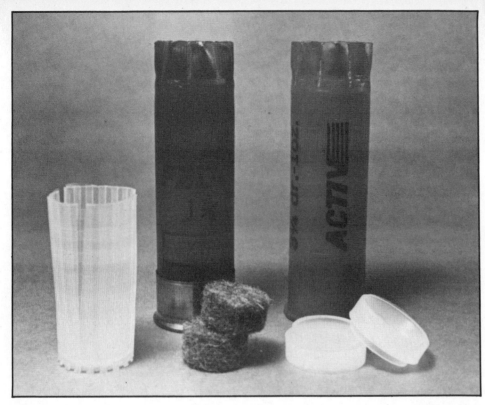

From left, the BP12 wad, felt wads and BPGS gas seals can be used to create light to long range loads.

originally as a long-range hunting wad, it is used in conjunction with the BPGS gas seal and felt wads. The wads are inserted into the base of the BP12 shot cup to raise the shot column height on the 1⅛-ounce charge to allow a proper crimp.

One of his favorite loads with that combo is assembled like this: Federal Gold Medal 12-gauge hull, one BPGS gas seal, a BP12 shot cup, two 20-gauge one-quarter-inch felt wads, Winchester 209 primer, 26.0 grains IMR PB powder, 1⅛ ounces of nickel-plated #7½ shot. Seat the BPGS over the powder, place both felt wads into BP12 and seat over BPGS. Pressure, 9500 psi; velocity, 1325 fps. Comments: Make sure BP12 is cut with four petals (instructions included with wads). It really reaches out and is a great long-range dove load.

Another wad Fackler favors is the G/BP International Target Driver, a special long-range, one-piece European wad commonly used by International trap shooters. Here are two loads for it:

1. Federal Gold Medal 12-gauge hull, G/BP International Target Driver wad, Fiocchi 616 primer, 27.0 grains Scott Solo-1250 powder, 1 1/16 ounces of plated shot. Pressure, 8300 LUP; velocity, 1300 fps. Comments: High speed load that performs well between forty-five and sixty yards.

2. Fiocchi 2¾-inch 12-gauge hull, International Target Driver wad, Fiocchi 616 primer, 26.0 grains Scott Solo-1250 powder, 1⅛ ounces of plated shot. Pressure, 6800 LUP; velocity, 1260 fps. Comments: Heavier shot charge with soft recoil, especially in warm weather. A good forty-five to sixty-yard load.

All of the components mentioned in the loads given here are available from Dave Fackler at Ballistic Products. So, too, is a far wider range of load data than space permits

Fast-burning powders are great for close range, but medium speed powders are best for long range loads.

here. Chances are there will be load data for your favorite hulls, powders and primers, using these specialized wads.

And there is certainly no reason not to use them. Once a shooter steps onto the station, analyzes the shot, then selects the appropriate load, when he pulls the trigger he will indeed be taking his best shot! — *Chris Christian*

THE HUNTER'S EDGE

These Advanced Reloading Tactics Give You A Big Advantage Afield

By reloading, shells can be tailored to hunting conditions, whether it be a hot dove field or a frigid duck blind.

Loading quality steel shot loads has been made much easier with the introduction of specialized Ballistic Products components made just for steel. Waterfowlers who reload will find they can better the performance of factory loads.

IF YOU are like many scattergunners who roll their own shells, you probably began with the intent of saving money. And that's a smart thing to do!

Factory shells are not inexpensive, and if you're feeding a pack of hungry skeet guns or even a single-barrel trap gun, it's not hard to run up an ammo bill that bears startling resemblance to the national debt.

By purchasing shot, powder, primers and wads in bulk, it is easy to shave forty to sixty percent off the cost of target loads, producing some highly effective loads in the process.

Some of those loads even manage to wind up in the field when "light loads" are needed, but when heavy, hard-hitting loads are required, many shooters simply opt for factory fodder under the assumption they won't be able to equal them at the loading bench.

According to Dave Fackler, that's not true. In fact, just the reverse is the case. At least, as long as the reloader is willing to take the time and utilize some of the more advanced reloading components and techniques.

"Factory loads are good," Fackler states, "but they may not be the best for a given time and place. The factories can't control how the shell is used, or under what conditions, so they must create an average load. Specialization is out, and the shooter is left with a load that will offer what is considered average performance.

"Reloaders," Fackler continues, "can create loads for the specific conditions under which they will be used, and thus be able to squeeze every bit of speed, power and lethality out of that shell under those specific conditions."

What types of hunting conditions might require such "designer" loads? "Extremely cold weather is one situation in which the hunter who builds special loads will improve his chances for success," Fackler says. "Cold weather robs power from powder, and average loads may not deliver enough lethality to take game cleanly."

Hot weather can be just as bad. Loads generally are pressure tested at a uniform seventy degrees. Yet, for each ten-degree rise in ambient temperature, that load can experience a 1000 LUP increase in pressure. A shooter using a load that tested at 10,000 LUPs in the lab may find the ninety-degree temperature common to a Florida dove field in October creates a really high pressure load! That's hard on the gun, the shooter and the patterns — not to mention chances of success.

"The hunter who understands advanced reloading techniques has the same advantage as does a rifleman," Fackler notes. "He can tailor his load to deliver all the performance characteristics he wants or needs under the exact conditions he will be using the load. That will give any hunter an advantage in the field."

Gaining a field advantage is something Fackler knows a

Spreader inserts or one-piece wads with integral spreaders create quick-opening patterns for close-flushing birds.

thing or two about. In fact, since 1975, he has been head honcho at Ballistics Products, Inc., (20015 75th Avenue North, Corcoran, MN 55340). Their innovative high performance shotshell reloading components are considered state of the art, and some of them are even used under license by major ammunition makers!

But if you think Fackler's brand of high-performance reloading is the same slap-dash-save-some-money approach used by many reloaders, think again.

"High performance loading for a shotgun is no different than loading match-grade ammo for a rifle," he explains. "You must use quality components to achieve a quality load, and you must be willing to test and evaluate those loads as part of the loading process. If you do that, you can create hunting loads that are far superior to factory fodder. If you're not willing to put forth that effort, then you might be better off using factory loads."

Here's how Fackler, and other savvy loaders, go about creating "designer" loads:

Hulls: It is common for target reloaders to squeeze as many loads as possible out of a hull, then take the beat-up hull and squeeze one more "field load" out of it. According to Fackler, this guarantees poor performing loads.

"The hull is the foundation of the entire load," he contends. "If it is old and weak, the load will be weak. Hulls must be in perfect shape, and it is best to start with once-fired hulls."

Fackler inspects his hulls carefully and will toss out any that do not have perfect mouths, or if the mouth is the least

bit brittle. A strong crimp is a must with slow- and medium-burning powders used in hunting loads in order to get a proper powder burn. Weak crimps make weak or "bloop" loads.

If the interior is pockmarked or scored by the heat of several firings, they, too, are discarded. Heavy loads of slow-burning powders score the hull interior far more than light loads of fast-burning target powders. A hull already showing signs of internal damage may burn through. Check the brass for cracks or loose fits.

The right series of hull also must be selected for the intended load.

Fackler has compiled years of high performance load data that he willingly shares. "We get requests all the time for heavy hunting loads using a certain type of hull, because the shooter has lots of them. Many times, I have to tell the shooter he can't make a high-performance load with that hull because of its characteristics."

One loading experiment should certainly point that out. In this test, the load was 1¼ ounces of buffered shot in a 2¾-inch hull, using the BPSG/BP12 wad-seal combination plus a one-quarter-inch wool felt 20-gauge wad, Winchester 209 primer and 27.0 grains of Dupont SR7625 powder. It then was loaded into the following hulls for pressure and velocity tests:

1. Federal Gold Medal Target hull; pressure, 8500 LUP/velocity, 1290 fps.

2. Fiocchi Hunting hull; pressure, 9000 LUP/velocity 1330 fps.

Reloading means a hunter has versatility, developing different loads for the hunt. Today, it is close-range quail for this hunter. The next day, the gun might see service on long-range ducks.

3. Winchester Poly, plastic disc internal base; pressure, 9000 LUP/velocity, 1330 fps. *Note:* This shell did not hold the load easily. Packed full, a good crimp was hard to obtain, and on some loaders, the hull would crush on crimping.

4. Winchester AA Target hull; pressure, 10,800 LUP/velocity, 1240 fps.

5. Remington Unibody hull; pressure, 15,000 LUP/velocity 1385 fps.

It is obvious this load is a good one in the Federal and Fiocchi hulls, mediocre in the two Winchester hulls and possibly dangerous in the Remington Unibody!

Once hulls are selected, Fackler takes the extra step of treating each one with silicone Super Slick. This is painted into the interior of the hull where it forms a glass-like surface and fills any pores. This prevents further scoring of the hull and, more importantly, improves the load.

"The silicone treatment generally increases the velocity of the load by ten to fifteen percent," Fackler says, "and it greatly increases the speed and pressure consistency of the load by providing a smoother, more consistent release of the internal components on firing. Every hull used for heavy loads — except paper hulls — should be siliconed."

Fackler also paints the outside of the hull near the mouth to prevent that from becoming crisp after a few firings.

Powders: Different powders have quite different burn rates and characteristics. Generally, they can be described as fast-burning (700X, Red Dot, et cetera) mid-range (PB, Unique, SR7625, et cetera) and slow-burning (HS-7, Blue Dot, SR4756, 800X).

"Fast-burning powders," Fackler notes, "are intended for light loads of small shot at modest velocities — target loads. They can make effective light field loads, but are not suited for high-performance heavy loads."

Mid-range and slow-burn powders are best for the field and which one to use can depend largely on the temperature at the time.

"Slow-burn powders can deliver the highest velocity

The special BP12 wad is intended to be slit by the user prior to loading. The number of petals created can alter the way the load patterns, giving the hunter another way to tune loads.

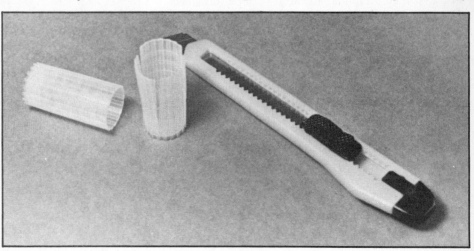

This 45-yard pattern of #5 shot is easy to create with the BP12-BPGS wad combination. It is just the right load a hunter needs to handle wild flushing pheasants.

"it's just that they are intended for light-pressure loads with light charges of small shot. In heavier loads, the petals are too thin and the structures too weak. You just beat the tar out of them and the shot charge, as well."

To counteract this, Ballistic Products has developed a "family" of tough, one-piece shot cups combined with a separate gas seal. Made in varying thicknesses, the wads allow the shooter to create lead and steel shot loads, choosing the appropriate wad. When seated over the BPGS gas seal, they have proved to be the most successful hunting wad available.

"The wads," Fackler explains, "are provided as one-piece, solid shotcups, but they are not intended to be used that way. The reloader must slit the cups to produce petals that will open the cup when it leaves the barrel. How many slits the wad requires is something the shooter will have to experiment with on his own."

The reason Ballistic Products doesn't slit the wads for the reloader is simple. "Every shotgun barrel is its own musical instrument. Two different barrels coming off the

Special, tough, one-piece hunting wad shot cups can produce dense patterns with larger shot sizes. Turkey hunters can really benefit from this special component.

and energy," states Fackler, "but they also can be the most difficult to ignite and burn properly in cold weather. If these powders are used in temperatures below the thirty to fifty-degree range, they may not burn properly, unless loaded into magnum shells with heavier shot charges. Performance can suffer.

"Under cold conditions, the advanced reloader can create special loads using mid-rate powders and smaller charges of larger shot to regain performance the cold robs from him."

Hot weather creates the opposite problem — too much burn and an elevation of pressures. Here, powder selection becomes less important, but the amount does. If you know you will be hunting in eighty-five to ninety-five-degree weather, powder charges should be reduced slightly — five percent or 2 grains, whichever is greater — and load pressures kept in the 8000 to 9000 LUP range.

Primers: The primer is critical in shell performance, and since each brand has a slightly different ignition/power level which may interact more effectively with various powders, it always is wise to use the primer recommended in the given load recipe.

That said, savvy loaders can switch primers in response to extremes of heat and cold to improve their loads. When cold weather inhibits powder burn, a load listed as using a mild primer (such as the Winchester 209) can be improved by shifting to a hotter primer, like the CCI 209M or the Federal 209. In hot weather, a hot primer can be replaced by a mild one to reduce pressures; just another way the reloader can fine tune for conditions.

Wads: High performance hunting loads require wads tough enough to stand up to the pressure and get the shot charge out of the barrel undamaged. One-piece, crushable target-type wads will not do that.

"It is not that they aren't any good," explains Fackler,

same assembly line may shoot quite differently. The use of our Driver wads allows each reloader to determine what type of slitting works best for the intended purposes. Different slitting configurations — two opposing slits versus three, for example — can produce different patterns from the same barrel and choke combination, and with different size shot.

"By allowing the reloader the means to experiment, we provide him with the greatest degree of pattern control. This is why high-performance hunting reloads will outperform factory loads," Fackler insists.

With one basic wad, reloaders can produce ultra-tight long-range patterns, or quick-opening, heavy-cover patterns. And there are even more fine-tuning aids available.

Ballistic Products offers several types of spreader inserts that increase quick-opening patterns. Felt wads in varying thicknesses also are available to allow the reloader to adjust the height of the shot column for a perfect crimp, or take up excess room in the shell when ultra-high velocity/reduced-shot charge loads are required.

For example, when felt wads — which weigh little and do not change the pressures or patterning of a load — are used, it is possible to make a 12-gauge, three-inch magnum deliver a 1¼-ounce shot charge at velocities approaching 1500 fps! This is with no more recoil than a standard 1¼-ounce, 3¾ dram, 2¾-inch 12-gauge load. As a long-range cornfield pheasant load, the possibilities are intriguing to say the least.

Such data is readily available from Ballistic Products, as are the required tools to trim and slit the wads. Using them is easy. The BPSG gas seal is inserted as an overpowder wad, followed by the custom-slit Driver wad, then whatever spreaders or felt wads are required to complete the load.

One additional high-tech trick Fackler uses is to coat the wads with Motor Mica dust, adding a teaspoon full to a bag of wads and shaking it up. That aids in a smooth, consistent release of components from the interior of the hull.

Shot: The last item Fackler considers is the actual payload. And, what comes out of the barrel is no better than what you put into the shell.

"Hard shot delivers the best and most consistent patterns," he says. "That is why I prefer nickel shot for any long range loads. It's expensive, but if you want maximum performance it is worth it."

Copper-plated shot also can be an effective choice, but industry standards for hardness are not what they should be. Some plated shot occasionally is offered that is no harder than soft, chilled lead shot. The buyer should test the shot.

If quick-opening, short-range patterns are desired, there is nothing wrong with plain lead shot, especially the harder brands like Lawrence magnum shot.

Adding buffer to shot charges often is desirable. "Buffer is a pattern tightening tool for longer ranges," Fackler claims. "Its purpose is to accommodate the individual spaces between the pellets and cushion them from each other and help prevent deformation of the shot.

"Nickel and good, hard, copper-plated shot do not require as much buffering, because they do not migrate around as much as lead. Steel shot and lead should be buffered in any size larger than #7½. If quick-opening loads are required,

Advanced reloading tricks, like buffered shot charges, ultra-hard nickel shot and tough shot cups, can create the type of dense patterning loads turkey hunters need.

buffering isn't needed."

Fackler recommends his Mix #47, a combination of ground plastics, and loads it by using a dipper to pour the buffer over the shot charge, then agitating the shell in the loading die with a small, hand-held vibrator. How much buffer to dip depends on the load and shot size, but the finished product should see the buffer level with the top of the shot column. A Tivex or thin paper overshot wad then is installed before the crimp in order to keep the buffer in place.

Loading high-performance shells may seem to require a lot of time and effort, and it does, but just as some riflemen will not be satisfied with a 1.5-inch group when they know that careful loading techniques may cut it to a .5-incher, there will be hunters who would consider this time well spent to gain performance in the field.

There is no doubt these advanced reloading tactics, combined with Ballistic Products' state-of-the-art components and wealth of load data, will give any hunter a big advantage there. — *Chris Christian*

CHAPTER 30

NEW SHOT FOR THE "GOOD, OLD DAYS"?

Bismuth Is Non-Toxic And Approximates The Performance Of Lead In Your Favorite Shotgun!

Bismuth's performance compares to lead shot. However, it may be years before waterfowlers can enjoy it afield.

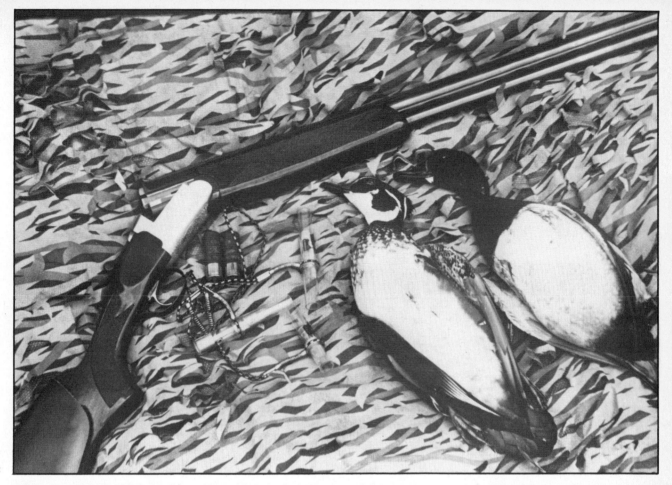

The much-debated requirement to use steel shot has forced many hunters to change the way they pursue ducks. Bismuth's development may bring back the "good, old days" when hunters relied on dependable lead shot.

"FOR FAST relief, take Pepto-Bismol." At least, that's what the TV commercial says. Never having used the product, I couldn't really comment on the truthfulness of that claim. I have, however, used one of the key active ingredients in that stomach relief preparation, and it would seem to provide a major measure of relief. However, that relief certainly is not as the pharmaceutical makers intended.

Bismuth, the active ingredient in the stomach soother, is an elemental metal that lies between lead and polonium on the periodic table. It is a crystalline substance that can be quite brittle and, in fact, is much like antimony. Obviously, it is a non-toxic substance, since it has long enjoyed Federal Drug Administration approval for medicinal purposes.

That's good news for those suffering from an upset stomach, and it may be especially beneficial if that upset stomach is brought on by the thought of having to shoot steel shot in your favorite smoothbore.

Bismuth, it would seem at the moment, may be the best possible choice for non-toxic shot pellets. In fact, in side-by-side field tests involving numerous species of ducks, doves, pheasants, and even turkeys, expert scattergunners were not able to determine any difference in performance between shotshells loaded with bismuth pellets and those loaded with lead!

The exception, of course, is that bismuth is non-toxic enough to be sold in an over-the-counter medicine, while lead — a proven toxin — is under fire currently from environmental groups across the country, and the move to ban lead from the environment is continuing to grow.

The importance of that last statement should not be overlooked. Those who would ban hunting, then guns, are quick to grasp at any straw that will lend crediblity to their ultimate goal.

Waterfowlers saw it first when a controversial study indicated that ducks were dying from ingesting lead pellets deposited in feeding areas as a result of hunting. Lead shot subsequently was banned for most waterfowl hunting across the country, and the anti-hunters got exactly what they wanted — major turmoil in the firearms industry, as gun and ammo makers tried to make non-toxic steel do a job for which it never was suited.

With one "victory" firmly in their grasp, the next step for the antis was to assault lead across the board. In fact, they've even gone so far as to demand that lead fishing sinkers be outlawed!

The possibility of their winning is real, and there may well come a time when lead is banned from many traditional uses. Already, a number of fine old gun clubs have had to curtail their operations or close down entirely, and

Hunters gunning wide open waters will appreciate bismuth shot. It offers ballistic performance far exceeding that of steel. In a side-by-side test with lead shot, hunters using bismuth could not tell the difference in its performance.

each year sees additional areas require the use of non-toxic shot for any form of wingshooting.

Since steel is the only currently approved non-toxic shot — and since it is virtually useless in any gauge smaller than 12-bore — this has caused many gunners to hang up some of their favorite smoothbores or give up the sport entirely.

That tickled the antis to death, because that's exactly what they have wanted all along. And that's why they probably are not going to be happy about bismuth.

Bismuth has the real potential to completely remove the only legitimate argument anti-gunners can muster against wingshooters — toxicity of the shot. Yet, when loaded and fired in shotshells, bismuth's ballistic performance is so close to lead that the vast majority of shooters won't know the difference, unless they are told.

Here's why that is so. In it's elemental state, bismuth (Bi) is eighty-six percent as dense as lead. Iron, the principle component of steel shot, is only sixty-eight percent the density of lead.

Steel shot is difficult to manufacture while bismuth is no more complex than lead. Its melting temperature is lower than that of lead (271C as compared to 327C), which means it will form easily in shot towers or Bleimeister operations into nice, round, little pellets.

While bismuth's elemental state is only eighty-six percent the density of lead, the finished product (ninety-seven percent Bi, three percent tin) becomes ninety-one percent as dense as the shot in common use, which has antimony added to it.

In terms of hardness, bismuth measures about eighteen on the Brinnell hardness scale, while lead shot (with a three percent antimony content) measures about ten. On the same scale, pure copper will measure about forty, and steel shot is so hard it cannot be measured on that scale. The actual hardness of bismuth shot is about the same as wheel-weight metal used to cast bullets.

That degree of hardness becomes a performance plus, because as any scattergunner knows — or should know — the harder the shot, with all other factors being equal, the better the load will pattern, because fewer pellets will be deformed upon firing. The three percent antimony lead shot measuring ten on the scale would be considered "soft" lead shot.

In terms of real world performance, bismuth's hardness rating compares well to the best premium hard-lead plated shot available. It's hard enough to resist deformation under normal firing, but not nearly as hard as steel and, therefore, will not damage even the finest old double-gun.

James Purdey & Sons, whose exquisite doubles can cost more than your average house, have determined that bismuth shot is perfectly safe in their guns and have given it their seal of approval!

What that means is that we now have a non-toxic shot that can safely equal lead shot performance in .410s, 28 gauges and 20 gauges, not to mention the big bores.

In the internal ballistics department, bismuth shot seems to perform almost identically to lead, and the same loading components are readily interchangeable. In contrast, steel shot requires special hulls, wads, primers, powders and buffers just to make safe and reliable ammunition.

Given the properties of bismuth, it certainly would seem logical that perhaps it should perform as well as lead. Early

Bismuth is already a legal non-toxic steel shot substitute in a number of other countries. Will our government reject its use in the United States? While there will be a delay, author believes it will be approved for waterfowl hunting.

tests conducted with bismuth pellets reloaded into conventional lead shot recipes did bear that out.

In one test, a researcher created two loads from identical components, using #5 lead shot for one, #5 bismuth for the other. Their velocity was about 1200 feet per second, with the bismuth shotshell having a twenty feet per second advantage. For comparison against steel shot, factory steel shells with the same size #5 shot were used. Their velocities averaged 1320 fps.

The test medium was wet phone books, and whether that does or does not duplicate animal tissue is a moot point. These penetration tests were intended only to compare one shot material against another.

After the rounds were fired, average penetration depth of each was computed by the number of pages penetrated by approximately fifty percent of the pellets in each charge. Since the point was to compare the penetrating abilities of bismuth and steel shot against lead, the depth of penetration of the lead shot was assigned a value of one hundred percent and the degree of penetration of the other two factored in in terms of how well they penetrated as compared to lead.

Penetration of the bismuth shot was 90.5 percent that of lead, while the steel pellets achieved only 67.2 percent. Those figures virtually mirror the differences in comparative densities between the three shot materials!

Shooting phone books, of course, only tells one how well the projectile will do on phone books. The same researcher continued the tests.

Loading #5 bismuth shot into a hefty 2½-ounce 10-gauge magnum load, the researcher dispatched a turkey gobbler at about fifty yards. The head and neck of the bird, according to the researcher, caught eleven of the pellets. The thinner parts of the neck vertebrae were completely penetrated. One pellet struck a heavy juncture of two bones and imbedded itself one-quarter-inch deep in the bone!

That's excellent penetration at that range and should show that, while bismuth may be a brittle material in its elemental state, it's not *that* brittle. The imbedded pellet still was completely intact with no evidence of shattering.

Subsequent tests in Argentina, where shooters mixed bismuth and lead shot throughout a four-day shoot, showed little difference in the performance of the two on a wide variety of gamebirds.

Although I did not participate personally in any of the described tests, I would not challenge the veracity of the individuals conducting them. I believe their results.

As mentioned, the previous testing was done using reloaded bismuth shot. Factory-loaded rounds were not available in any real quantity. That has changed, however.

At the 1993 SHOT Show, the Bismuth Cartridge Company, (3500 Maple Avenue, Suite 1650, Dallas, TX 75219) unveiled a line of factory bismuth-loaded fodder.

Initially available in 12-gauge only, with smaller gauges to follow, there are four 2¾-inch loads currently available: two long-range magnum loads featuring 1¼ ounces of shot in sizes #5 or #6 and two Premium Upland Game loads carrying 1 1/16 ounces of either #7½ or #8 shot. The former loads are 3¾ dram equivalents with an advertised velocity of 1330 fps, while the latter are 3 dram/1220 fps loads.

Author believes bismuth is the logical evolution of the shotgun projectile. It is environmentally safe, yet offers field performance rivalling proven lead loads.

With the elimination of lead for hunting, a significant effort has been made by major manufacturers to develop a shotgun load that would perform like lead.

If the shot charges sound light, remember that bismuth is lighter than lead and there are approximately fifteen percent more pellets in an ounce of bismuth than an ounce of lead. Bismuth Cartridge Company loads their shells by weight, meaning that the 1¼-ounce load is equivalent to a 1⅜-ounce load, and the 1 1/16 version equals a 1¼-ounce lead shot charge.

This publication was able to obtain a box of each for testing. Unfortunately, feathered game seasons had passed for the year, limiting the testing to paper targets. Results of those tests, however, were quite encouraging.

Given the limited number of rounds available, only a few were expended to duplicate previous penetration tests in wet phone books. The results of those mirrored earlier tests by other researchers. Bismuth shot penetrated about ninety percent that of lead shot, while penetrating about twenty-six percent farther than steel shot pellets in the same size.

Chronograph tests using my Oehler 35P and a 30-inch-barreled Ruger Red Label Sporting Clays over/under showed velocities close to those advertised. The two 3 dram loads averaged 1210 fps (ten fps below manufacturer-claimed velocity) while the 3¾ dram loads cranked out 1309 fps, falling twenty-one feet per second below their advertised velocity of 1330.

For comparative patterning tests, I choose to rely exclusively on the Red Label, because during the previous six months I had fired, measured and recorded over five hundred test patterns that covered a wide range of currently available 12-gauge factory loads, and had built a large data base as to what that gun and interchangeable choke tube system would do.

Grouping shotshells by type, collected data showed the Red Label would perform as follows:

Top-quality, hard-shot target loads, like the Winchester AA Trap Load and the Federal Gold Medal line, would deliver forty-yard patterns averaging eighty-two percent full choke, seventy-one percent modified, sixty-two percent improved cylinder and forty-nine percent skeet choke. They were the tightest patterning shells in that gun and patterns tended to be distributed uniformly.

The next best fodder was the premium buffered, copper-plated 3¼-dram field loads like the Federal Premium line. They almost equaled the target loads, patterning about three percent points lower across the board. The same Premium loads in the 3¾ dram version patterned about six percent below the target loads, as did most brands of pigeon loads tested. Most of the buffered loads tested showed a tendency to stack up a large proportion of pellets in the pattern center and were not as uniformly distributed as the target loads.

Due to their softer, unprotected shot, the less expensive black shot loads in the 3¼ and 3¾ dram sizes would average right around industry standard choke percentages: seventy percent, full; sixty percent, modified; fifty percent, improved cylinder; and forty-three percent, skeet.

One-ounce promotional loads (often referred to as dove and quail loads) were, as usual, the worst performers.

216

This full-choke pattern at 40 yards with a bismuth 1 1/16-ounce, #7 1/2 field load shows a dove-downing, evenly distributed pattern.

Bismuth acts so much like lead that components are interchangeable. Below, a dissected bismuth round reveals the use of standard Gualandi one-piece wad.

They came in at around five percent less than the black shot loads and those patterns often were patchy and full of holes.

It is important to understand the pattern figures listed above when evaluating performance of the bismuth shot, because even though the Red Label Sporting Clays gun has all the "high-performance tricks" — lengthened forcing cones, back-bored barrels and long choke tubes — shot hardness still plays a major role in its ability to deliver effective patterns.

Patterning the bismuth loads showed them to be quite effective. The 3 dram loads in sizes 7½ and 8 delivered pattern percentages equalling the 3¾ dram buffered, copper-plated loads: sevety-five percent, full choke; sixty-four percent, modified; fifty-five percent, improved cylinder; and forty-two percent, skeet. While the percentages were virtually identical with the Premium 3¾ dram loads, patterns were much more uniform without any tendency toward excessive center density. In terms of uniform distribution, they rivaled the best target loads!

The 3¾ dram #6 and #5 loads were even better. They delivered seventy-eight percent, full choke; sixty-nine percent, modified; fifty-eight percent, improved cylinder; and forty-six percent, skeet. The patterns were distributed uniformly with only the slightest indication of center stacking. They were some of the prettiest patterns I have ever achieved with a hunting load!

There is not a doubt in my mind that these shells can deliver real field performance that will approximate that of the best copper-plated, buffered hunting loads available today.

That's the good news. The bad news is that this type of ammo has not been approved yet for use on waterfowl in the United States. It has been certified for use as a non-toxic steel shot substitute in Europe, England, Canada and Australia, but our bureaucrats have established a complex and costly — about three years and $750,000 — testing requirement for any non-toxic shot, with the exception of steel shot.

There is some hope that the U.S. Fish & Wildlife Service might cut some slack in that area. Scientific testing by Dr. Glen C. Sanderson of the Illinois Natural History Survey already has found bismuth non-toxic to ducks, and the FDA has ruled it non-toxic to people. Given its acceptance by other countries, I think it would be somewhat difficult for the U.S. to ignore or reject the new shot.

As for cost, raw bismuth is considerably more expensive than lead. Some also have questioned its availability. Much of the world's supply, it seems, is in countries that could be considered politically unstable. Still, good old Yankee dollars and an export market do tend to have a stabilizing effect.

Because of that, I would expect to see bismuth shotshells ultimately priced equivalent to the premium grades of plated, buffered lead shells. I don't consider that unfair, because they seem to deliver about the same level of performance. At present, bismuth shotshells are priced at $19.50 per box. Increased demand may bring that price down somewhat.

With any luck, the new shot may be approved by the 1993/1994 waterfowl season. Bismuth shot presently is legal for use on all species but waterfowl. At the worst, it should be legal by the following year.

I can't wait for the "good old days" to return. — *Rod Hunter*

CHAPTER

31

AMERICA'S SHOTGUN: THE UPLANDER

Hatfield Gun Works' checkering is 20 lines per inch to produce the maximum practical grip on the stock.

This Hatfield Side-By-Side Is The Real McCoy!

AMERICAN WING SHOOTERS never have been accused of disguising their love for finely crafted fowling pieces. For most such connoisseurs of quality firearms, ownership often means purchasing such pieces that were crafted in England, Spain, Italy or some other scattergun-making Mecca. The few American-made fowling pieces that have achieved lofty status in the past now are closely guarded treasures.

Bearing this in mind, it is something of a grand mystery how the exquisitely crafted shotguns made by Hatfield Gun Works of St. Joseph, Missouri, have remained largely unknown to most knowledgeable shotgunners. In fact, Hatfield's Uplander shotguns have been a well-kept secret of such magnitude as to rank second only to the legendary covert operation: the nuclear-developing Manhattan Project of the early 1940s!

Since 1985, when Ted Hatfield and his company first branched out their muzzleloader rifle manufacturing business to include shotguns, they have produced what many of those familiar with their work consider America's finest side-by-side 20-gauge shotgun, the Uplander.

After shooting one of these bantamweight doubles, one can only ask, "Where did such a piece of workmanship come from, and why is this the first time I have heard about it?"

The Uplander 20- and 28-gauge shotguns from Hatfield Gun Works come in premier grade (top) and field grade.

That is a fair question according to company president Ted Hatfield. He is the first to admit that over the course of the last decade, Hatfield Gun Works has focused virtually all of its resources, time and capital on creating the Uplander as opposed to expanding the budding company's abilities to make the availability of this side-by-side shotgun known to the shooting world.

Located in the one-time frontier town of St. Joseph, Hatfield Gun Works is known nationally for manufacturing high-quality frontloader, Missouri-style (or Kentucky-type) rifles. Available in .32, .45 and .50 caliber bores, each of these graceful smokepoles features a full stock made of extremely durable, select number five grade "curly" maple. Widely regarded as one of the finest ready-to-shoot, primitive-style firearms marketed in recent years, Hatfield's long rifles feature browned barrels and are available with percussion cap ignition, as well as the more traditional, flintlock system.

Except for the company's insistence on using the rock-hard maple for all stocking, Hatfield's slender, slim-lined 20-gauge Uplander double bears no similarities to the muzzleloader rifles. The Uplander side-by-side is a lightweight work of art. Doubles with lines of this caliber rarely have been produced in this country by anyone, other than a handful of famed — and expensive — low-production cus-tom fowling pieces.

Tipping the scale at a mere 5¾ pounds, it is a full pound under the weight of any domestically produced shotgun even remotely comparable to the Hatfield Upland, although it is slighty heavier than the lightest English-made doubles. The Upland features a seductively trim English-style stock and a durable break-top boxlock frame of the type that has long been preferred by American shotgunners.

Producing these strikingly beautiful frontloader firearms came about almost as a lark, says Ted Hatfield, a direct descendent of the famous Hatfields of West Virginia, who along with the McCoys, engaged in our country's most remembered family feud.

"I grew up in a family that peddled and dealt in firearms as well as a little gunsmithing throughout the state of Missouri. However, except for a handful of long rifle muzzleloaders we know were made by my great-great-grandfather sometime between the mid-1840s and the late 1850s, I can lay no claim to gunmaking lineage.

"Ironically, though, my great-great-grandfather's gunmaking did have an influence on me. One of his muzzleloader rifles — an heirloom squirrel gun stocked in curly maple — was passed on to me. This 150-year-old rifle served as an inspiration for my current rifle making. It also was used as the design for the frontloader shooting pieces

Left, unlike other shotgun makers in the U.S., Hatfield selects curly maple as its standard stocking material. Below, nearly all of the gun's engraving is done before the gun undergoes the case-hardening process.

the company now produces," says Hatfield.

Luckily for Hatfield, when starting his venture, he had ready access to the knowledge of several gunsmiths who lived in Missouri. Most notable among them was John Crow, the renowned gunsmith who held many patents, including the Crow Safety found on the old Winchester Model 12. Another talented member of his team was John Thornton. This self-taught gunsmith once created a match-quality frontloader rifle by milling out a barrel from a discarded axle from a Model A Ford!

During the company's early years, Hatfield Gun Works was literally a "shade tree operation." All of the key gun-making machinery was stored under a tarpaulin that was stretched beneath a grove of trees in Norbourne, Missouri. Later, Hatfield moved to an old store in St. Joseph, then to a metal building. Finally the Hatfield Gun Works found its current location in a new building in that city.

During the last decade, the growing muzzleloader market was eager to obtain Hatfield's finely crafted frontloaders which, according to some, have no equal among mass-produced domestic or imported rifles. From its start with five panagraph machines that were operated under the trees only on sunny days, the company soon found itself involved in investment or "lost wax" casting. During the start-up years, the company — known then as Hatfield Rifle Works — produced a grand total of twenty-five guns. Some years later, when the first shotguns were manufactured, the firm was using computers and state-of-the-art technology to produce 2500 muzzleloader rifles per year.

A lifelong wingshooter and collector of finely made side-by-side shotguns, Ted Hatfield had long harbored a desire to try his hand at crafting such a shotgun that might meet his own expectations and exacting requirements. Growing up shooting only side-by-sides, Hatfield developed a definite prejudice for these scatterguns at a young age, but confesses this came about with a little help.

"When I was still a youthful shooter, my grandfather explained to me that a shotgun has two barrels that are arranged side-by-side," says Hatfield. "When I queried him about semi-autos, he informed me these were really 'machine guns' unfit for use by true sportsmen. I then asked him about those scatterguns that have dual, stacked barrels — over/unders. He said when I was old enough to

understand that type of sordid arrangement, he would gladly explain all of the details to me."

Prior to designing the Uplander, Ted Hatfield owned Purdy, Holland & Holland, L.C. Smith and Parker shotguns. One of his hobbies was working on these guns, a craft he eventually mastered to a high degree. While sawing stock blanks for rifles, Hatfield discovered an especially

The engraving on the Uplanders is superb, most of it done by artists at the Hatfield manufacturing plant in Missouri.

nice piece of leftover maple that was too short for use on a rifle. He decided to use it for restocking his favorite L.C. Smith shotgun. Despite the fact that his five-man production team was back-ordered for over five hundred front-loaders, he soon was obsessed with his new project.

The result was a stock comparable to nothing any U.S. wingshooter had ever seen. This, in turn, led to the inevitable decision for Ted Hatfield to attempt to manufacture classic side-by-side shotguns at his facility in Missouri. American gunmakers long have catered to the mass market rather than the wants of more discriminating shooters and gun owners. Probably the biggest reason low production-run shotguns are so rare in this country is the fact the big-time gunmakers find it unprofitable to fill small orders. Over the years, they have steadfastly refused to accommodate this segment of the market.

After settling on the notion that he would attempt to provide quality double shotguns to this slice of the shooting market, Ted Hatfield opted to use trouble-free, break-top Anson and Deeley-style boxlocks that were pioneered in England almost one hundred years ago. Using this double-locking mechanism and an underlug system developed by Holland & Holland, this style of boxlock was chosen over the sidelock mechanism found on most English-made side-by-side shotguns. Boxlock frames are more durable and trouble free in regard to how sidelocks fit to the stock, a tidbit that is important to Americans who shoot more and use heavier loads than do European shotgunners.

Decades ago during the heyday of Winchester's Model

21, John Olin is said to have conducted a test wherein he had thousands after thousands of rounds shot through his Model 21, as well as Purdy and Holland & Holland shotguns. The Winchester Model 21 has a boxlock mechanism, while the foreign-made shotguns used in the tests had sidelock frames. At the end of Olin's experiment, only the boxlock of the Model 21 showed no signs of structural failure.

The boxlocks used in the construction of the Uplander are produced at Hatfield's Missouri operation using the old lost-wax casting method. One of the first things Ted Hatfield discovered when looking into making the Uplander was that much of the manufacturing process could be done in Missouri, but no U.S. Company would supply him with the quality of barrels he sought. Stevens, one of the last producers of side-by-side shotgun barrels in this coun-

Hatfield's still soft white boxlocks are sent to Italy for fitting with 20- and 28-gauge barrels. The barrel lugs are wedge-cut so they actually fit tighter as wear occurs. Being made specifically for upland bird shooting, this side-by-side is designed to enhance the shooter's ability to down flushing birds such as bobwhite quail, ringneck pheasant or ruffed grouse.

The right barrel — the first to fire — features an improved cylinder choke. The second-shooting, left barrel has a modified choke. Barrels of the Uplanders are regulated — or aligned — to provide a forty/sixty pattern. That is, sixty percent of the shot pattern occurs above the barrel while

Notably easy to handle in the field, Hatfield's 20-gauge Uplander was given a thorough workout by author.

the remaining forty percent of the pattern hits beneath an imaginary line extending from the center of the barrel.

Only after their return to the Show-Me State are the completed boxlock frames and barrels designated for engraving and case-hardening that separates these shotguns from the rest of the field. However, this is preceded by the stocking process. As pleasing as is the performance of the barrels of the Uplander, the stock is the first thing most of us notice about these shotguns.

"Stocking is the aspect of the Uplander that I take the greatest pride in accomplishing," explains Hatfield.

"Unlike most makers of quality shotguns, walnut is not our standard stocking material. When select curly maple was generally available to gunmakers in this country, it was preferred. Extremely strong, yet light weight for its strength, select grades of maple also offered the added bonus of being the world's most eye-pleasing wood."

Hatfield goes to great effort to obtain sufficient quantities of the most difficult-to-find, premium-grade curly maple. Traditionally, such grades of this seemingly abundant species of hardwood came from Pennsylvania. However, only those maples growing on the north-facing mountains that are beaten by high winds furnish wood that exhibits the "curly" grain. Even where the conditions are right, foresters say only about one out of every five hundred maples grows in such a fashion.

"Two years ago we visited a sawmill in Canada. The owners told us they had a tractor trailer load of gun stock-grade curly maple," Hatfield says. "We went there, and ended up buying the entire load. At our Missouri plant, we hand-planed each piece of wood to judge its quality.

It turned out that only one-third of the wood in that load had any value for making gun stocks. Of the entire flat-bed

Impressive craftsmanship is present on Hatfield's side-by-side Uplander.

The 20-gauge Uplander was easy to handle in the rough, heavy cover typical of Eastern grouse hunting.

load of maple, I found just over 1000 pieces that were suitable for use as full stocks on our muzzleloader rifles. Another five hundred pieces were suitable for use as shotgun stocks and forestocks, but only forty percent of these were of premium-grade maple. Of the latter, we found thirty to forty pieces of super-super fancy-grade wood. Most important to understand, though, this wood represented several years of accumulation by the sawmill owner. It was a coup we may never again be able to duplicate."

Once the wood for the stock is selected, Hatfield's long stocking process begins. Stock blanks are cut and fitted to the frames of the shotguns. Then starts the slow process of filing the stocks in shape. Each stock is worked individually to fit the frame.

In terms of design, the Uplander stock is neither strictly European (although the grip is best described as an English straight-style), nor anything else that ever has been produced over the years by American shotgun makers.

"The unique style of our shotgun stock and forearm occurred more by mistake than actual design," according to Hatfield. "When we first decided to create our own side-

by-sides, we had an idea of what we wanted, but little else. One day, while experimenting and filing on a stock blank, with the L.C. Smith side-by-side as a model, I worked the wood down to where it looked identical to the stock of the older shotgun.

"Without thought, I started planing and rasping, taking off a little here and little more there and so on. Knowing the premium-grade maple is incredibly strong, I kept removing wood until all that was left was a slender forestock and a lithe butt stock. It resembles the European style, but boasts American practicality," says Hatfield, who is justly proud of this contribution to shotgun making in this country.

After the stock is worked to its final form, the wood is sanded to perfection while still on the frame. Next, three separate coats of stain are applied to the wood, including an acid-base type that brings out the rich, fullness of the maple grain. This technique is used not only for its ability to add beauty, but also because it soaks deeply into the wood and serves as a protecting agent. If accidentally dropped and scratched, the resulting abrasion will not show up as a scratch as it would on other shotgun stocks.

The staining process also involves hand-rubbed coat-

SPECIFICATIONS

Barrel:	26 inches.
Gauge:	20, standard; 28, available.
Chamber:	3-inch.
Choke:	Improved cylinder/modified.
Action:	Anson and Deely boxlock; single non-selective trigger, selective ejectors, doubling locking underlugs.
Stock:	English straight-grip, hand checkered 20 lines per inch; created from select grades of (or, curly) maple.
Model Options:	The Uplander is available in five grades; I, II, III, IV and V. Grade I is an economically priced field grade side-by-side. Grades II through V feature progressive levels of engraving and 24-karat gold inlays.

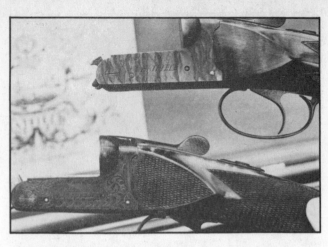

Hatfield produces and case-hardens its own boxlocks. While some would consider the method used a bit primitive, it provides the unique and desired results.

The frame of the Uplander field grade (top) reflects the effects of case-hardening done at the Hatfield plant.

ings of linseed oil, turpentine and varnish. This task is repeated up to thirty times. Keeping the wood of one of these fine shotguns in like-new condition is as simple as occasionally rubbing the stock with warm linseed oil. All of this stock work is done with the wood on the frame and barrels, which by this time have a dull, ugly brown look. The wood is worked and later stained while attached to the metal to ensure these two components mesh perfectly. During the staining process, the wood swells when absorbing the liquid, then shrinks. It's a tough way to make a shotgun, but it takes only a few seconds to appreciate the results.

Next, the largely finished butt and forestocks are removed from the frame and sent to one of two craftsmen located near the company's facility to be hand-checkered. Almost a lost art in the United States, hand-checkering is done at twenty lines per inch, despite the fact much of the checkering on many of the world's finest shotguns is twenty-five to thirty lines per inch. Ted Hatfield believes twenty-line checkering is much more practical for a true wingshooting piece. This configuration provides the best grip, the real reason checkering is done.

Engraving is done while the stocks are being checkered.

This artistic touch comes on the better grades of Uplander shotguns. Most engraving is done by craftsmen at Hatfield's manufacturing operation, but a portion is sent out. Frames and barrels are engraved while the metal still is in its soft stage. Gold inlay work, which is available on the top grades of the Uplander, is only done after the frame has been case-hardened.

Hatfield Gun Works is the last firearms manufacturer in the United States that still does the labor- and skill-intensive job of on-site case-hardening. Technically shallow, its purpose is to reduce surface wear and provide coloring.

"We spent a considerable amount of time researching possible methods for case-hardening or tempering our boxlock frames. Old-timers offered a variety of time-tested recipes that call for adding everything from a plug of tobacco to firing up the works only during a full moon," Hatfield reports.

"We currently use a fifty-five gallon barrel, packing the parts in bone charcoal. Air is injected through the mixture by using a mechanized compressor pump system. The entire barrel is placed in our forge at about 1600F. At that temperature, steel readily absorbs carbon from the bone charcoal.

Hatfield takes extra steps to guarantee the closest fit between metal and stock.

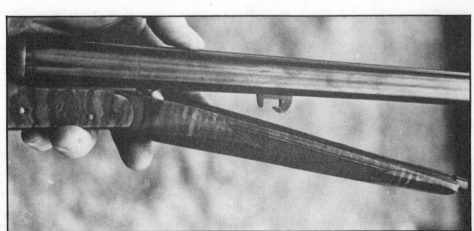

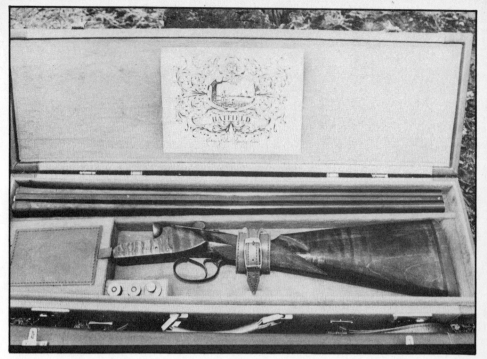

Hatfield's 20- and 28-gauge Uplanders are delivered in distinctive carrying cases.

"After holding the barrel in the forge at that temperature for a couple of hours, the entire mess — barrel, charcoal and boxlock frames is dumped into water. To get the desirable brilliant mottled reds, blues, browns, grays and yellows, we have to get the contents into water before it is touched by air. It's a tricky affair with plenty of high magic. And, to make it interesting, the gods can turn on you without warning," says Hatfield.

"Until recently, I was concerned that we were embarassingly primitive. However, a few months ago I toured the manufacturing facilities of one of England's best known shotgun makers and observed their case-hardening procedure.

"They did their case-hardening in the alley behind their gun works, using a trash can. Air is fed into it by using a hand-powered bicycle pump!" Hatfield says. The case-hardening recipe used in his Missouri operation is traditional, and calls for nothing that is especially exotic or odd such as a dead cat or excessive chanting.

Following case-hardening of the frames, barrels of the Uplander double are refitted and finished in one of four blues or other finishes that include browning, coin or my personal favorite, French gray, which accents engraving and especially the gold inlay work done by Hatfield Gun Works.

Lastly, the finished shotgun is placed in a special, all-leather break-down carrying case.

The natural question is how does it shoot? I have had an Uplander double for the last four shooting seasons. I have used my personal shotgun on a variety of upland gamebirds ranging from ringneck pheasant, mourning dove, bobwhite quail, woodcock, ruffed grouse and Wilson snipe. My usual shooting proficiency on mourning dove is nothing to brag about. Quail and pheasant, on the other hand, are usually in serious trouble when they are within range, while grouse and snipe have a better than even chance of seeing another day following an encounter with me.

Using the Hatfield Uplander, I average shooting about thirty percent better on dove, and even better on quail and grouse. I'm the first to admit this is less than scientific. With this in mind, I requested a second shotgun for testing.

Taking the second Uplander to a trap range near my home in eastern Tennessee, noted trap shooting expert Hal Glasgow and I ran two hundred rounds of factory-loaded ammo through this pristine work of art. On two occasions, Glasgow went fifty for fifty, then forty-six of fifty. I also shot forty-six of fifty, which for the record, equals my best trap shooting score with any shotgun, much less a lightweight 20 gauge.

Glasgow was astonished at how well the Uplander handled. Rather than test the gun by shooting in traditional trap style, he used the sporting clays approach. During his career as a serious shooter, which spans over four decades, he said, "I never have had a shotgun that seemed to leap into my shoulder as quickly or as comfortably as this little side-by-side 20-gauge."

My observations are identical to Glasgow's. Asking Ted Hatfield what it is about the design of this shotgun that imparts that real or imagined affect, he said the lightness of the gun is certainly a factor, but stock design is the key. It allows you to shoulder faster which, in turn, allows your brain to make the necessary adjustments needed to make a successful shot.

"We offer off-the-shelf models, but buyers can visit our facilities for a custom fitting that includes measurements to ensure your new shotgun fits you like a glove. Included is a trip to the trap range to fine-tune how your stock should be modified to accommodate individual shooting habits," Hatfield explains.

Despite the loving care that goes into creating these works of beauty, the Uplander is first and foremost a shotgun designed by a wingshooter for hunting gamebirds.

For more information, contact Hatfield Gun Works, 2028 Frederick Avenue, St. Joseph, MO 64501. — *Don Kirk*

AN ALL-PURPOSE SHOTGUN?

The Red Label Is Ruger's Only Model, But The Variations Meet Virtually All Shooter Needs!

A straight English grip and a slenderized forend offer field shooters a lighter and quicker version of the Red Label.

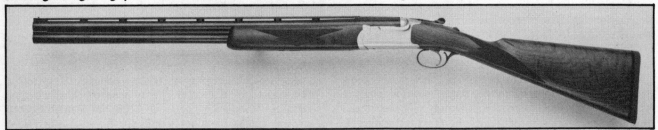

The author contends the redesigned balance point makes the Ruger Sporting Clays Model a positive handler.

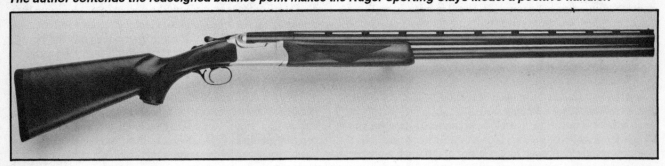

THERE WAS a time when American-made over/under shotguns in the medium price range appeared to be heading the way of the passenger pigeon. In a market where relatively inexpensive pumps and semi-autos achieved the lion's share of sales, few American gunmakers seemed willing to compete in the over/under market long dominated by European guns.

Bill Ruger, fortunately, wasn't one of them. And when he introduced the first Ruger Red Label, in 20-gauge, most observers were surprised when it became an instant success. That was followed shortly by a 12-gauge version

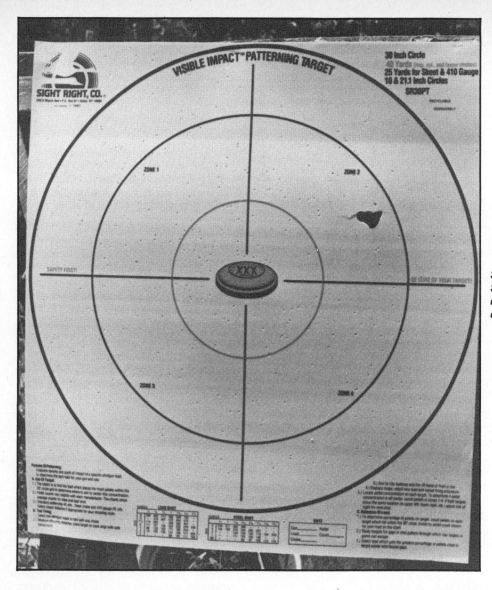

VISIBLE IMPACT™ PATTERNING TARGET

Skeet chokes from Ruger's Sporting Clays Model O/U delivered these excellent open patterns at 25 yards.

whose acceptance was equally gratifying.

Unfortunately, for those of us who were hoping a 28-gauge would follow, things stopped there. The two guns remained steady sellers in the Ruger line, with the only major model changes being the addition of interchangeable choke tubes a few years after their initial introduction.

Many observers thought Bill Ruger was content to rest on his laurels, but in 1992 he created a noticeable stir among afficionados with the introduction of two new models: one a slimmed-down version of the popular 12- and 20-gauge field guns, featuring a sleek, English straight grip, the other a highly refined 12-gauge intended for the demands of sporting clays. Here's a look at Ruger's latest offerings:

Ruger English Field Model — Upland gunners, who do far more walking than shooting, often show a decided preference for slimmed-down versions of the standard-weight field guns. Ruger's entry into this market utilizes the proven Red Label action in a redesigned stock featuring a more slender forearm and a straight "English-style" buttstock.

Available in 12- and 20-gauge in barrel lengths of twenty-

six and twenty-eight inches, the 12-gauge model tips the scales at 7.5 pounds while the 20-gauge weighs in at a petite seven pounds.

All English Field Model guns come with five interchangeable choke tubes (two skeet and one each in improved cylinder, modified and full, with extra tubes available), and feature a free-floating ventilated rib with a single brass bead front sight.

The action is straight Ruger: an investment cast stainless steel receiver, automatic ejectors, single selective trigger and an automatic safety (which can be converted to manual by the factory). Barrel firing selection and safety are combined in a single tang-mounted lever, a quick, positive system.

All English Field Model guns are chambered for both 2¾- and three-inch shells. The forearm and buttstock are of American walnut with eighteen-line-per-inch checkering and a new checkering pattern to accommodate the new stock design. On the 20-gauge, twenty-six-inch barrel test model, wood to metal fit was excellent and the checkering crisp and well executed. A standard red rubber butt plate with a black spacer was fitted.

One of the most enduring arguments in stock design is

The English Field Model gun comes with two skeet tubes installed. Additional chokes include improved cylinder, modified and full.

the advantage — or lack of it — for the English straight grip. It's also one of the most misunderstood aspects of stock design, because if the truth were to be known fully, the straight grip is nothing more than a crutch that aids in the correct execution of the English-style of field shooting.

The typical English style (a most useful and realistic field style, I might add) has the head erect, eyes level and the gun coming to the shoulder with little, if any, movement of the head canting to meet the gun.

Once the gun is mounted, virtually all gun movement is controlled by the non-trigger hand (the pointing or, as Churchill called it, the "kill hand"). When making points on quick, erratic targets (which certainly includes about every species of upland game bird) it is generally conceded that it is quicker and more positive to move the barrels with the hand on the forearm than it is with the hand on the trigger.

What the straight English grip does is deliberately put the wrist and arm in a bind and reduces the amount of gun control that can be produced by the trigger hand, forcing the shooter to rely more on the forearm hand.

Additionally, this binding effect causes the elbow of the grip hand to be pulled higher on the mount, which tends to pull the gun more firmly into the cheek, making it easier to keep the head down on the stock. English-gripped guns also tend to come to the shoulder with a slightly higher point than pistol-gripped stocks. This is a decided advantage on rising birds, or incoming birds, which is what most of the English gentry were shooting in those days. In short, the straight grip was created to facilitate a particular shooting style. The fact that it is one of the most attractive stock designs is just icing on the cake.

It does not particularly lend itself to American-style clay target games where a smooth swing is infinitely preferable to a quick point. Experts at this style find trigger hand control is an aid, especially on horizontally oriented targets like those encountered on skeet and sporting clays ranges. Indeed, in skeet the forearm hand becomes nothing more

SPECIFICATIONS

Model:	Ruger Red Label English Field
Gauge:	12 or 20
Chamber:	3-inch
Choke:	Interchangeable screw-in tubes in skeet, improved cylinder, modified and full. Extra full tube available in 12-gauge
Stock:	Straight English style. American walnut with 18-lines-per-inch checkering. Red rubber buttpad with black spacer.
Length of Pull:	14⅛ inches
Drop at Comb:	1½ inches
Drop at Heel:	2½ inches
Overall Length:	26-inch bbl., 43-inch; 28-inch bbl., 45-inch
Weight:	12-gauge, 7.5 pounds; 20-gauge, 7 pounds
Standard Accessories:	Instruction manual. Five interchangeable choke tubes (two skeet, one each in full, modified and improved cylinder. Choke tube key. Extra full tubes available for 12-gauge.
Suggested Retail Price:	$1157.50

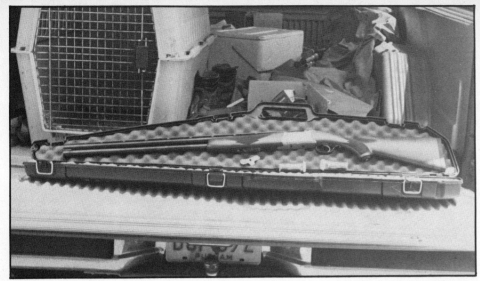

Woodstream's Field Locker gun case provided a secure and convenient means of transporting the sporting clays gun to range for testing.

than a glorified barrel rest.

In the field, however, many experts feel the English grip is a decided advantage.

Ruger Sporting Clays Model — No self-respecting smoothbore maker can afford to be without a sporting clays model in their line these days. Sometimes, these "new models" are nothing more than standard field models with a tad more barrel length and a radiused recoil pad. Ruger's approach, however, is an extremely well-thought-out design.

Available only in 12-gauge, the sporting clays model utilizes the standard Ruger action featuring automatic ejectors, automatic safety and a single selective trigger. In deference to competitive shooters, the factory will convert the safety to manual and the ejectors to extractors. Serious competitors will appreciate that.

Externally, three obvious changes distinguish the gun from the standard field model. Gone are the solid filler strips between the barrels, nor is there any provision to mount them. My experience has been that most competitve shooters using the older Red Label remove them anyway to help promote barrel cooling, and they're certainly not missed on the new model.

Instead of the single front bead sight, the sporting clays gun boasts the popular two bead system, a mid and front bead that results in more positive mounting alignment.

Lastly, in comparing the new gun to my personal Red Label, I find the forearm to be a bit slimmer than on my gun. I like the feel a little better.

The sporting clays model also features thirty-inch barrels instead of the twenty-six- and twenty-eight-inchers found on the Red Label field guns, and it is within these barrels that real innovation is found.

Maximum pattern control is important in any wing-shooting game, but doubly so in the demanding field of

SPECIFICATIONS

Model:	Ruger Red Label Sporting Clays
Gauge:	12 only
Chamber:	3-inch, lengthened forcing cones
Barrel Length:	30 inches, backbored to .741-.745
Choke:	Interchangeable stainless steel. Special 2-7/16 length tubes. Not interchangeable with standard Red Label tubes.
Stock:	Pistol grip style. American walnut with 18-lines-per-inch checkering, black rubber buttpad, metal pistol grip cap.
Length of Pull:	14⅛ inches
Drop at Comb:	1½ inches
Drop at Heel:	2½ inches
Overall Length:	47 inches
Weight:	7.7 pounds
Standard Accessories:	Instruction manual, four interchangeable screw-in choke tubes (two skeet, one each improved cylinder and modified). Choke tube key. Full and extra full choke tubes available as accessories at additional cost. Convert automatic safety to manual, $12 plus shipping. Automatic ejectors to extrators, $20 plus shipping.
Suggested Retail Price:	$1285

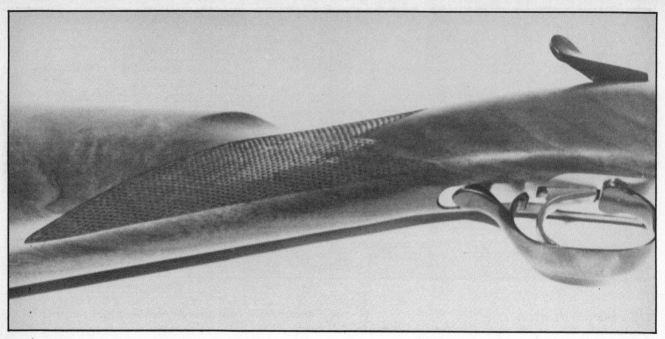

The straight grip on the English Field models features a new checkering pattern to accentuate the shotgun's design.

sporting clays. Here competitors are faced with targets at widely varying distances, and experts have found it is often more advantageous to alter their pattern desity by changing their shells, instead of choke tubes.

By varying shot hardness and velocity, they can alter their patterns up to one full degree of choke simply by selecting the appropriate shell.

Accomplishing that, however, requires a properly dimensioned barrel. Contemporary research into the baffling field of internal shotshell ballistics indicates that maximum pattern control (as well as minimal shot deformation and shot stringing) is achieved with the following:

1. A lengthened forcing cone that allows the shot cup/payload to enter the barrel smoothly and with a minimum of disturbance.

2. An overbore (backbored) barrel that lets the shot get down the tube with little deformation.

3. Long choke tapers that prevent a sudden compression of the shot charge as it is slammed through the tighter choke.

Such custom barrels were previously available only through a handful of top gunsmiths, and on some frightfully expensive European guns. They're standard on the new Ruger!

The sporting clays model offers backbored barrels at .741-inch to .745-inch, lengthened forcing cones and extra. long (2-7/16-inch) choke tubes of stainless steel. These are not interchangeable with standard Red Label tubes.

The gun is supplied with four tubes (two skeet plus one improved cylinder and modified, with full and extra full tubes available). And, unlike older tubes that use a system of notches to denote choke, these have the markings engraved on them.

Another noticeable change in the new model is the balance. My personal twenty-eight-inch-barrel Red Label

balances right at the junction of forearm and receiver. The sporting clays model balances three-eighths inches forward of that, giving the gun a more muzzle-heavy feel. Despite that, the sporting gun "feels" lighter and livlier, even though both weigh in at about the same 7.7 pounds.

On The Range — Prior to engaging aerial targets, both guns were patterned on my backyard range using Federal's one-ounce #8 Game Load in the 20 and their 1⅛-ounce #8 Extra-Lite target load in the sporting gun. Skeet chokes were patterned at twenty-five yards and the other tubes at the traditional forty yards.

As expected, the little 20 placed its pattern center slightly high (about a fifty-five/forty-five distribution). Patterns were evenly distributed, consistent and well within choke/percentage specifications.

The sporting model shot perfectly flat (fifty/fifty) just what I would want for sporting clays, and patterns were equally well-distributed, tending to run to the tight side of the choke specs. That's not uncommon, when using top-quality hard shot target loads at modest velocities.

I no longer get overly involved in figuring pattern percentages down to the umpth point, because it has no real meaning. There are too many variables within the shell itself to take such figures as gospel. Instead, I simply look for even pattern densities that fall within accepted percentage specifications for the choke used, and both guns performed admirably.

With all bird seasons closed, and the nearest sporting clays range a half-days drive away, I opted for the local skeet range, where I ran into 46-year-old Jim Hutchinson who agreed to help wring the guns out. I view that as fortunate, since Hutchinson is an avid bird hunter who also carries a ninety-seven percent competitive skeet average. More importantly, he owns and shoots a standard twenty-six-inch, 12-gauge Red Label, making his impressions of the new guns even more poignant.

Expert shooter Jim Hutchinson ran 25 straight clays the first time he put the Ruger Sporting Clays Model into action.

I went first with the 20-gauge and, given its field gun intent, I elected to shoot from the International skeet position, with gun butt touching the hip until the target appears. I knew the little gun would be quick and snappy, but as it turned out, it was a bit too quick for me. I promptly missed the first two targets as the lightweight little gun seemed to be running a good bit faster than my mind is capable of operating.

Forcing myself to slow down, I finished the round with only a couple more misses for a 21x25.

Jim Hutchinson hefted the gun and remarked that you would have to concentrate a little more than you would with a heavier gun, but proved it's not impossible. Shooting from a sporting clays low gun, he quickly ran 25 straight!

Hutchinson was quite impressed with the little gun, noting it was only the second time in his life he has picked up a strange gun and run 25 straight. Both of us felt it would be an excellent grouse, woodcock and quail gun.

Shifting to the sporting clays gun, I could see Hutchinson's eyes light up as he made a few practice mounts.

Reserving his comments, he again stepped to the line and ran another 25 straight.

"This is the best feeling Ruger shotgun I have ever picked up," he noted, as he returned the gun. And when I stepped up to Station 1, I immediately understood what he meant.

Sticking with the International position, I promptly inkballed the first four targets. There was no sense of haste, urgency or indecision. The gun just flowed to the birds and left a black puff hanging in the air. Station 2, however, is the real test for me.

Every skeet shooter has his personal demon and mine is high house 2. Even when I was competing regularly (AA average) this bird always required a lot of concentration, real attention to foot position and a conscious effort to drive the barrels through the bird. Even then, I never was sure of that bird until I saw it break. I hate that house, because it has cost me a number of 100 straights.

I got even with the Ruger. The bird came out, the gun came up and I knew it was history before I slapped the

The Sporting Clays model features longer choke tapers than the standard Red Label interchangeable chokes.

trigger. It was a tremendously "positive" feeling.

I think I understand how some of our Gulf War F-15 drivers felt when they got a perfect "missile tone" and knew their Sidewinder was going right up that MIG's tailpipe!

I also knew the last twenty targets were as good as dead, and even a fumbling gun mount on my second low house 8 didn't save it from becoming yet another inkball — 25x25!

I'm always a bit hesitant to apply superlatives regarding the handling characteristics of any shotgun. There are so many variables involved with individual build and shooting style that this truly can be a case of "one man's meat being another's poison." So, I'll just simply state that the new sporting clays model is without a doubt the smoothest, most positive handling smoothbore I have ever picked up. And that includes a number of high-grade Italian guns that I'll never be able to afford.

I also wouldn't confine this gun just to the sporting clays ranges. Jim Hutchinson opined it would be an excellent gun to tube for four-gauge skeet events. My thoughts are that it would make an excellent field gun. The same dynamic handling qualities required for sporting clays are no handicap in the field, and indeed, many expert sporting shooters use their guns on birds!

One thing about the sporting model that Hutchinson and I noticed after our range session was the recoil. It was definitely less than we expected. In fact, it was noticeably less than the 20-gauge gun.

I'm sure the barrel dimensions play some role in that, but I'm inclined to give equal credit to the balance. I suspect the slight weight-forward balance is producing less upward whip and keeping the gun coming back in a straighter line.

Regardless, I count that as just another plus on what should prove to be a sterling performer on range or afield. — *Rod Hunter*

Author found the English Field Model such a fast handler that he had to slow his rhythm before he could take targets.

LURE OF A RECORD

This Guiness World Title Holder Tells How He Did It!

I T WAS at high noon on August 30, 1992, that John Cloherty set a new world record — a mark that is not likely to be broken soon or easily. In a single hour, he broke an official 4551 flying clay targets with 12-gauge shotguns.

Why did he do it?

"Because they keep such records," Cloherty chuckled after he set the new Guiness World Record at the Paul Bunyan Rifle Range in Puyallup, Washington. This was during the second annual Sports Afield Sports Fair produced by Mike Raahauge and Dick Haldeman.

However, there was a much more serious reason why Cloherty went to all of the trouble — and pain — to set a new high in shotgunning.

"I always felt confident I had a good shot at attaining a new record," Cloherty explains, "and with my new post at the National Rifle Association as sporting clays representative, I had hoped to demonstrate to the public that the NRA was out there, getting involved with the recreational shooter, and wasn't strictly involved with Second Amendment right to keep and bear arms issues and competitions."

I had the opportunity to go dove hunting with Cloherty two days later for the season opener in Southern California where Cloherty calls Pasadena home. Except for a rather large bruise on his right leg, the champ was in top form, puffing darting doves with his Remington Model 870 pump .410 shotgun.

Cloherty and partner Rick Kennerknecht use a lot of targets during exhibitions, including ones that go bang.

Left, Cloherty (left) used his .410 Remington 870 to dove hunt two days after he set a new world record. At right is Mike Conway with Bernardelli 28-gauge.

Cloherty has done much to promote sporting clays as an NRA director.

During that hunt, Cloherty, fellow shooting buddy and industry personality Mike Conway, and the author had plenty of time to discuss what the shotgunner had accomplished. By then, he was known as the Iron Man of shotgunning.

The raw statistics of the world record shooting session were breathtakingly awesome all by themselves. Cloherty had bested the previous record set nearly three years earlier at Raahauge's Sports Fair in Norco, California. That record was establihsed by former Olympic shotgunner Dan Carlisle. It was 3172 targets in an hour. What that meant was that Cloherty broke 1379 more targets than did Carlisle. He didn't just set a new record, he literally blew the old one out of the water!

During that fateful hour, Cloherty shot twenty-two different Benelli Super 90 Model 1 12-gauge shotguns which had been Lazer-Ported and tuned at The Shotgun Shop in the City of Industry, California.

In all, Cloherty fired 6599 Winchester AA Lite 1⅛-ounce, 2¾ dram equivalent shells — or one every half-second. Six Beomat skeet target throwing machines launched a new world record 10,741 White Flyer clays targets (eighty cases) during the hour.

Actually, Cloherty broke 6316 clays during the sixty minutes, but Guiness rules preclude counting multiple breaks with a single shot.

Helping Cloherty during the record event were more than forty local club members, headed by Ed Cole, president; and Mike Servey, vice president. Official timer and judge was Dave Workman, editor of *Hunting & Fishing News*. Other officials included Tom Forbes, Mike Hadley, Butch Hulit, Olympic shotgunner Matt Dryke, and Dick Haldeman. Staff for the event included Rick "KK" Ken-

Charlton Heston (right) joins with Cloherty (left) and Rick Kennerknecht, also a world class sporting clays shooter.

nerknecht, Pat Raahauge, Bruce Polley, Sten Nielson and Ron Tree.

"I felt privileged to have had the opportunity to attempt the record," Cloherty explains. "I was a great deal more aware of what was going on around me than I thought I was going to be. I felt a great deal of control. It was actually enjoyable."

Cloherty indicated he never doubted he could do it.

"I just felt confident," he recalls. "I never really had any major doubts it was possible, or I wouldn't have tried it. I had three months to train: cycle work and weight training. As much as the training paid off, I also spent a lot of time thinking about how best to do it.

"And having seen two unsuccessful attempts and the record itself before me, I just had a real strong opinion of how the best way to do it would be."

Cloherty had been present three years before when Dan Reeves attempted to set a new world record. At that time, Reeves would have had to break 2313 targets in an hour, but fell short. The record at that time had been set in 1988 in England by Colin Hewish, who broke 2312 targets in sixty minutes. Also, Cloherty was there in 1990 when former Olympian Dan Carlisle actually did set a new record. Cloherty also watched as Alan Owens tried to best Carlise's record. That was in May, 1992, at the Sports Fair in Norco, Calfornia, the same place where Carlisle had been successful two years before.

If something is flying, Cloherty can hit it with a gun. Here he uses a Phelps .45-70 revolver to break clays.

As a trick shooting entertainer, Cloherty makes many odd shots, including this over-the-head clay-buster.

"I started thinking about it back when Reeves attempted it and didn't do so well," Cloherty notes. "It's so easy from the sidelines to sit there and watch what is going on and think of ways to improve upon target presentation, technique, training, method of shooting; the whole setup.

"It's easy to sit there on the sidelines and figure another way to do it, that you hope will be a better mouse trap," he continues. "I had the advantage of doing that three times. My game plan from the time I saw Carlisle do it until the time I did it never really changed. After the idea came into my head, nothing ever really came up to change my mind."

But why would a Southern Californian go to the state of Washington to set a shooting record?

"The place of choice for myself obviously would have been at Raahauge's in Norco," Cloherty states. "I'm from that local area and have so many acquaintances, and there always is a big crowd there. But at the time I was putting that record attempt together, another effort had been promised for the next May in Southern California.

"So the next alternative was the Sports Fair in Washington," he explains. "It took the showmanship and the showboat nature of the Sports Fair. By going to Washington, we showed some more people in a new area what sporting clays and clay target shooting is all about. After all, we did have a sporting clays course set up there, too. And that's been my idea all along: to take clay target shooting and sporting clays to the people who don't normally get to see it."

A professional instructor, Cloherty enjoys helping increase the number of sporting clays students hit.

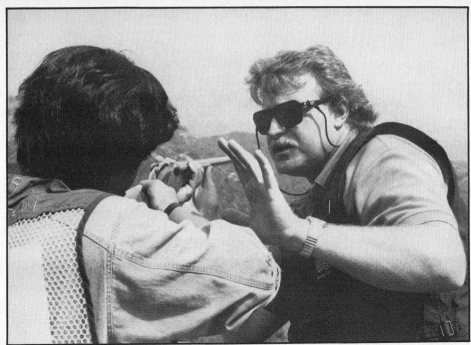

Cloherty is intense about shotgunning and does all he can to improve a shooter's technique and confidence.

Cloherty gives shooting tips on a sporting clays course to actor Jameson Parker.

Sponsors for Cloherty's record attempt were the National Rifle Association, as well as James Baker, head of the NRA's Institute for Legislative Action. That was totally consistent since Cloherty was head of the NRA's sporting clays development effort at the time.

However, allow me to inject a side note here about Baker, himself. He is a lot more than just an NRA official. He has a personal passion about firearms, and does not hesitate to donate his own money (not the organization's) to benefit shooters and shooting interests.

There were all kinds of threads tying things together during the period before Cloherty's record-setting shoot. He first decided he wanted to try it when he watched Carlisle set the record several years before. Cloherty saw it well, because he was a member of Carlisle's support team.

But I saw it coming even before then. Cloherty started shooting shotguns as a youngster, going hunting with his father.

"I started shooting as a kid, probably 12 or 13 years old," the 38-year-old champ explains. "Basically, I just

Two days after he set the new world record, Cloherty showed no ill effects from the marathon performance. He was again shooting, this time for doves during the opening of the season. He was joined by Mike Conway.

Cloherty is a champion shooter. For competition, he uses a Beretta over/under 12-gauge for sporting clays.

went out twice a year or so. I went dove hunting on opening day and maybe one or two pheasant hunting trips a year with my dad.

"As a tune-up for those annual sojourns, I started going down to Pachmayr's shooting facilities." The facility was called International Trap and Skeet at the time, and was located in suburban Los Angeles County. "I would get used to shooting the gun after a whole year. Then I discovered you didn't have to wait a whole year until hunting season to shoot your shotgun.

"I started shooting quite a bit of skeet with a trap and skeet club," he explains. "The club made a trip to a sporting clays course, where I tried sporting clays, and I've been hooked since. That was about six or seven years ago and I've been at it since."

Quickly, he skyrocketed to AA status, and served as an official instructor. Eventually, Cloherty also became a trick shooter, performing before crowds all over the country.

But even when he earned a living as a drywall contractor, John Cloherty's real aim in life was to make a livng by shooting. To that end, he also took notes as he watched Carlisle shoot. After all, Carlisle also is an accomplished trick shooter.

Unlike many trick shooters of the past, however, Cloherty also is a real entertainer. He loves performing in front of crowds, and was well on his way to establishing himself as a trick shooter when the NRA job, and later, the world record shoot, developed.

During that time, his partner in the trick shooting demonstrations was Rick Kennerknecht — one of Cloherty's

As an exhibition shooter, Cloherty is a goodwill ambassador for the shooting sports. Following his trick-shooting demonstrations, he enjoys talking with the audience, especially youngsters. They often ask for his autograph.

long-time buddies and fellow shooter. He and "KK" performed at all kinds of shoots and other shooting-related events.

Once it was decided he would indeed shoot for the record, Cloherty went into serious training. He not only made certain he was in top physical condition, but he studied the problems others had had before him — and he had seen several attempts firsthand.

Common among the other attempts were problems with the shooting hand. Those shooters had hands that looked like hamburger at the end of the hour of non-stop firing.

So Cloherty assembled all the right stuff. He had padding in the right places. He made certain the targets were in the right place in the air. And, he was in good enough shape to do it all — nonstop! Unlike all of the shooters before him, Cloherty never took a break. He never wiped sweat off his brow, nor did he even take a drink of water during the shoot. All he did was grab guns, pull triggers and break targets. Cloherty attacked the record as though his job depended upon success. Perhaps it might have. However, that consideration is moot now.

What has happened to him as a result? Not a lot, according to Cloherty. Yet, there have been effects. After all, he does hold the record. It may be difficult to quantify these sorts of things, but there are benefits.

For Cloherty, however, the biggest benefit has been that the record-setting shoot has helped the cause of the NRA in that it has helped show a positive aspect of firearms shooting. It is something a non-shooter can see and understand.

Cloherty doesn't compete as much as he did at one time, but he still is a most credible and serious shooter. Meanwhile, he also continues to do shooting exhibitions which always include what has come to be known as his "signature" shot. For that shot, Cloherty holds a shotgun upside-down over his head and breaks clays in the air. It's fun to watch.

Meanwhile, Cloherty and the NRA are in the process of finalizing their NRA clays program which will involve fun shoots and local competitions. Some of the events will involve a multi-trap NRA Clays Demonstration Unit which looks somewhat like a Jungle Jim apparatus covered with clay target throwers.

"The NRA will be offering two different size units," Cloherty explains. "The fun shoots will revolve around them, more or less, and hopefully we'll have it culminate with a national-type event with the potential of a car give-away or something like that."

Would he ever consider going for the world record again?

"Not unless somebody else breaks more than I did," he chuckled. — *Steve Comus*

WHAT'S HAPPENED TO TRAPSHOOTING?

Here's A Rundown On Recent Events — And What Is Ahead!

Trapshooting, oldest of the clay target sports, continues to draw new shooters, young and old, to its ranks each year.

RECREATIONAL SHOOTERS still can take their hunting or game guns to the range and shoot a round of trap. But to be really competitive, it takes a lot of time, specialized gear and green — as in money.

What has happened to trapshooting? To answer that question, one must investigate where it has been, and what

the future of the sport will likely see. Only then can a shooter understand where it is today.

Starting at the beginning is usually a good idea for any subject, and trapshooting is no exception. Trapshooting had its roots in a bloodsport — live pigeon shooting. To put it bluntly, all of the clay target shotgun sports are bloodless alternatives to the killing of living, feathered flyers.

Top bunker shooter Derek Partridge uses a Kemen over/under to break fast-moving clays in this growing sport.

To this day, vestiges of its origin permeate the trapshooting game. For example, clay targets still are referred to commonly as "birds." And, a broken clay routinely is termed "dead." One of the old-line clay target makers continues to call its clays White Flyers. In an historic sense, a true white flyer would have been a white pigeon. Although it is not so common now, within the past couple of decades, it was common for many people to refer to shotgun target games like trap to be "clay pigeon shooting."

In fact, the designation of the game of trapshooting points to the origin of the sport. In the original live pigeon shooting discipline, the live birds were placed in "traps" in the field in front of shooters, and when the shooter called "pull," the "trapper," or person operating the traps, would pull a cord which would open the trap containing the pigeon, and the bird could fly off. To this day, when a trapshooter calls for a target, he or she says "pull." This despite the fact most target-launching machines now are electronically operated and require only that the trapper push a button to release the target.

Certainly, live pigeon shooting continues to be conducted around the world. In the United States, it is done in a semi-secretive manner for a number of reasons. The greatest of these is that a sizable amount of public sentiment against such activities as being "barbaric" result in protests and harassment. But there is another sub-rosa factor which keeps some of the live bird shoots on the shadowy side of

things. It's called gambling. Large sums of money change hands at some of the live bird shoots, and in most states, such activities are not totally proper.

Currently, the more open live bird shoots occur in places like Mexico and Spain. Curiously, these also are two countries where another animal/human sport still is practiced: bullfighting.

More than a century ago, however, live bird shooting began to fall out of social favor in a number of places around the world, including Great Britain and the United States. Add to the list some of the continental European countries, and there was ample desire to replace pigeon shooting with a bloodless alternative.

The game of inanimate-target "trap" shooting evolved. But it didn't go directly from live pigeons to the shooting of clay (actually, they are made from a form of pitch, not clay, now) flying saucers as is practiced currently. Nor was there merely a brief period which saw the launching of cow patties from the pasture as targets.

A simple catapult was pressed into service in the early days, starting in 1877. These catapults would launch glass balls into the air, and gunners would attempt to break the flying orbs with their shots. Although supplanted by clay targets, the shooting of glass balls continued for a while, tapering off until it virtually disappeared during the early years of the Twentieth Century.

Shortly after the introduction of glass ball shooting came

Gene Lumsden, now an executive with Interarms, spent years as a serious Olympic trap competitor.

the clay target — a saucer-shaped disc of actual clay. That was in 1880, and by 1885, clay target shooting had become popular. Hence, the term "clay target shooting" was born, and remains in effect today. However, the advent of clay targets necessitated a new design of mechanical launcher. A catapult, as used with the glass balls, simply didn't work well.

In operation, modern clay target throwing machines are little different from their original ancestors. A spring-powered arm or flipper holds the target in place in a cocked position, and when the shooter calls for a target, the arm is released, accelerating through a wide arc and spinning the target into the air in the process. This spinning launch sends the inverted saucer-shaped target into a relatively straight flight pattern. When the shooter fires, the target is generally hit on-edge as it flies away.

With more than a century of evolution, trapshooting has become a highly technical game with extremely specific field measurements, target flight limitations and rules of conduct for both shooters and trappers. It is in these refinements that the game of trap changed from a predominantly recreational pastime to serious competition. Now it is often the games played by shooters within the game of trap which can decide the outcome of a shoot. And it is the practice of these "games" which have retarded the recruitment of some new shooters, as well as caused the drop-out of others.

Competitions are what they are, and true competitors go through life with a win-at-any-expense attitude. Both concepts are alive and well in the trapshooting game today. But before going too far into the subject, it is necessary to note that there are basically two major and distinct forms of trapshooting conducted around the world. One form is commonly termed American Trap, or ATA Trap. The Amateur Trapshooting Association (ATA) is headquartered at Vandalia, Ohio. For most shooters in the United

States, the term trapshooting means ATA trapshooting. There are, however, other smaller trapshooting associations, but the bulk of trapshooting involves the ATA. Currently, there are slightly more than 36,000 active ATA shooters, and more than 1100 affiliated clubs.

The ATA was formed in 1923, and has been headquartered at Vandalia, Ohio, since 1924. The organization's major shoot each year is the Grand American at the Vandalia headquarters, and more than 6,000 shooters compete in that event each summer.

But internationally, there is a different breed of trapshooting which is growing in the United States — slowly, but steadily. It is the form of trapshooting which is conducted at places like the Olympics. Hence, it is interchangeably referred to as Olympic Trap, or, simply, Bunker. It gets its "bunker" designation from the fact that the trap fields for that brand of shooting have bunkers in which fifteen traps are located.

Bunker is the world's most challenging form of the game due to the fact that, in this discipline, the targets go faster and at a greater number of angles horizontally and vertically than in the other forms of trap. Also, in bunker, the shooter is permitted two shots at each target.

During recent years, bunker has dictated some major ammunition changes. First, the shot payload was limited to 28 grams (almost exactly one ounce), but now the legal limit has dropped to 24 grams (seventh-eighths-ounce) for international competition.

By contrast, ATA trapshooting is simpler. Rather than a bunker with multiple traps, there is a smaller trap "house" covering a single trap machine. It is the simplicity of the trap field setup here which afforded the game its level of popularity across the country during the formative years. Literally, trap facilities can be established just about anywhere it is safe and legal to shoot, and a regulation field can be put into operation for relatively little money. Hence,

Trap is a sport where there's no distinction between wheelchair and standing competitors. Each year, the California Paralyzed Veterans Association holds an international trapshoot that draws shooters from throughout the country.

trapshooting always has been the most prevalent of clay target games in the United States.

The basic rules of ATA trapshooting not only give the game its distinct personality, but they foster practices among competitors which are criticized often. One of the most often-cited such practice is that of target refusal, due to a "slow" pull.

Since ATA rules do not provide for any built-in delay between the time the shooter calls for a target, and when the target is launched, hard-core shooters have come to expect the target to be launched immediately when called for. Although this may not sound like a critical matter to the casual observer, it literally can make or break a shoot for some. The reason is that, when they call for the target, they simultaneously begin their gun movement. If the target is not launched immediately, the gun will have moved too far by the time the target appears, and the shooter may not be able to recover in time to hit it.

Timing is everything in shooting, and especially in shooting moving targets. In fact, serious shooters take the timing aspect to other levels, as well. Some insist on competing solely or primarily with the same squad. The important dynamic there is that squads of shooters who shoot together often create a tempo of their own, and it is the timing of the shot to shot to shot which actually does give a measurable edge.

Traditionally, there was another reason for squad tempo to be considered essential. It was part of a practice called "reading the trap." Since the trap machines would oscillate mechanically and predictably, shooters could deliberately time their calls for targets at moments when the targets would be launched in known directions within the permitted arc.

So what? So everything. Someone who could time the release of the target to those moments when the target would go in a known direction, could determine the direction for the easier shots, and preclude a target going in a direction for the harder shots. A squad which could shoot at an established tempo could help each of its members know more or less where the target would be when released.

That, in turn, meant it paid a shooter to begin gun movement at the time he or she called for a target, knowing full well the gun would be heading in the direction needed to break the target in the predetermined flight zone. Yes, this has been one of the many games within the game of trap.

And there are many more games shooters play. Some are no more imaginative than mind games, intended to interrupt another shooter's game. Although some of them can be experienced during normal competition, a study of them can be made during high stakes shootoffs.

As much as timing and teamwork may have gotten a shooter into the shootoffs, the reverse is likely to take place when it is shootoff time. There, a shooter purposely may call for targets differently each time — one time giving a quick call, another time maybe taking a moment to adjust the gun mount, then giving a delayed call. Subtleties prevail here. It even can go so far as a shooter changing the way he or she calls for a target. For example, for one target, the shooter may shout a quick "pull" command. Next time, it may be an elongated "p-u-l-l" statement, or it might be nothing more than a guttural utterance in betwen — anything to keep the next shooter off balance and out of synchronization.

The mind game is not limited to the firing line itself. Before going onto the field, shooters have been known to do things ranging from one shooter moving the safety on another shooter's gun in an effort to interrupt the other shooter's concentration and game on the field, to engaging the other shooter in a conversation which will inject doubt or uncertainly into the mind of the competitor.

However, the mind game in trap transcends any high jinks one could imagine. Some competitors become so involved in playing mind games with others that they end up giving themselves a mind game, as well. It is in this aspect that some of the more humorous traits of the game emerge.

Some shooters go through elaborate rituals before taking the field each time, and then before mounting the gun. Or shooters will become so convinced there is some kind of magic in ammunition or other gear that, unless they use only that kind, their game literally falls apart.

Trapshooting definitely has become an equipment game. The rules of the game itself dictate that equipment be of critical concern to serious shooters. But first, a look back to the roots.

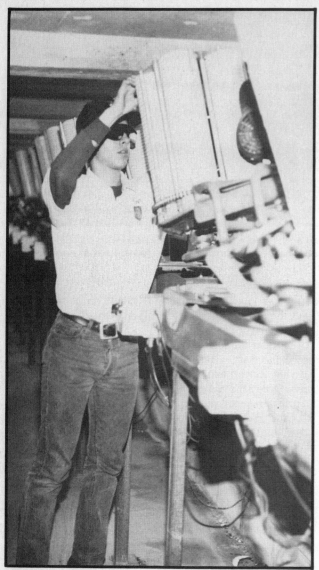

A scorer loads one of 15 clay target throwers inside a trap bunker. There're three throwers for each station.

Initially, live pigeon shooting was conducted with side-by-side shotguns — the same shotguns used for hunting game birds. For that discipline, where the actual flight pattern of the bird was unknown to the shooter, the gun needed to fit and swing in a wide range of movements — just as it would be when hunting game birds.

However, when the inanimate target game evolved into one where the targets always were released on a predictable level of rise, and where the targets always were going away, the advent of a more thoroughbred configuration of gun was inevitable.

Among the early gun modifications was the flat sighting plane — at first between the barrels of side-by-side guns, and later atop single-barrel and over/under guns. Later, solid, raised ribs gave way to ventilated ribs. This was done to help preclude the annoyance of heat waves from a hot barrel interfering with sight picture and visual target acquisition.

Next came the relatively high comb of the butt stock. Since the targets always rise when launched, there is no need for a lower hunting-style stock. And, a high comb puts more of the pattern above the line of sight than below — another advantage when shooting targets which are going upward.

Smooth swings are critical in trapshooting, even though accomplished shooters use little gun movement. To that end, trap gun barrels normally are long — thirty inches or longer.

Barrel choking is critical in trapshooting. Again, a hunting gun routinely is called upon to engage birds at varying distances. Too tight a choke will grind up the game bird at close ranges, and too open a choke will give inconsistent results on live birds at longer range.

But in a controlled atmosphere like a trap field, the distance at which a shooter takes the target is determined ahead of time. Also, the fact that the clay targets are taken on edge requires a rather dense pattern to assure that several pellets hit the target. To that end, trap guns typically have tight chokes which deliver high percentage patterns.

As trapshooters become more accomplished, they learn how to take targets with a minimal amount of gun movement. This means there comes a point when the configuration of the butt stock and forend take on radical personal dimensions. These dimensions serve two simultaneous purposes. First, they contribute to repeatable and predictably precise gun mount. Also, they allow just enough of the right kinds of movements, but preclude the shooter from moving too much or in too radical a direction. Again, the slight edge rears its head.

This phenomenon is translated into things like adjustable butt pads, adjustable combs or adjustable grips. Some guns even have adjustable ribs which can be fine-tuned for specific loads or for specific conditions.

All of these things, and more, are designed to help the shooter break targets time after time after time — enabling them to run hundreds of targets without a miss.

Serious clay target shooters shoot a lot of targets. Although recoil may be a minor annoyance to a hunter or recreational shooter, it becomes the nemesis of serious target shooters. In the same way a boxer becomes punch drunk after a lifetime of being pounded senseless in the ring, clay target shooters eventually receive counter-productive messages from their bodies, which are reacting to being pounded by the recoil of the gun against the hands, face and shoulder.

Subconsciously, the mind knows that when the index finger pulls the trigger, trauma will be inflicted. Instinctive mental defense mechanisms come into play, and shooters find themselves flinching — at first from time to time, and later routinely.

This is not a case of anyone being wimpy. After taking tens of thousands of hits, the body simply refuses to engage cooperatively in prolonged masochism.

To prolong the inevitable and minimize the effects of recoil which build over time, further refinements are found on trap guns. There are the rubber recoil butt pads, and even internal recoil absorbers which range from miniature versions of an automobile shock absorber to mechanisms which divert the direction of recoil down and away to metal vials of substances like mercury to afford a static inertia

International clay targets are hurled from the bunker twice as fast as ATA trap.

which delays and diminishes the felt recoil.

Such changes even involve the barrel or barrels of the gun itself. Ports, or holes, in the barrel near the muzzle represent one system. As the shot payload goes down the barrel, hot powder gases bleed off through the ports, forcing the gun downward and/or slightly forward. Eliminating muzzle jump precludes trauma to the face in recoil.

And there are other internal barrel features used by serious trapshooters. One of the basic alterations is the removal of sharp and short forcing cones. Traditionally, the bore in a shotgun is smaller in diameter than is the chamber which holds the shell. The transition from the chamber to the main bore was abrupt — ranging from a ninety-degree ledge to a sub-inch ramped constriction. And when fiber wads were used in shells, the abrupt transition helped preclude powder gas blow-by and improved performance.

However, with the advent of the plastic wad with a shot cup and skirted base, the abrupt transition from chamber to bore was not only obsolete, but actually counter-productive. By extending the distance of the transition, the shot could be launched much more smoothly. Since the design of the plastic wad with the skirted base allowed it to expand and seal the gases, there was nothing lost by lengthening the "forcing cones" or transitional dimensions.

In addition to precluding damage to the shot cup or shot itself, due to an abrupt forcing cone transition, the longer the restriction, the less the hammering effect when the shot went off. This meant less felt and softer recoil.

This phenomenon has been taken to great lengths, literally. Some gunsmiths offer the lengthening of the forcing cones to an inch or two, while others have reamers which will extend the transitional restriction to four inches, or more.

And, since perfect patterning and recoil reduction both are critical concerns of serious trapshooters, the gun game has gone another notch up the equipment ladder. It is a phenomenon known as "overbore" or "backbore." This is

a simple matter, actually. It simply means that the inside diameter of the bore is larger than normal.

For example, a shotgun gauge was determined by the precise diameter of the bore. Measurement was the number of lead balls of that diameter that it took to make a pound. Hence, it took twelve lead balls the diameter of the bore to make a pound for a 12-gauge shotgun. Or it took sixteen lead balls the diameter of the bore to make a pound for a 16-gauge, and so on.

In trap, or 12-gauge terms, that diameter happens to be .729-inch. So a 12-gauge gun would, by definition, have a bore .729-inch in diameter. Manufacturing plus-and-minus tolerances have resulted over the years in a fairly wide range of actual bore diameters for a given gauge, but technically, the bore should be .729-inch wide.

Again, with the advent of skirted plastic wads, options were expanded, allowing the actual bore diameter to be increased without sacrificing velocity, due to gases blowing by a hard paper or fiber wad.

Hence, the practice of overboring evolved. Again, it accomplished two positive goals simultaneously. First, it offered a softer felt recoil, but it also contributed to enhanced patterning.

Internal barrel dynamics are complex, but essentially what overboring permits is a greater degree of massaging and fine tuning of the shot charge as it goes down the barrel and through the choke.

So far, however, the design efforts involved to help reduce the effects of recoil have been static. But even all of those factors cannot preclude flinching, which means missed targets. In a game where breaking long strings of targets is essential, even an occasional flinch can lose a match for a shooter.

How does a person sidestep nature and minimize the occurrence and effects of flinching? In the trigger, of course. Traditional triggers work when the shooter pulls or squeezes them to the rear. This movement releases the sear; this, in turn, allows the hammer or striker to spring forward and

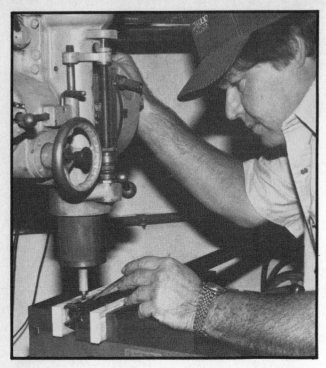

Stan Fitzgerald, shotgun gunsmith and avid shooter, polishes the monoblock on a set of over/under barrels.

force the firing pin into the primer, which then ignites the powder charge. The expanding gases created by the burning powder then accelerate the shot charge out the barrel and toward the target.

Shooters discovered, however, that a flinch would cause them to pull the gun off target via a twitch which involved the trigger hand, finger and even shoulder. Translated, this means that the muscles which constrict in the shooting sequence can be short-circuited by the nerves and twitch the gun off target.

Virtually all of this problem can be eliminated if the shooter doesn't have to restrict a series of muscles at the moment of truth. This reality gave birth to what is known as a release trigger — something which is encountered almost exclusively in trap, and for good reasons, including the fact that they are inherently unsafe in most other shooting activities.

A release trigger works simply. When the shooter has shouldered the gun and prepares to call for the target, the trigger is "pulled" in the same manner as any traditional trigger. However, the gun doesn't go off. Rather, the trigger is cocked or "set," and will disengage the sear only when the trigger finger "releases" it or lets go. Hence, the term "release trigger."

This system functions well in ATA-style trap where the shooter has control over precisely when a target will be launched, and where a single-shot is taken at a single target. And that is why many of the accomplished and veteran trapshooters have their guns equipped with such trigger devices.

Certainly, some of them even use the mechanisms for shooting trap doubles. However, such practice is not universally effective, nor universally applauded.

Rules and course of fire in trap also foster further special-

ization on the equipment front. In ATA-style trap, there are actually three distinctly different games. There is sixteen-yard trap, handicap trap and trap doubles.

The basic game is sixteen-yard trap, which is so-named because shooters stand at shooting stations which are located sixteen yards from the target launcher, or trap. To keep interest higher among the broad spectrum of shooters abilities, a classification system was injected into the trap game. Typically, these are AA, A, B, C and D, with AA being the best shooters. There also are other classifications encountered, including juniors and women. The object of such classifications is to allow shooters to compete directly against others of similar skill or abilities.

Ideally, the classification system makes the game more fair. However, for fierce competitors who have a win-at-all-cost attitude, the system can be and sometimes is abused. The practice is called "sand bagging." It is simple in its practice: The shooter purposely misses just enough targets to keep himself or herself in a classification lower than actual ability. By doing so, he or she is competing against other shooters who are not as skilled, and the chances of winning are enhanced. Although rules exist which are intended to minimize such practice, it cannot be eliminated.

In an effort to spread the winning around a bit more, handicap trap was invented. The object is to make the better shooters stand farther from the trap in an effort to equalize all of the shooters' prospects of winning, because as the distance from the trap increases, the degree of difficulty in hitting targets is enhanced.

For women and sub-juniors, the handicap distance starts at eighteen yards, and continues to a maximum of twenty-seven yards. For juniors, the handicap yardage starts at nineteen yards, and for men, it starts at twenty yards, and continues to a maximum of twenty-seven yards.

Taking male shooters as examples, the shooter competes at handicap from the twenty-yard line until he "earns" yardage. This happens when he wins or ties at a competition, and depending upon how many competitors there are in the event, a half-yard or yard is earned each time, until the shooter is started at the twenty-seven-yard mark. Specific rules account for adding or subtracting yardage, based on performance.

Since the distance to the trap for accomplished shooters is significantly longer than it is for the sixteen-yard events, shooters routinely have separate barrels or completely different guns for the handicap shoots than for the sixteen-yard competition.

Still another gun, or other set of barrels, often is pressed into service for the trap doubles shoots. As the name would imply, a simultaneous pair of targets is launched in doubles. This calls for a gun capable of shooting two quick shots, thus ruling out any of the thoroughbred single-barrel trap guns.

In practice, doubles guns are choked differently and even have differently configured stocks than do guns used specifically for either of the singles events. Unlike the practice in singles, the target launcher in doubles does not oscillate. Rather, it is stationary and throws each pair of doubles in exactly the same divergent directions. This means the shooters know exactly where the targets will be going.

Hence, it is common practice to take the first target quickly

John Dickman, owner of the Shotgun Shop, installs a recoil pad as part of an overall upgrade conducted on an over/under trap gun.

— in ambush fashion for some shooters — then swing over to the other target and take it. It is not odd, therefore, for guns with two barrels to have noticeably different chokes in each barrel, and for the shooter to use two different types of ammunition — one kind of shell for the first target, another kind for the second shot.

Since the first target can be taken almost immediately, a more open bore will suffice, as it offers a wider pattern in case the shot is a bit off. And, since the second target will have had time to get fairly far away by the time the shooter gets to it, a tighter choke generally is preferred for the second shot. Shooters using a single-barrel gun like an autoloader generally opt for a modified or improved modified choke, splitting the difference for the two targets.

The proliferation of interchangeable choke tubes for shotguns has precluded some of the perceived need for two or three separate guns for the various games, but even with them, shooters routinely change barrels because of the differences in swing dynamics of barrels of different lengths.

For example, a shooter with a two-barrel set for the two singles games might use a thirty-inch modified choke barrel for the sixteen-yard event, and a thirty-two-inch full choke barrel for the handicap shoot.

The point is that the more serious and accomplished shooters become, the more they demand specific performance characteristics out of their equipment. And there is another factor which comes into play at some point in a shooter's career. Trapshooters use their guns enough to wear them out. There comes a point where guns which can take hundreds of thousands of rounds of use become relevant.

Yet these things do not evolve singly or separately. They progress in concert, which means that shooters can play an escalating equipment game for years — even for life.

It is in this context that one begins to appreciate why some of the full-on thoroughbred trap guns are so expensive. First, they have to be able to hold up under extended use. They have to handle flawlessly, and their mechanisms have to be totally tuned. That is why veteran trapshooters can be seen walking to the line with outwardly outlandish-looking guns that cost thousands of dollars.

Cost, however, is both relative and subjective. By the time a shooter becomes accomplished, he or she has and is investing large sums of money for ammo, targets, entries and travel to events. This also presupposes a commitment of mega amounts of time and energy. Hence, a $5000 or $10,000 shotgun which will last for years and retain most, if not all (because of inflation), of its value over time is not so out of line, if one also factors-in a similar amount of money, or more, for all of the other trapshooting-related expenses each year.

At the least, however, one fact is clear. Trap has come — or gone — a long way since it began. It no longer has any meaningful tie to hunting. It has evolved technically far beyond that point.

In becoming a total discipline unto itself, trap has taken on a character which is liked by many, but which tends to intimidate some would-be newcomers. It is difficult for anything to have everything every way. And so it is with trapshooting.

Meanwhile, the numbers of active, registered trap shooters is on a gradual increase, and has been during recent years, expanding at the rate of about three to four percent a year.

Indeed, it has become a game of specialization. — *Steve Comus.*

CHAPTER 35

YOU CAN SHOOT THE GRAND AMERICAN

All You Have To Do Is Join The Amateur Trap Association And Get To Ohio!

Author shoots the Ithaca 4E single-barrel trap gun at the Grand American. The shotgun has a 32-inch barrel with a .043-inch choke. This translates to no mercy shown for targets. Author considers the Ithaca 4E a real clayseeker.

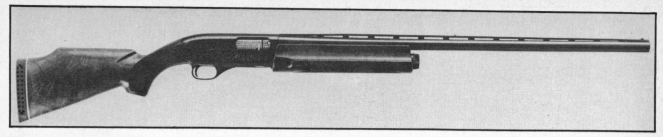

During the doubles events at the Grand American, author elected to use a Winchester Super-X Model 1 trap gun.

ALL IT TAKES to shoot in the Grand American is the desire to do so, and the decision to make it happen. There is no need to be a long-time trapshooter. There is a mile-long field of dreams in Vandalia — and they can come true for anyone who simply shows up.

After four decades, the dream for me still was alive. Separated by more than simply time, there had been literally worlds of experiences flown by — experiences on several continents and in scores of countries which were punctuated by the witnessing of major global events.

Yet, the dream persisted. It would not be denied. And it wasn't. Finally, I stepped up to the line and shot the Grand American. The fulfillment of a lifelong dream? Certainly. But it turned out to be so much more. It truly was worth the wait.

Maybe it is true a person never can go home — really. But in spirit, it can and does happen. It happened there in Vandalia, Ohio, on that muggy August day. I had come home, and it was a good feeling.

The world was a much different place in 1952. A mere fifty miles north of the Amateur Trapshooting Association headquarters, as a youngster I openly wondered what it would be like actually to shoot in the Grand American! It was, after all, the main event — the largest shoot in the world, and it was close enough for an 8-year-old mind to envision as possible.

But it may as well have been a million miles away, at least when it came to doing anything about it. It took forty years, but I finally decided to make it happen. Once the decision was made, even I began to change as a person.

Anticipation leading to shooting the Grand American for the first time continued to build from the first moment I decided to go for it, hitting fever pitch whenever the thought of it crossed my mind.

"It's really going to happen," I told myself. Several of the deepest childhood dreams and fantasies would become reality. Soon, I would step up to the line, call for a target and actually break a clay at the Grand American!

I may have been approaching the half-century mark in my life, but that didn't mean some of my innermost thoughts as a young shooter in the early 1950s were any less vivid — or valid for that matter.

Those were different times. Then, the "dream" trap gun was an Ithaca 4E single-shot. Most shooters used Winchester Model 12 pump guns at the time, but the single-shot Ithaca captured my imagination, because it was so expensive, comparatively speaking.

A regular single-barrel hunting shotgun retailed then for less than $30, and a full-on Model 12 trap gun could be bought for a couple hundred dollars — $250 if it had a really high grade stock.

Yet, the Ithaca 4E went out for more than $400! It had to be special, not just because it was so expensive, but because many of the serious competitors at the Grand American shoot such guns. At least, that was the message relayed in shooting publications of the time.

As a youngster who grew up a scant fifty miles from

The straight-forward style of the Ithaca 4E trap gun makes it a thoroughbred. The design provides total comfort, even in full recoil from a three-dram load.

Unlike some modern, space-age trap guns, the Ithaca 4E is totally basic, complete with a long, open pistol grip stock.

Vandalia, Ohio, home of the Grand American, I had always taken it for granted that eventually I would get around to shooting in the big event.

High school came and went, as did college and the Army. There was always some logically understandable reason why I could put off going to the Mother of All Shooting Events.

I never even got around to becoming a serious trap shooter. Oh, I'd shoot an informal round or so a year some years, but there were blocks of years during which I never set foot on a trap field.

Hunting had been my forte with a shotgun, and I did that, even if only ceremonially some times, during most of the years. Decades passed, and still those unfulfilled dreams lay dormant somewhere in the recesses of my mind.

Sporting clays came along in the 1980s, and a number of factors fell together which resulted in my writing about that new game, shooting it quite a bit and even co-authoring a book about it.

Yes, the game of sporting clays is a lot of fun, and yes, it is in some ways more challenging for an all-around shooter than trap shooting ever could be. But, frankly, there is no direct comparison possible. Trap and sporting clays are two distinctly different games, and each embodies its own set of challenges. Each offers its own brand of enjoyment. I realized that fact, and the more I shot sporting clays, the more I really wanted to do what sages through the ages have asserted cannot be done: I wanted to go back home in a spiritual way, and shooting the Grand American was a necessary part of living out that lifelong fantasy.

I could fly to Ohio from my West Coast home and cover the event as a writer, taking in the wonder of it all. But that would be hollow somehow. To complete the dream and set my mind at ease, I actually would have to shoot in the Grand American.

All of these emotions welled up in August, 1991, as I talked with some fellow sporting clays shooters, and one of them mentioned that an acquaintance was "back at the Grand."

Without thinking, I retorted: "I've always wanted to do that."

It was a dispassionate statement of fact rather than a declaration of any importance. But it triggered the dream.

As I walked from one sporting clays station to another that day, my mind replayed the dream. There I was, on the trap field at the Grand American, breaking clays with an Ithaca 4E. I could even see myself opening the gun, ejecting the spent shell and loading another when it was time to shoot again. In my mind, I could smell the burned powder.

At the next shooting station that day, I made a second matter-of-fact utterance: "I think I really will shoot the Grand next year."

I never had shot a registered trap target in my life, and I didn't have any idea what it took to compete in the Grand, but I knew I had a year to put it all together. So, I asked around, and some of the trap shooters I knew told me what I should do was to join the ATA (Amateur Trapshooting Association) and spend the ensuing year shooting at all kinds of tournaments so I would be up to speed for the following Grand American.

Certainly, that was good advice, but it didn't have to be that demanding. After all, none of my dreams ever saw me winning the Grand, or anything like that. They merely showed me shooting in the big event. Trap shooting had

The Ithaca 4E is a study in simplicity. The single-shot action does all that it was designed to do and keeps doing it for generations.

Of the Ithaca single-shot trap guns, the 4E was a more elementary grade. Engraving is tasteful but no precious metals are used to decorate this basic grade.

been considered more like a way of life than a particular series of challenges.

In order to be classified, I would have to register a whole lot of targets, and frankly, there wasn't that kind of leisure time, because during the same period of time, I was going from full-time employment to working on my own.

Fortunately, the ATA takes such situations into account. If a shooter is not classified properly, then that shooter must "compete" in the A Class, and must take handicap targets from the twenty-five-yard line. That sounded totally reasonable. It wouldn't have mattered to me if the class was AA, and if the handicap yardage was twenty-seven.

Winning for me, after all, was all in the shooting of the event. A high score would be nice, but was not at all necessary to validate the dream. I wouldn't want to embarrass myself during the shoot, but there was little likelihood of that. I'd done enough shotgunning as a hunter and sporting clays participant to be able to hit at least a fair share of targets, and to handle myself on the line with some modicum of decorum.

Joining the ATA was a pleasantly painless procedure.

For the price of a couple of big burgers, fries and a chocolate shake, I was a card-carrying member of the organization. It was all handled conveniently through the mail.

The original plan was to shoot a few dozen rounds of trap during the year, including at least a handful of doubles, just to get a feel for everything. But procrastination prevailed.

Before I realized it, the month was May and I was covering the big annual shoot put on by the California Paralyzed Veterans Association. It's a trap shooting proposition, and it was the first round of trap for me in nearly a decade.

I used my sporting clays over/under, and broke twenty-two or twenty-three targets from the sixteen-yard line. The handicap event was from the twenty-yard line, and I matched my score from the sixteen-yard distance. And there was a doubles event.

It was the first time in my life I had ever attempted trap doubles. As the squad headed for the field, I asked one of the veterans of the shoot what that game was about, and how one might want to shoot it. He explained it briefly, and we began to shoot.

Doubles in sporting clays are the most normal presen-

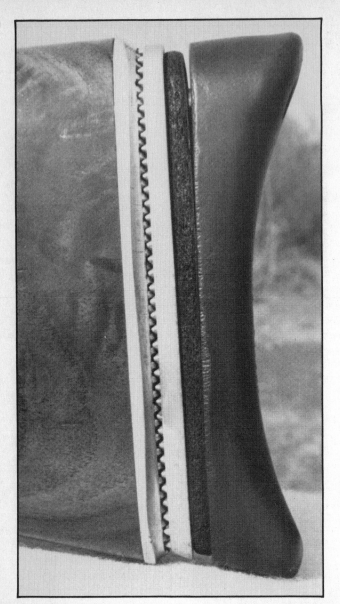

Above, the adjustable butt pad is the only non-original part of author's Ithaca 4E.

tations, so any apprehension about two targets in the air simultaneously had long since been erased from my mind. I merely called for the targets, visually spotted them, then shot. It may not have been the typical approach, but again, I shot the same percentage as I had at singles from either the sixteen or twenty-yard line.

Hence, in one day I had learned where my abilities put me in the trap game: I could expect to break, on average, about eighty-eight to ninety-two targets out of every one hundred. That's not enough to make waves in the trap game, but it's not so bad as to be a total embarrassment, either.

A month later, I was covering a police/fire department shoot put on by the Los Angeles Police Department and other local officers and firemen. A couple of years before, I had acquired a Winchester Super-X semi-auto trap gun — initially with the thought of using it for duck hunting with steel shot. The Monte Carlo stock precluded effective duck shooting for me, and I had not gotten around to swapping stocks for one with a straight comb.

The gun still was in the vault, so I decided to use it for the wobble trap event at the police shoot. Unceremoniously, I broke my "normal" twenty-three with it. And it became instantly obvious that trap is best shot with a trap-configured gun. It was not only more fun that way, but the targets broke with authority. That felt good.

By the time that shoot was over, I knew I had the gun I wanted to use for doubles at the Grand. Since the boyhood dreams had not involved doubles, the gun I would use for doubles was irrelevant, and I already owned one that would do the job well — the Super-X.

But for singles, my mind was not so at ease. I could shoot the singles with the Super-X, but it wouldn't be the same. The singles gun simply had to be a vintage Ithaca 4E, which, of course, would be the only proper handicap gun for the rookie appearance at the Grand.

During the year of planning (or, more appropriately, procrastination) for the Grand, I had discussed my thoughts with a number of fellow shooters, and learned that one

Right, this side view of the Ithaca 4E action shows one of the reasons the design has been so durable. It is beefy and bold in the right places without being clunky.

The Knickerbocker-action 4E Ithacas are the most sought-after, because they are the strongest. They can handle a steady diet of the latest loads. The twin-lug lockup on breech end of the barrel is super strong.

shooting and hunting buddy just happened to have a spare 4E. Actually, I think he had two spare 4E guns, but that situation never was really spelled out or pursued.

The fact of the matter was that he had one, and was willing to part with it for a reasonable sum. That, in itself, was a fortunate break. I merely sold one of my several side-by-side hunting shotguns and turned over that exact amount for the 4E.

By the time all of that took place, it was a scant two weeks before the Grand, but every single detail was falling into place. I already had my airplane tickets in hand, and was ready to go.

I could have borrowed any number of trap guns to take to the Grand, or I could have used the Super-X for everything, or I could have shot with my sporting clays gun. But I found myself on a mission to do it right.

Some folks openly wondered whether I was planning to become a serious trap shooter. Maybe, maybe not. I honestly had no idea, and it really didn't matter that much to me. I was in the process of fulfilling a lifelong dream, and I would worry about other things when their time came.

I didn't have the slightest idea if I would ever shoot the 4E following that Grand American. The question was moot. It just didn't matter, because for me, if that gun got me through the Grand, it would have fulfilled its purpose in my life. Anything else would be gravy.

It had taken me decades to come to such an introspectively induced realization. In life, some things are important. Other things are not. And life simply is too short to worry about those things which are not important.

Yes, I was on the verge of "going home" as a shooter. And, I was doing it for all the right reasons, and precisely

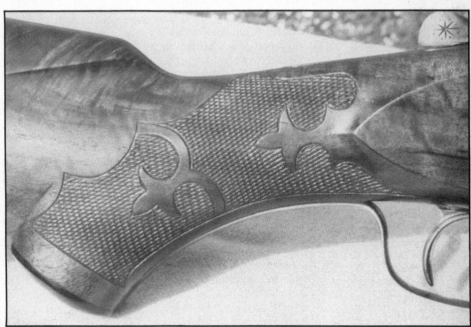

Adding to the quality of the 4E Ithaca, the checkering on the stock is hand-cut.

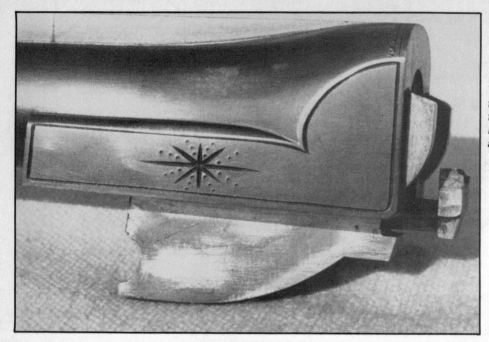

The rear of the barrel on the Ithaca 4E is bold. Note the gun's massive locking lugs which are located just above the automatic ejector.

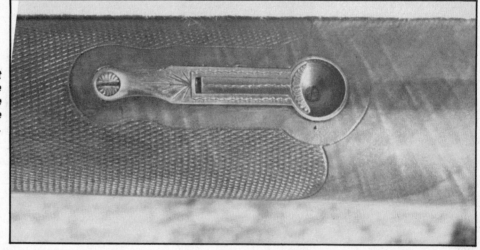

There's a generous amount of detail surrounding the forend release latch. Note how it fits nicely into the stock's checkering pattern.

the right way for me. Frankly, success would come when I broke my first target at the Grand American. That would mean I would have shot the Grand, and broken a clay in the process.

As procrastination continued to rule, another reality became apparent. Not only would this be my first, and perhaps only, Grand American, but I would be shooting my first registered targets at the Grand. What a way to start!

Although there had been no plan to do so, starting in registered shooting at the biggest and most prestigious event of its kind in the world is really the ultimately proper way to do things.

After all, from that day forward, all of my percentages of registered trap shooting would be couched in a setting starting with the biggest and best that sport had to offer.

Will I become a rabid trap shooter? Right now, I honestly have no idea. It could happen. But it likely will not. Rather, I suppose I'll shoot registered trap somewhat infrequently. From now on, you see, I will be shooting trap for the pure enjoyment of the sport.

I have no need to compete with myself or anyone else. I have, after all, realized my dream. All that is left is pure fun. It's strange how life works out sometimes.

Having experienced all of those emotions, desires and trepidations, I would not have been surprised if, when I actually walked to the line and called for a target, I would fall apart. But it wasn't that way.

I may not have shot a registered trap target before in my life, but I had broken many thousands of the flying disks. Shooting, after all, had become not only a way of life, but my means of making a living.

That first morning at the Grand actually felt nice. It was quite pleasing as I loaded the gun, mounted it to my shoulder and called for the target in a rote manner. And the target broke. It was totally crunched!

By the time I completed the first twenty-five targets, I'd hit most of them, missed a few. The score was essentially unimportant.

It was the opening sixteen-yard singles event, and that meant shooting twenty-five targets at each of four adjacent fields. By the time I completed that first one hundred

Even the bottom of the Ithaca 4E receiver 4E shows it has proper lineage. It's heavy enough without being chunky.

targets, I had managed to run all twenty-five of them straight on one field. That didn't diminish the glow which would have been there even if I'd walked off the line after breaking that first target.

As much as the bulk of the dream had been fulfilled, it was not yet an accomplished feat. The Ithaca 4E single-shot, after all, was the handicap gun, and that event would come the following day.

It did, and the dream was complete. It still was good, and anything after that would be little more or less than icing on the cake. Dessert is great, and I was going to hog it all!

With a little coaching from some friends, I duplicated the twenty-five straight once more during the Grand. I didn't set any records on that one hundred-target event,

and that's fine. I shot at least one field flawlessly with my dream gun. What more in life is there, really?

During the week-long course of the Grand American, myths crumbled upon occasion, and new realities were made evident.

Through the years, I had heard many times about the "crusty" and "grumpy" trap shooters. I found the opposite to be true of those I met at the Grand. They could not have been friendlier nor more helpful. Maybe it is different at some shoots in some places, but at that place and at that time, it was great.

Top shoots bring together top people. And, in the shooting industry, the Grand is no exception.

One day I found myself on the same squad with Jess

Although the 4E is a rather standard grade of Ithaca single-shot trap gun, the basic design allows enough room for artists to express themselves. The huge wood panel above the trigger can be enhanced with a carving or elaborate checkering.

The receiver's two vertical slots are where the barrel lugs lock up. The cut-out at the bottom accepts the huge hinged section of the barrel

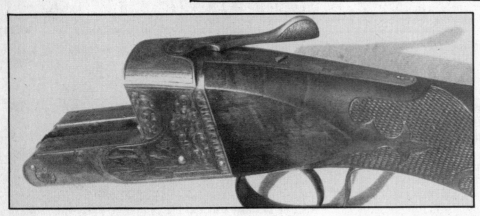

It wouldn't happen today, but in the 1930s when the author's gun was made, there was no need to put a safety device on a trap gun. When it was not on the line to be shot, it was kept open.

Briley from Texas. He's the Briley after whom the company which makes interchangeable chokes is named. He and I were a sort of nostalgia squad — he with his vintage Parker single-barrel trap gun from the 1920s, and me with my Ithaca single from the '30s.

At one of the practice traps, I found myself waiting in line behind Al Ludic, maker of trap guns with the same name.

And it was nice to talk with Rudy Etchen, one of the winningest trap shooters of all time. I knew Rudy from other places, and even had the pleasure of hunting with him in Texas a couple of years before, and shooting sporting clays with him in Kansas the preceding fall.

At the Grand that same year, Rudy Etchen and his son, Joel, took the father/son honors. Rudy Etchen shot a 199, and Joel broke all two hundred targets in the event. The younger Etchen went on to take it all in that singles competition, but it meant going until almost midnight and another 175 targets to do it.

George Haas, who shot on the U.S. Olympic trap team in 1988 in Seoul, Korea, was there, and we talked about things on various occasions throughout the week.

Karl Lippard and Lucio Sosta were in the Perazzi building every day, and once when I stopped by for a chat, Art Bright of Collectible Arms was there, as well, talking to both of them.

Danielle Perazzi also was there, but frankly it was more impressive to be around Lippard and Sosta. They both speak English, and there is an undeniable American flair to the Grand.

Mike Jordan did well for Winchester ammo at the Grand. He took most of the industry awards. I had hunted upland game, waterfowl and big game with Jordan over the years, but this was the first time I had seen him shoot serious targets. Yep. He's good!

Bud Fini at the Remington building was justifiably proud of the single-shot trap gun he had helped nurture all the way from the drawing boards to reality a couple of years ago, and Frank Kodl at the *Shotgun Sports* magazine tent was a pleasure to meet, as always.

So even from a professional standpoint, the trip was outstanding. I guess that's the way things go when dreams actually come true.

If I ever am fortunate enough to shoot the Grand again, my personal agenda will be much different. It will be, out of necessity, a matter strictly about business.

But that never will alter the fact that, for a number of separate, yet brief, moments in 1992, I found myself experiencing the fulfillment of a forty-year-old childhood dream — a dream which really did come true.

Meanwhile, I also always wondered what it would be like to shoot rifles at Camp Perry? Hmmmm! — *Steve Comus*